Conversations With St. Philomena

Anchor of Hope from Heaven

By Janie Garza

Published by St. Dominic Media
P.O. Box 345
Herndon, VA 20172-0345

Conversations With St. Philomena

Declarations

Since the abolition of Canons 1399 and 2318 of the former Code of Canon Law by Pope Paul VI in AAS 58 (1966), p. 1186, publications about new apparitions, revelations, prophecies, miracles, etc., have been allowed to be distributed and read by the faithful without the express permission of the Church, providing that they contain nothing that contravenes faith and morals. This means no imprimatur is necessary. However it is welcome!

In Chapter II, No. 12 of the Second Vatican Council's *Lumen Gentium,* we read:

"The Holy Spirit... distributes special gifts among the faithful of every rank... Such gifts of grace, whether they are of special enlightenment or whether they are spread more simply and generally, must be accepted with gratefulness and consolation, as they are specially suited to, and useful for, the needs of the Church...Judgment as to their genuineness and their correct use lies with those who lead the Church and those whose special task is not indeed to extinguish the spirit but to examine everything and keep that which is good." (confer 1 Thess. 5: 19-21)

"That private revelations occur in all times is evident as appears from the testimony of the Sacred Scripture and tradition. To stamp these testimonies as untruths gives scandal and bears witness to impiety."

Cardinal Bona

Published by ST. DOMINIC MEDIA
P.O. BOX 345, Herndon, Virginia 20172-0345
Phone 703-327-2277 / Fax 703-327-2888

www.sign.org

Library of Congress Catalog Card Number:
ISBN: 1-892165-09-0
Cover Design by Carolyn Robel

TABLE OF CONTENTS

TABLE OF CONTENTS

Messages

1997

Pages

1998

*I come as the "Anchor of Hope"
from Heaven*

*to help families in these troubled
times, especially to help the young
children and the youth: to help
them to understand that God wants
them to remain pure and holy. I
am the wonderworker of God for
those who believe in my
intercession.*

St. Philomena: May 1, 1996

Acknowledgments

Thank you to all the friends of St. Philomena who made
possible the publication of this book.

Roger and Linda Broz
Margie Cristofaro
Carmine Darcangelo
Ruth Mary Demere
Doris Frommell
Mr. and Mrs. Ralph Hoffmann
Diana Jaeger
Peter and Lucille Lamy
Thomas Lieser
Roger and Rosalie Lucas
Amado Montalvo
J. Paul and Veronica Rodriguez
Harold and Margaret Schachtner
Mrs. Bernadette Settelmeyer
St. Jude the Apostle Catholic Church
Lillian Timma
Mr. and Mrs. Patrick Toole
Mary Worley

Introduction

I do not think that anyone who has ever asked something of St. Philomena with faith has ever been disappointed. Certainly, we have to be persevering in our prayer as Christ the Lord tells us, but there is no question in my mind or heart that this young, fourth century martyr-saint is very powerful and quick to answer.

Mrs. Janie Garza of Austin, Texas is a wife, mother, and grandmother and was chosen by our Lord to be a vessel of simple and holy messages for the sanctification of the family of today. She has been receiving messages and visions since February 15, 1989 and has two volumes of messages published and dedicated to the holiness of families. She has received messages and visions from our Lord Jesus, our Blessed Mother, St. Joseph, the Three Archangels, and a number of Saints and heavenly Friends of God. In the latter part of 1995, Janie began hearing a voice who identified herself as "St. Philomena". Janie could not see her, but could hear her in the form of an inner locution.

Time went on. At the beginning of 1996, St. Philomena again came to Janie and told her that she would suffer much during Lent, more than the usual accentuated Lenten suffering. St. Philomena told Janie that she would intercede for her. At this point, Janie knew nothing about St. Philomena, nor had ever heard of her.

On February 2, 1996, St. Philomena came to Janie while she was praying her rosary. The young Saint told Janie that she had come to tell her not to be discouraged during her suffering, but to offer it up consistently for poor sinners. Because Janie could not see but only hear her and wanted confirmation that the voice was truly that of St. Philomena, Janie asked for a confirmation indicating that it was truly St. Philomena herself. Janie requested firstly that a St. Philomena medal would somehow reach her, secondly that a statue of St. Philomena be sent to her, and lastly that a first class relic would somehow make its way to Janie. Janie felt like she was asking too much but she greatly desired an obvious confirmation of the Saint of which Janie knew nothing.

A week later Janie received a medal of St. Philomena and one of St. John Vianney from a friend in Chicago. This was on a Monday. On Tuesday, Janie met a man who was very ill. Janie asked St. Philomena to pray for him, and although he was not a Catholic, she felt moved to give her medal of St. Philomena to the sick man (overcoming a hesitancy to do so since she had just received the medal as a direct request from St. Philomena). The man gladly took the medal. The gift of the medal was joined by a rosary that Janie offered for the man, asking for St. Philomena's intercession to Jesus that this man would be healed. At this point, Janie began feeling the special presence of the young Saint.

On Wednesday (which was Ash Wednesday of 1996), Janie was praying in her living room when a UPS truck stopped to deliver a package. When she opened the package, she found a first class relic of St. Philomena in a small box. Janie conveyed to me how she cried with joy, thanking God and St. Philomena. It had come from some friends of hers in Cleveland, Ohio.

The next day, Thursday, Janie called the sick man whom she had been praying for and told him that St. Philomena would indeed help him. The family had asked her to pray that the medical test examining him for serious illness would come back negative. On Friday, he received the results of his medical test and they were in fact negative.

A week later, after Janie had given a talk in Denver, Colorado, a friend handed her the oil of St. Philomena which had come from St. Philomena's shrine in Mugnano, Italy. One week following this gift, a beautiful statue of St. Philomena arrived for Janie in the mail. In fact, all of her requests for the authenticity of the little princess Saint were fulfilled.

As Janie's spiritual director for over eight years, I can personally verify the authenticity of Janie's supernatural experiences, particularly in light of the discernment and criteria offered by the great Carmelite mystics St. Teresa of Avila and St. John of the Cross, the spiritual tradition in which I have been formed as a Carmelite. Janie receives supernatural messages in three major ways:

1) *Three dimensional apparitions*, where she is able to see, hear, and touch the grandeur of the vision, whether it be Our Lord, Our Blessed Mother, or St. Joseph.
2) *Interior visions*, which Janie likens to "seeing a television show in her heart." These interior visions are something that she can see but cannot touch. The apparitions of St. Philomena to Janie Garza are interior visions.
3) *Interior locutions*, which she describes as inner voices whereby she is able to recognize whose voice is speaking to her heart.

In regards to the messages contained in this volume concerning St. Philomena, the vast majority of the messages would fall into the category of interior visions, whereby she could see and hear St. Philomena who is often accompanied by the archangels, St. Michael, St. Gabriel, and St. Raphael. Although these messages would not be considered "dictational" in the strict sense, her immediate recording of the message following the event, coupled with the special grace she is granted to be able to remember and write down the words spoken by the heavenly visitors, constitute a clear and accurate conveyance of the supernatural messages given.

Conversations With St. Philomena

The messages Janie has received from St. Philomena beginning in 1996 and extending to December 1997 are messages intended for the entire world in a heavenly effort for the Church and all mankind to have a greater understanding and, most of all, a greater love for her who has been called by the popes, "St. Philomena, powerful with God." She is a fourth century martyr who has been returned to the heart of the Church by both the Papal Magisterium of the last two centuries and the ongoing prophetic dimension of the Church as well. St. Philomena also has an intimate relationship with Our Lady, Mediatrix of all Graces, as well as a historical and spiritual relationship with the Patron Saint of parish priests, St. John Marie Vianney.

It is clear to me that at this important time in human history and in the Church, Our Lady desires a greater knowledge and greater love and devotion to St. Philomena, her "little princess saint". It is my personal and priestly prayer that all will have the grace to receive these precious and supernatural words of St. Philomena with an open heart.

Fr. Henry Bordeaux, O.C.D.

Foreword

The following oral address was delivered by Dr. Mark Miravalle, S.T.D., Professor of Theology and Mariology at the Franciscan University of Steubenville, to a large number of the student body at Franciscan University on April 9, 2000 and appears here in transcribed form.

It is a true joy for me to introduce you to the life and devotion of a Saint that, in some sense, has been a well-kept secret, though through no desire of Heaven. She is a Saint who has been called the "thaumaturga", the miracle-worker, of the 19th century. She was declared by the soon-to-be Blessed Pope Pius IX as the Patroness of the Children of Mary. She is the Saint of whom the great St. John Vianney, a mystic and priestly giant of the spiritual life in his own right, said, "I have never asked for anything through the intercession of my Little Saint without having been answered."

She is a Saint to whom numerous Saints themselves have shown tremendous devotion, including Pope St. Pius X, the Pope of the Eucharist; Blessed Anna Maria Taigi, the mother-mystic; St. Peter Julian Eymard, who was cured through the intercession of St. Philomena; Blessed Pauline Jaricot, foundress of the Propagation of the Faith; Blessed Damien of Molokai, the leper-priest, who consecrated his first church to St. Philomena; and St. Peter Chanel, the first Saint of Oceania. In addition, the popes of the 19th and 20th centuries so lavished indulgences on devotion to her, especially on the Cord which carries numerous plenary indulgences.

Conversations With St. Philomena

Finally, I can say that devotion to St. Philomena is making a return and spreading like wildfire throughout the Catholic world in this day, in this age. She is not just the "thaumaturga" for the 19th century. Heaven desires her to be the miracle-worker for the 21st century, for our own times.

Let me begin with a brief history of St. Philomena, from the discovery of her tomb in 1802 to the time she is raised to the altar in 1837. Then we will glance at the appreciation of the 19th and 20th century popes for this Little Princess Saint, followed by an examination of the relationship between St. Philomena and St. John Vianney, Patron Saint all parish priests; and finally the major forms of devotion offered to St. Philomena today.

Where does this Saint come from? Who is this Saint who, uniquely in the history of the Church, has been canonized solely on the basis of her intercession? On May 24, 1802, excavators of the Catacombs of St. Pricilla in Rome (designated as the "Greek Chapel") found a new grave. This grave had three tiles on the front of it that were painted with the following symbols: the palm, which is a symbol of martyrdom, an anchor and a number of arrows. Inscribed in red on the tiles were the following Latin words: on the first tile was the word, *Lumina*; on the second tile, the combined words, *Pax Te*; on the third tile, the words, *Cum Fi*. If you begin with the second tile, which was a custom found in catacomb inscriptions, with the words "Peace to you", you have "Pax Tecum Filumina", "Peace to You, Philomena."

Upon anatomical examination of the bones, it was determined that this was a young girl of approximately 13 years of age. In the grave was also a vial of blood, which was typically found in the graves of martyrs of the early Church. Immediately, Msgr. Pouzetti, Vatican custodian of holy relics, sought historical records for "Filumina" from Roman martyrology sources, but nothing substantial was found.

Meanwhile, there was a humble little priest from Mugnano,

a small town outside Naples, named Fr. Francesco di Lucia, who was concerned about his parish which he said had grown "spiritually weak." He was going to Rome to obtain relics of a martyr from the Catacombs to help revitalize his parish. He asked for the help of his Bishop-elect, Msgr. DeCesare, and through his intercession and the help of the royal ambassador of the King of Naples, Pope Pius VII gave Fr. di Lucia permission to take the sacred remains of "Filumina" back to his failing parish in Mugnano in 1805.

Immediately, the young Miracle-Worker began her intercession. Within the first months of the relocation to Mugnano of this unknown Saint, numerous miracles took place and were officially recorded by the bishops and priests of the region. For example, a local woman suffering for twelve years from a disease declared "incurable" by the physicians of her day was healed as she was dressing the sacred remains. On the same day, an attorney was carried into the chapel suffering from sciatica. Immediately upon entering into the vicinity of the sacred remains, he was cured. Further, a noble lady who was scheduled for an amputation of a leg with a cancerous ulcer was instantly cured. Perhaps the most remarkable incident occurred just as the remains of the Saint were brought into the parish church of Our Lady of Grace. The bells of the church rang and the town paralytic, Angelo Bianco, was suddenly and unexpectedly healed. He ran into the church screaming that he was cured, to the amazement of all. This was quite a dramatic and supernatural entry for the young martyred Saint into a small parish. There were numerous other miracles officially recorded by the diocese.

Over the next few years, from 1805 to 1810, word of these numerous miracles spread throughout Italy and beyond. Hundreds of pilgrims traveled from Rome to Mugnano. Reports of these numerous miracles reached Pope Gregory XVI. For example, Anna Maria Taigi, the housewife, mother and mystic who had cardinals waiting to see her because of her prophetic gifts, prayed daily to St. Philomena. On her deathbed, she commended her family and children to the care of St. Philomena. Sometime before her death, her granddaughter, Peppina, had an accident in which the pupil of her eye had been irreparably damaged. Blessed Anna Maria took some of the oil that burns at the tomb of St. Philomena and applied it to the eye of her granddaughter. By the next morning, Peppina had perfect sight, as confirmed by numerous medical examinations. The use of the oil originated when the relics of this unknown Saint were brought to the little church of Our Lady of Grace. At the time, a mother with a blind child went to the oil lamp, dipped her finger into the oil, applied it to the eyes of her young son and immediately he was cured and his sight was given him.

Another curious phenomenon occurred when Bishop DeCesare began to send out the dust from the bones of St. Philomena to neighboring parishes and dioceses. He found that although he sent out more and more dust, he still had the original amount of dust from the bones as when he began. This was brought to the attention of the Vatican Congregation of Rites, and they then decided to conduct an experiment. First, they sent out bone dust from the relics of another Saint and expectedly found that the remains diminished. When they then sent out the dust from the bones of St. Philomena, they found that inexplicably there was a miraculous multiplication of bone dust. As confirmed by the Congregation of Rites, truly this was a Saint whom God wanted to be known, and known quickly!

Perhaps the best known miracle of St. Philomena concerned the Frenchwoman, Blessed Pauline Marie Jaricot. Blessed Pauline Jaricot was a remarkable young woman, daughter of an aristocratic family, and close friend of the Cure d'Ars, St. John Vianney. She started what is called today the Propagation of the Faith for the missionary activity of the Church. In 1834, at the age of 35, she became gravely ill with a serious heart disease which made her an invalid. She was encouraged by St. John Vianney to make a pilgrimage to the tomb of St. Philomena, which she did against all medical counsel. She stopped at Rome on her way to Mugnano, but was so gravely ill that she was unable to make a papal audience she had previously arranged with His Holiness, Gregory XVI. Out of respect, Pope Gregory XVI went to see her at the Sacred Heart convent where she was staying. Seeing her deathly state, Pope Gregory asked her to pray for the Church and its Head "as soon as you arrive in Paradise." However Pauline responded, "Yes, Holy Father, I promise you. But if I walk on foot to the Vatican upon my return from Mugnano, would your Holiness deign to proceed without delay to the final inquiry into the cause of Philomena?" Gregory XVI responded, "Of course, for in that case it would be a first-class miracle." But as he left the room he told an Italian sister, "We will never see her again."

On August 8, 1835, Pauline arrived in Mugnano looking, according to witnesses, "more like a corpse than a living person." Word had gotten out that Pauline Jaricot was going to ask the intercession of St. Philomena and the people in the streets were cheering her on her way. The citizens of Mugnano called out, "Don't worry, our Saint will take care of you!" On Saturday evening, Pauline went to the Chapel of St. Philomena, but nothing happened. On Sunday, she went to several Masses, received Holy Communion, but again, nothing happened. She returned to the chapel Sunday night and again on Monday morning, still very weak, and again, nothing happened. By Monday morning, the townspeople, in a particularly southern Italian manner of intercession, began to bang on the grave of St. Philomena, reminding her that her reputation was at stake. "Do you hear us, Philomena?" they cried. "If you do not cure this pious lady, we will pray to you no more. We will have nothing to do with you. Return her to health right now!"

Pauline tried to kneel, but she collapsed. She later explained that as she lay in front of the tomb she began to feel a certain healing power. That afternoon, August 10, precisely when our Eucharistic Lord was raised high in Benediction, Pauline was completely and miraculously cured. The next day she walked with a huge crowd in processions through the streets of Mugnano, through Naples, all the way up to Rome.

Conversations With St. Philomena

The Pope had not yet heard of the miracle. Pauline asked permission to enter the Vatican chambers of the Holy Father without being announced and thus she entered the audience room of Gregory XVI. The Holy Father exclaimed in astonishment, "Is it really you or an apparition? Is this really my dear daughter? And has she come back from the grave, or has God manifested in her favor the power of the Virgin-Martyr?"

The Holy Father had her walk, and then *run*, through the Vatican halls. Pope Gregory had her stay in Rome for a year so he could see her as often as possible to be certain that it was really a miracle. Finally, on January 30, 1837, Gregory XVI kept his word and raised St. Philomena to the honors of the Altar of the Church. The Pontiff made this solemn decree, for the first time in Church history, *based solely on the power of her intercession, solely in light of the undeniable miracles.* It is moreover the only instance of a martyr of the Catacombs of whom nothing is known being granted a proper Mass and Office.

But Heaven was not to keep this Saint unknown for long. During this remarkable period, three separate individuals in different parts of Italy, and completely unknown to each other, began receiving details of the life of St. Philomena through various modes of private revelation. The most well-known of these were locutions received by Mother Luisa di Gesu in August, 1833. These locutions were granted the official *Imprimatur* by the Holy Office that same year, December 21, 1833.

Mother Luisa had been praying before a statue of St. Philomena when she thought she heard a voice tell her the specific date of death (August 10) of Philomena and specific details of her journey from Rome to Mugnano, details as yet unknown to the public. Mother Luisa, fearing she was experiencing an illusion, increased her prayer and fasting. Under obedience to her Superior in whom she had confided, she observed complete silence during the revelations. Mother Luisa's Superior then wrote to Fr. Di Lucia, reporting the revelations and asking him to confirm the veracity of the specific details reportedly revealed by St. Philomena. Fr. Di Lucia confirmed every detail and requested that the nun "be open" to any additional revelations pertaining to the life of St. Philomena. Again under obedience, Mother Luisa prayed to St. Philomena for further information and immediately the "same voice" began revealing the historical facts of the life of the 4th century martyr.

The following is the account of the life of St. Philomena as taken from the official account of Fr. Di Lucia's *Relazione Istorici di Santa Filomena* and subsequent annals.

My dear sister, I am the daughter of a Prince who governed a small state in Greece. My mother was also of royal blood. My parents were without children. They were idolaters. They continually offered sacrifices and prayers to their false gods. A doctor from Rome, named Publius, lived in the palace in the service of my father. This doctor professed Christianity. Seeing the affliction of my parents, by the impulse of the Holy Spirit, he spoke to them of Christianity and promised to pray for them if they consented to receive Baptism. The grace which accompanied his words enlightened their understanding and triumphed over their will. They became Christians and obtained the long-desired happiness that Publius had assured them as the reward of their conversion. At the moment of my birth, they gave me the name of "Lumina", an allusion to the *light* of Faith of which I had been, as it were, the fruit. The day of my Baptism they called me "Philomena", *Daughter of Light*, because on that day I was born to the Faith. The affection which my parents bore me was so great that they would have me always with them.

It was on this account that they took me to Rome on a journey that my father was obliged to make on the occasion of an unjust war with which he was threatened by the haughty Diocletian. I was then thirteen years old. On our arrival in the capital of the world, we proceeded to the palace of the Emperor and were admitted for an audience. As soon as Diocletian saw me, his eyes were fixed upon me. He appeared to be prepossessed in this manner during the entire time that my father was stating with animated feelings everything that could serve for his defense. As soon as Father had ceased to speak, the Emperor desired him to be disturbed no longer, to banish all fear, to think only of living in happiness. These are the Emperor's words, "I shall place at your disposal all the force of the Empire. I ask only one thing, that is the hand of your daughter."

My father, dazzled with an honor he was far from expecting, willingly acceded on the spot to the proposal of the Emperor. When we returned to our own dwelling, Father and Mother did all they could to induce me to yield to Diocletian's wishes and to theirs. I cried, "Do you wish that for the love of a man I should break the promise I have made to Jesus Christ? My virginity belongs to Him. I can no longer dispose of it."

"But you were young then, too young," answered my father, "to have formed such an engagement." He joined the most terrible threats to the command that he gave me to accept the hand of Diocletian. The grace of my God rendered me invincible. My father, not being able to make the Emperor relent, in order to disengage himself from the promise he had given, was obliged by Diocletian to bring me to the Imperial Chamber. I had to withstand for sometime beforehand a new attack from my father's anger. My mother, uniting her efforts to his, endeavored to conquer my resolution. Caresses, threats, everything was employed to reduce me to compliance. At last I saw both of my parents fall at my knees and say to me with tears in their eyes, "My child, have pity on your father, your mother, your country, our country, our subjects."

"No, no!" I answered them. "My virginity, which I have vowed to God, comes before everything, before you, before my country. My kingdom is Heaven."

My words plunged them into despair and they brought me before the Emperor who, on his part, did all in his power to win me. But his promises, his allurements, his threats, were equally useless. He then got into a violent fit of anger and, influenced by the devil, had me cast into one of the prisons of the palace, where I was loaded with chains. Thinking that pain and shame would weaken the courage with which my Divine Spouse inspired me, he came to see me every day. After several days, the Emperor issued an order for my chains to be loosed that I might take a small portion and bread and water. He renewed his attacks, some of which, if not for the grace of God, would have been fatal to purity. The defeats which he always experienced were for me the preludes to new tortures. Prayer supported me. I ceased not to recommend myself to Jesus and His most pure Mother.

My captivity lasted thirty-seven days. Then, in the midst of a heavenly light, I saw Mary holding her Divine Son in her arms. "My daughter," she said to me, "three days more of prison and after forty days you shall leave this state of pain."

Such happy news renewed my courage to prepare for the frightful combat awaiting. The Queen of Heaven reminded me of the name I had received in Baptism saying, "You are Lumina, as your Spouse is called Light or Sun. Fear not, I will aid you. Now, nature, whose weakness asserts itself, is humbling you. In the moment of struggle, grace will come to you to lend its force. The angel who is mine also, Gabriel, whose name expresses force, will come to your succor. I will recommend you especially to his care."

The vision disappeared leaving my prison scented with a fragrance like incense. I experienced a joy out of this world. Something indefinable. What the Queen of Angels had prepared for me was soon experienced. Diocletian, despairing of bending me, decided upon public chastisement to offend my virtue. He condemned me to be stripped and scourged like the Spouse I preferred to him. These were his horrifying words. "Since she is not ashamed to prefer to an Emperor like me, a malefactor condemned to an infamous death by his own people, she deserves that my justice shall treat her as he was treated."

The prison guards hesitated to unclothe me entirely, but they did tie me to a column in the presence of the great men of the court. They lashed me with violence until I was bathed in blood. My whole body felt like one open wound but I did not faint. The tyrant had me dragged back to the dungeon expecting me to die. I hoped to join my heavenly Spouse. Two angels shining with light appeared to me in the darkness. They poured a soothing balm on my wounds, bestowing on me a vigor I did not have before the torture. When the Emperor was informed of the change that had come over me, he had me brought before him. He viewed me with a greedy desire and tried to persuade me that I owed my healing and regained vigor to Jupiter, another god, that he, the Emperor, had sent to me. He attempted to impress me with his belief that Jupiter desired me to be Empress of Rome. Joining to these seductive words promises of great honor, including the most flattering words. Diocletian tried to caress me. Fiendishly, he attempted to complete the work of Hell which he had begun. The Divine Spirit to whom I am indebted for constancy in preserving my purity seemed to fill me with light and knowledge. To all the proofs which I gave of the solidity of our Faith, neither Diocletian nor his own courtiers could find an answer.

Then the frenzied Emperor dashed at me, commanding a guard to chain an anchor around my neck and bury me deep in the waters of the Tiber. The order was executed. I was cast into the water, but God sent to me two angels who unfastened the anchor. It fell into the river mud where it remains, no doubt, to the present time. The angels transported me gently in full view of the multitude upon the riverbank. I came back unharmed, not even wet, after being plunged with the heavy anchor. When a cry of joy rose from the watchers on the shore, and so many embraced Christianity by proclaiming their belief in my God, Diocletian attributed my preservation to secret magic.

Then the Emperor had me dragged through the streets of Rome and shot with a shower of arrows. My blood flowed but I did not faint. Diocletian thought that I was dying and commanded the guards to carry me back to the dungeon. Heaven honored me with a new favor there. I fell into a sweet sleep. A second time the tyrant attempted to have me pierced with sharper darts. Again the archers bent their bows. They gathered all their strength but the arrows refused to second their intentions. The Emperor was present. In a rage, he called me a magician and, thinking that the action of the fire could destroy the enchantment, he ordered the darts to be made red in a furnace and directed against my heart. He was obeyed. But these darts, after having gone over a part of the space which they were to cross to come to me, took a quite contrary direction and returned to strike those by whom they had been hurled. Six of the archers were killed by them. Several among them renounced paganism. The people began to render public testimony to the power of God that protected me.

These murmurs and acclamations infuriated the tyrant. He determined to hasten my death by piercing my neck with a lance. My soul took flight towards my heavenly Spouse who placed me with the crown of virginity and the palm of martyrdom in a distinguished place among the elect. The day that was so happy for me and saw me enter into glory was Friday, the third hour after mid-day, the same hour that saw my Divine Master expire.

What is noteworthy from a historical perspective is not only that this revelation was confirmed by two other individuals unknown to each other (one a priest, the other an historian), but these other confirmatory historical facts: 1) Diocletian was known for executing Christians by the use of arrows, as exemplified by St. Sebastian; 2) Diocletian was also known for killing Christians by tying anchors around their necks and throwing them into the water; 3) The reference to "Lumena" -- the name given to her at birth, "Light" -- and then at Baptism, *"Fi Lumena"*, "Daughter of Light", may explain the arrangement of the tiles found at the grave ("Lumena", her first given name, was on the first tile).

Why is St. Philomena making such a comeback today? Why is our Lord and our Mother wishing this to take place? I believe, first of all, because she was pure without the support of her family. This young Saint remained pure against the wishes of her family, and is that not sadly the case so often today? Secondly, she persevered under persecution with a remarkable strength enduring, what were in fact, several martyrdoms. Has not our Holy Father, Pope John Paul II, spoken more than ever about Christian Martyrdom, especially in this last year? Has he not encouraged the faithful to be willing to offer everything for our Lord in whatever ways we are called to do that? Who better than this young, pure Saint to give us a true example of that kind of strength and courage?

Let us also examine the cherished relationship between St. Philomena and the Cure' of Ars, the great St. John Vianney. From the first moments that the Cure' heard of this Saint there was a "union of heart" which led to consistent, direct supernatural experiences. St. Philomena appeared to St. John Vianney on numerous occasions. One documented occurrence was May, 1843, when John Vianney was sick, given up for dead from double pneumonia. He had received Last Rites. With his last words, he asked that a Mass be offered for St. Philomena on his behalf. At that moment, St. Philomena appeared to him, cured him, and gave him personal information that gave him strength for the rest of his life. In May, 1859, Vianney confided to a friend, "I had a hard time discovering the will of God concerning an enterprise that bothered me (the need for funds for a new church and his assistant pastor was encouraging him to take the money from a separate fund for missionary activity). I asked to know the will of God. St. Philomena appeared to me; she had come down from Heaven and she was beautiful, luminous, surrounded by a white cloud. She told me twice, 'Your works are more perfect, because there is nothing more precious than the salvation of souls.'"

The Cure' was the first to erect a chapel to St. Philomena in France, and habitually attributed all miracles that came through him to the young martyr-saint. The spiritual effects of the combination of St. Philomena, "Miracle-Worker of the 19th century," and St. John Vianney, reader of souls and patron of parish priests, were awesome to behold. The records at Ars document as many as *14 miracles a week* as people flocked to Ars for both St. Philomena and the Cure'. The Cure's practice was to direct people who needed any physical cure to St. Philomena by recommending they make a novena of prayer, or by sending them oil from the lamps burning at the tomb of St. Philomena. Here are but a few testimonies.

A gentleman had traveled from a distant town and told the Cure' that he had come because he had heard there were extraordinary things happening in the parish. The Cure' responded, "What do you mean, extraordinary things in my parish? You must not believe everything you hear." The man said, "Well then, Father, when I get back to Cusance, I will say nothing is happening in your parish." The Cure answered, "In that case, you would be lying. You must not do that. Tell them that everything is happening through the intercession of the Blessed Virgin and St. Philomena. The deaf, the dumb, the blind, the paralyzed and the possessed are healed. But it is only through the intercession of the Blessed Virgin and St. Philomena."

In another example, St. Peter Julian Eymard, the founder of the Society of the Blessed Sacrament, was taken to Ars in a serious condition. The Cure' saw him and said, "Pray a novena to St. Philomena and you will be cured, but not here, when you are further away." St. Peter was miraculously cured when he arrived home. So numerous were the miracles performed through St. Philomena's intercession at the parish of Vianney leading to the ubiquitous flocking of pilgrims that the Cure' was once heard to say in a Catechism class, "Couldn't she work miracles elsewhere?!!"

A hotelkeeper at Ars, Francois Pertinand, related the following case: "This is what happened to me. I came down with a serious illness which caused terrible swelling, to the point that it had reached my chest. I was taken to Villefranche for medical care. The doctors declared that my blood was contaminated and there was no remedy for it. With that, my parents absolutely wanted to take me back home. The Cure' came to see me. He told me that I had only two days to live, but if I were willing to have confidence and follow his advice, I would be healed. 'If you make a novena to St. Philomena with your parents and me,' he said, 'when it is over, you will go to Fourviere in thanksgiving.' This seemed impossible to me, but I followed his advice anyway. On the fourth day I was able to get up; and on the ninth, I harnessed my horse myself and went to Lyons with my family."

Mrs. Marie Robert relates the following incident: "Fr. Vianney was teaching his eleven o'clock catechism class. I can still see him in his little stall next to the Blessed Virgin's altar. The coach arrived. All of a sudden the church door opened abruptly, causing us to turn our heads to look. Three people were there by the holy water font: a woman, and a man holding a child in his arms. Looking at these newcomers, Father Vianney said to them with a sigh, 'Poor people! You came so far to seek something here that you have at home! Your faith is great!' Then he went on with his catechism lesson. At the end, after reciting the Angelus, he spoke again to the father and mother in a loud voice, saying, 'Take your child to St. Philomena, over there to the left!' The unfortunates crossed the church and went to kneel before the statue of St. Philomena. Suddenly we heard a loud noise of moving chairs: the father had passed out *on hearing his son speak for the first time*. The six-year-old boy had been paralyzed, deaf and dumb from birth! 'Nice Papa, nice!' the child said in his native dialect, and he began to walk. The man explained to us, weeping with joy, 'We came to Ars to ask for the healing of our son, who has never talked and never walked.'" The accounts and documented testimonies of miracles truly goes on and on and on.

The union of heart between this old French prelate and this young Roman martyr is beautifully conveyed in the words of the late nineteenth century English prelate, Cardinal Manning, who wrote: "Mysterious and wonderful is the sympathy which thrills through the communion of saints, unbroken by distance, undimmed by time, unchilled by death! The youthful saint went forth from her mother's arms to die for Christ; the lictor's ax cropped the budding lily, and pious hands gathered it up and laid it in the tomb; and so fifteen centuries went by, and none on earth thought upon the virgin martyr who was following the Lamb withersoever He went, till the time came when the Lord would have her glory to appear; and then He chose a champion for her in the lonely toil-worn priest to whom he had given a heart as childlike, and a love as heroic as her own; he gave her to be the helpmate of his labors, and bade her stand by him to shelter his humility behind the brightness of her glory lest he should be affrighted at the knowledge of his own power with God."

The nineteenth and twentieth century Popes also manifest generous and consistent tribute and proper veneration to our Princess Saint. It begins with Pope Leo XII, who first gave permission that altars would be dedicated and chapels erected in her honor. Pope Gregory XVI, as we have discussed, declared her a Saint, raising her to the altar of the Church and granting her a special Feast of August 11. He also approved a special Mass in her honor.

Blessed Pope Pius IX also manifested a remarkable devotion to St. Philomena. In fact, the mother of Pius IX prayed to St. Philomena because Pius IX, as a child, had a problem with epilepsy. Her prayers were answered and, of course, much more. As bishop, Blessed Pius IX made many pilgrimages to the tomb of St. Philomena, and declared her "the patroness of the children of

Mary." At a critical time in the history of the Church, when this Holy Father had to flee Rome because of the Revolution of 1849, he made a pilgrimage to the tomb of St. Philomena. He went two hours south to Mugnano and knelt before the tomb of St. Philomena and begged the grace to return to Rome. He later confided that when kneeling before her bones he received "an interior certainty of his soon return to Rome" which took place. At the moment of his death, Blessed Pius IX had the pectoral cross removed from his chest and placed on the sacred remains of St. Philomena.

Pope Leo XIII, not be outdone, started the Archconfraternity of St. Philomena and with almost unprecedented generosity, he approved several plenary indulgences for the wearing of the Cord of St. Philomena. The Cord is white and red-colored in honor of the virginity and the martyrdom of St. Philomena. It was strongly promoted by the Cure', and some attribute to the Cure the origins of the Cord. Not only did Pope Leo XIII grant a plenary indulgence for the first moment of wearing the cord and three other times during the year, but he granted that anyone who wears the Cord of St. *Philomena will receive a plenary indulgence at the moment of death.* It is hard to imagine a better time to receive a plenary indulgence than at the moment of death!

Pope St. Pius X also had a tremendous devotion to St. Philomena. He beatified the Cure. He also advocated the wearing of the Cord and declared, "All the decisions and declarations of his predecessors regarding St. Philomena should in no way be altered." This is the remarkable papal and ecclesial support which this young Saint attained based solely on the power of her intercession. Such is the testimony of Popes and Saints alike of the real and miraculous intercessory power of this thirteen-year-old martyr of purity and Christian courage under persecution.

With so much devotion and support from Saints and Popes, it came as a significant surprise when in 1961 the Congregation of Rites, in a "historical purging" of the liturgical calendar, and without any question to her canonization, nor to the indulgences,

Conversations With St. Philomena

removed the feast of St. Philomena from the universal Church calendar. During the liturgical adjusting, the Congregation dropped a number of feasts of our Lord and the Blessed Mother and other Saints as well. A real irony of the reason given for dropping this feast was a lack of "historicity" concerning St. Philomena, and yet she was raised to the altar precisely *when there was no historical knowledge of her, but solely on the documented evidence and papal approved fact of the power of her intercession.*

What was behind this liturgical action? There was a Professor Marucchi who, in 1903, came up with some questionable archeological conclusions. In essence, Marucchi claimed that the three tiles on her grave were not in the correct order and this proved that the tiles had been taken off, St. Philomena's bones removed, and some other Martyr's bones had been put in their place. These claims were comprehensively countered and overturned by a number of historians and archeologists, particularly the Jesuit archeologist, Bonavenia, in 1907. He stated that it was a frequent custom in the catacombs to begin the epigraph on the second tile with the "Pax Te Cum" in the middle. Two recent archeologists, Praneli and Mistillo, after examining the actual tiles in 1963, claim that the position of Marucchi had no foundation for "during the process of going from first to second usage, chips would have very likely been made to the edges of the brick tiles... [these tiles] still have sound and undamaged matching edges along the line of fracture." Marucchi had not personally examined the tomb nor the tiles, but made only an abstract hypothesis without archeological research or evidence. The Austrian historian, Markhof, strongly criticized Marucchi's conclusions as "superficial and lacking historical objective."

How, then, are we supposed to respond to this liturgical directive? Pope Paul VI, Pope of the Second Vatican Council, gives us the answer. In an audience with Pope Paul VI, His Excellency Bishop Fernaneles of Mysore, India and head of the Cathedral of St. Philomena in India, asked the Holy Father how this liturgical directive was to be incorporated. The documented

xxviii

response of Paul VI was as follows: "Continue as before and do not upset the people." Let us follow that papal wisdom in union with an endless line of Popes and Saints and appreciate how the Church continues to bless devotion to a Saint, not an "historical abstraction" whom St. John Vianney spoke to and experienced as true, real, personal , and powerful.

Finally, let us look at the major forms of devotion to St. Philomena. First, there is the Cord of St. Philomena. The Cord is worn under one's clothing, tied around the body. The Cord is of wool, linen or cotton and is white and red in honor of the virginity and martyrdom of the young Saint. At one end of the Cord are two knots, again symbolizing our Saint's roles as virgin and martyr. No ceremony is required for conferring or wearing the Cord. The Cords can be obtained from St. Philomena Centers or you can make your own. There is a priestly blessing in the Roman Ritual for the Cord and a prayer that is recommended to be said daily:

"O, St. Philomena, virgin and martyr, pray for us that through your powerful intercession, we may obtain that purity of mind and heart which beats to the perfect love of God. Amen."

The Congregation of Rites has granted a plenary indulgence (the full removal from temporal punishment under usual conditions of 1) confession, 2) Eucharistic Communion, 3) prayers for the Holy Father, and 4) detachment from sin for wearing the Cord on the following days: the day on which the Cord is worn for the first time; on May 25 (the anniversary of the discovery of her body); on August 11, the Feast of St. Philomena; on December 15, the anniversary of the approval of the Cord; and, most remarkably, *at the moment of death* (without need to fulfill the other criteria, for obvious reasons).

The second form of devotion is the Oil of St. Philomena. There is an oil lamp that burns at the tomb of St. Philomena and oil coming from that lamp continues to be the physical instrument of countless cures throughout the world. I recently heard of one mother who had a child with night terrors. She started blessing the child with the oil of St. Philomena and they stopped entirely. One night she forgot to bless the child with St. Philomena's Oil and the terrors returned. The next night she blessed the child with the Oil again and they stopped. The Oil once again is a very powerful sacramental for healing and protection.

The third form of devotion is the Chaplet of St. Philomena. Initiated by St. John Vianney, it is an easy way to offer consistent prayer to St. Philomena. The Chaplet consists of praying the Creed, three Our Fathers in praise and glory to the three Persons of the Trinity, followed by 13 Hail Mary's in honor of the 13 years of St. Philomena's life. It ends with the invocation, "St Philomena, pray for us!"

The fourth mode of devotion is the Novena of St. Philomena, a method strongly recommended by the Cure' d'Ars. One Novena prayer reads:

"Oh faithful Virgin and glorious Martyr, St. Philomena, who works so many miracles on behalf of the poor and sorrowing, have pity on me. Thou knowest the multitude and diversity of my needs. Behold me at thy feet, full of misery, but full of hope. I entreat thy charity, O great Saint! Graciously hear me and obtain from God a favorable answer to the request which I now humbly lay before thee. (Here specify your petition.) I am firmly convinced that through thy merits, through the scorn, the sufferings and the death thou didst endure, united to the merits of the Passion and Death of Jesus, thy Spouse, I shall obtain what I ask thee, and in the joy of my heart I will bless God, who is admirable in His Saints. Amen."

Although answers to these Novenas manifest themselves in a great variety of favors, most common concerns include the special grace of purity and chastity, the spiritual and physical needs of families and especially children, physical cures of all types, and financial needs, especially at difficult times. All items of devotion -

- cords, oil, novenas, prayers and literature -- can be obtained directly by contacting the Sanctuary of St. Philomena at the following address:

> Sanctuary of St. Philomena
> Mugnano del Cardinale
> Avellino, Naples
> Italy

Their website is www.philomena.it. You may also contact one of the authorized St. Philomena Centers in the United States which acts as extensions of the Sanctuary.

In conclusion, I want to add a final encouragement, one that is the least objective: my own personal experience of this Miracle-Worker Saint. Indeed, I can echo the words of St. Augustine, "Late have I loved Thee," in reference to St. Philomena. This "Little Sister of the Mystical Body" has come late into my life, but with tremendous power. Her presence in my spiritual life and that of my family has brought great graces to our marriage, new peace and grace of purity into our family life, and newly resolved striving for courage under persecution and commitment to Christian holiness. Through her intercession, we have an almost tangible presence of this Saint for us in our home.

I invite you to welcome St. Philomena into your families, into your marriages, into your priestly and religious lives, into your hearts. Trust in her friendship. She and the Blessed Mother, who always accompanies her daughter, will not disappoint you.

St. Philomena, powerful with God, pray for us!

> Dr. Mark Miravalle, S.T.D.
> Professor of Theology and Mariology
> Franciscan University of Steubenville

Conversations With St. Philomena

Conversations
With
St. Philomena

Anchor of Hope from Heaven

Janie Garza

1996

Your Suffering Will Intensify

February 9, 1996

This morning I was awakened by my guardian angel. He guided me to our prayer room where I immediately felt the presence of St. Philomena. I do not know how I knew, I just did. Her presence was so strong that I was moved with deep emotion. I had been praying a novena to her for her intercession. I said the following prayer:

St. Philomena, please tell me what you want of me, if indeed you want anything. Then I prayed to the Holy Spirit:

O Holy Spirit, enlighten my heart, help me to discern clearly that this is truly St. Philomena. Holy Spirit, I cannot see anyone, but I truly know that there is a heavenly presence with me in this prayer room.

After the prayer, I heard these words:

St. Philomena: *Dear Janie, I am St. Philomena. Our Master has sent me to come to help you in your suffering. Know that I am truly here with you.*

Janie: St. Philomena, is there something that you wish me to do for you?

St. Philomena: *Dear Janie, I am here to help you to draw closer to Our Master.*

Janie: St. Philomena, I cannot see you. I can only hear you. Please

2

let me see you.

St. Philomena: *Dear Janie, it is not up to me to grant you this request. Only Our Master can do this.*

Janie: But won't you ask His permission?

St. Philomena: *Dear Janie, remain quiet and you will see me in your soul.*

I saw a young girl with ocean blue eyes and curly black hair, a very pretty girl who appeared to be about twelve or thirteen years old. She was wearing a long white dress with embroidered designs on it. It had long sleeves that were puffed from the shoulders to the elbows; then the sleeves became straight. From the waist up, the dress was gathered in little pleats.

St. Philomena: *Dear Janie, Lent is approaching. Prepare! During Lent your suffering will intensify. Our Master will visit you to comfort you. Know that it is a great heavenly privilege to be united in the Passion of Our Master. Do not doubt this suffering. The painful shoulder wound, which you have been experiencing, is also from Our Master.*
Dear Janie, during Lent abandon yourself completely to Our Master. Offer much sacrifice and many acts of mortification. Try to give up the things which you like so much in reparation, for your own purification, for your family and for poor sinners. During Lent, spend time praying more as a family, reflecting on the Passion of Our Master. Our Holy Mother and St. Joseph will help you much during Lent.

Janie: St. Philomena, will you help me to visit your shrine?

St. Philomena: *Dear Janie, you will be granted this favor. Our Master will help you in believing that I am truly coming to you. Trust Him, dear Janie. I must go now. I will intercede for all your petitions.*

Conversations With St. Philomena

Janie: She was gone and my heart was filled with joy.

Remain Loving During Difficulties

April 30, 1996

I only heard these words:

St. Philomena: *Remain loving, my little sister, Janie, especially in times of difficulty and suffering. In doing this you will not offend those who are causing you sadness.*

Then the Holy Spirit spoke these words: *Remain confident and determined and do all that God orders you to do.*

Anchor of Hope

May 1, 1996
Feast of St. Joseph the Worker

The Holy Family greeted me and I greeted them. The Archangels, St. Michael, St. Gabriel and St. Raphael, accompanied the Holy Family.

St. Joseph: *My little one, today is a special day for you. Today, you will see St. Philomena with the eyes of your soul. She will help you to embrace the call to holiness. She will be a very close friend and you will learn to love her very much.*

Janie: Beloved St. Joseph, I am most grateful to God for this great privilege.

Our Lady: *My angel, know that little St. Philomena will help you to desire purity more and more. Trust in her intercession. To St. Philomena God denies nothing, for she gives her all for love of Him. Embrace your little sister whom God has given as your Heavenly little sister.*

4

Our Lord: *My humble servant, my little sweet St. Philomena will help you to embrace Me, your Eucharistic Savior. Go to her with love in your heart.*

Janie: St. Michael, St. Gabriel and St. Raphael remained quiet.

St. Joseph: *My little one, you will also help St. Philomena. The more you know her, the more you will spread devotion to her. Many souls know of her and have devotion to her. You, my little one, will bring thousands of souls to St. Philomena. St. John Vianney had great love and devotion to her. You will also have great love and devotion to her.*

Janie: St. Joseph, how long will she be with me?

St. Joseph: *My little one, she will come every day to visit you and help you. She will also give simple guidance for families and their children. St. Philomena will delight you and fill you with heavenly surprises.*

Janie: Like what, St. Joseph?

St. Joseph: *My little one, in time you will know. Are you ready to see St. Philomena with the eyes of your soul?*

Janie: Oh, yes! Please hurry!

I saw a great light with angels all around and in the center stood a beautiful young girl dressed in a long white dress

Janie: St. Philomena, you are so beautiful and so young! Please tell me what it is you are coming for?

St. Philomena: *I come as the "Anchor of Hope" from Heaven to help families in these troubled times, especially to help the young children and the youth: to help them to understand that God wants them to remain pure and holy. I am the wonderworker of*

5

Conversations With St. Philomena

God for those who believe in my intercession.

Janie: Why did you come to me?
St. Philomena smiled and responded.

St. Philomena: *Why not you, dear Janie?*

Janie: Well, I don't know you nor do I have a devotion to you.

St. Philomena: *Do not be concerned about that. I shall tell you what you need to know about me later on as we continue to visit. My sweet Janie, I have given you all that you asked of me to help you to believe that I would be coming to visit you daily. Recall that in your prayers you asked me to give you a first-class relic of myself. You prayed with some doubt, thinking that your request would be hard to obtain. Recall how surprised you were and how you cried with great joy when you received my relic on Ash Wednesday. I continued to give you everything that you asked me as a confirmation of my visits to you. Know that Our Master chose you because you have great love for children and youth, for you suffered much during your own childhood and your youth. You understand what it is like to feel unloved or unwanted. You know about being abandoned and neglected as you were growing up. Nobody knew of your great suffering except God. You kept everything to yourself. As a child, you promised God that you would help all the children that suffer in the world by praying for them. You kept your promise to God, and you have dedicated your life to working with children and the young.*

My sweet Janie, know that through our prayers, many prayers will be answered. Through my relic, God will grant miracles to many. Many will recover from sicknesses, including mental illness. Many will return to their faith.

My little sister, this is enough for today. Until tomorrow, farewell!

St. Philomena said to pray for a pure heart, for a pure heart has no desire to sin. Today, we prayed for young pregnant mothers who

6

were contemplating abortion. St. Philomena said that our prayers saved 100 babies. Praise God for ever and ever!

St. Philomena's Prayer to God

May 2, 1996

St. Philomena offered this prayer to God during our visit.

St. Philomena: *Heavenly, Almighty, and Good God, please, we beseech Thee, hear the prayer that we entrust into Thy care.*

Today we implore Thy help to guide poor sinners to return to the sacraments. Good and Almighty God, reach out to these poor sinners who have lost their way and now live in darkness.

We know that Your mercy has no limit. Through our poor humble prayers, send these poor sinners Your Holy Spirit to enlighten their way and to help them to turn away from sin, to return to Your mighty love and mercy. Amen.

We prayed for all who reject God. St. Philomena has such a great love for poor sinners. During our visit all we did was pray together.

St. Philomena wants to be a friend to all who invoke her intercession. She especially loves all children and youth. She is much concerned about the killing of the unborn babies. This makes her very sad.

I feel so much closer to St. Philomena and I thank God for her.

God Wants Spouses to Love and Forgive One Another

May 3, 1996

St. Philomena: *Greetings from Heaven!*

Janie: Greetings, St. Philomena!

We prayed for special intentions and for broken marriages.

Conversations With St. Philomena

Janie: St. Philomena, how does God feel when people who are married by the church get a divorce?

St. Philomena: *It hurts God when a family suffers any problems. He loves His children with immense love. It is not God's desire that families suffer. He wants the family to trust Him. In this way, He can help them; then there will not be any reason for divorce. God wants spouses to love and forgive one another.*

Janie: St. Philomena, I am so grateful that God loves me and our family. I know now that God loves all people. Please pray for us.

St. Philomena: *My little sister, I will intercede for your special intentions. Remember, give God all your concerns with trust in your heart. Until tomorrow, farewell, little sister!*

Janie: Farewell, St. Philomena!

Pray for the Young

May 4, 1996

St. Philomena: *My little sister, today pray for all young people who do not believe in God. These young people have given themselves to Satan through the lifestyles that they have chosen.*

Little sister, please introduce me to all the young people that you know and who ask for your prayers and to those young people that you meet. Tell them that purity is pleasing to God, and when a soul loves purity, that soul has no desire to sin.

Today, offer all your prayers for all the young people in the world. Until tomorrow, farewell, little sister!

Janie: Farewell, St. Philomena!

The Suffering of Youth

May 5, 1996

St. Philomena: Greetings from Heaven, my little sister!

Janie: Peace to you, St. Philomena.

St. Philomena: *My little sister, today I ask you to continue to pray for the young people. There is so much sorrow in so many young people because they do not know God. These young people are so in need of much prayer and love. Poor little souls, how they suffer! Embrace them through your prayers and sacrifices, and let us both intercede for their conversion. Until tomorrow, farewell, little sister!*

Janie: Farewell, sweet St. Philomena! I will pray with you. The youth are most dear to my heart.

St. Philomena: *Little sister, I know that you love the young people with a special love. God will hear your prayers because your prayers are offered with love in your heart. God loves a loving heart.*

Dedicate May to Our Lady for Young People
May 6, 1996

St. Philomena: *Greetings from Heaven, little sister!*

Janie: Peace to you, St. Philomena.

St. Philomena: *Little sister, dedicate the rest of this month to the intercession of Our Lady for young people. This is the month in which Our Most Holy Queen and Virgin Mother is honored by recommending young people and children to her, she will take them all under her motherly protection. She will take care of all young people.*

Janie: St. Philomena, I will recommend all the children and youth to Our Most Holy Mother.

St. Philomena: *Until tomorrow, farewell, little sister!*

9

Conversations With St. Philomena

I was inspired to pray the following prayer to Our Lady:

"Prayer to Our Lady for Children and Young People"

Mother of Compassion and Love, Our merciful Queen, I recommend all the children and youth in the world to you, keeping in mind also the unborn. Pray for them, O Holy Mother, and protect them through your motherly mantle.

Let no harm touch them. Hold them tenderly to your bosom. Crush the head of Satan and drive him and his evilness far away from these precious souls. I place them all in your care, asking this in the name of your Son. Amen.

Pray for the Unborn, Children, Young People
May 7, 1996

St. Philomena: *Greetings from Heaven, my little sister!*

Janie: Peace to you, St. Philomena.

St. Philomena: *Little sister, continue to pray with your family for all the unborn, the children and the young people. Much goodness is already coming from your prayers. Many young people are returning to their faith. Many expectant mothers have decided not to abort their babies. Many parents are being better parents because of your prayers recommending all the unborn, the children and young people to Our Most Holy Mother.*

I, St. Philomena, encourage you to continue with these good intentions. Until tomorrow, farewell, little sister!

Janie: Farewell, St. Philomena!

God Will Be Your Strength
May 8, 1996

St. Philomena: *Greetings from Heaven, my little sister!*

Janie: Greetings, St. Philomena!

St. Philomena: *My little sister, I know that you are tired this morning. Be at peace. God will be your strength. I shall not stay long so that you may spend quiet time with Our Master in prayer.*
I shall return this afternoon after you put your little grandson down for his nap. Until then, farewell, little sister!

St. Philomena returned this afternoon and we spent quiet time praying for our Holy Father.

Encourage Parents to Ask for My Intercession
May 9, 1996

St. Philomena: *Greetings from Heaven, little sister!*

Janie: Peace to you, St. Philomena.

St. Philomena: *My little sister, today I ask you to continue to recommend my powerful intercession to all parents. So many parents have problems loving and accepting their children with all their shortcomings. Encourage parents to ask for my intercession and together, with their prayers united with mine, we will help their children.*
Pray also, dear little sister, for all the parents who physically and verbally abuse their children. To abuse these souls is most displeasing to God. There is so much violence and hatred in the hearts of families. This is one of the many reasons why parents abuse their children so much. Pray for these special intentions, little sister. Until tomorrow, farewell!

Janie: Farewell, St. Philomena!

My Powerful Intercession
May 10, 1996

St. Philomena: *Greetings from Heaven, my little sister!*

11

Conversations With St. Philomena

Janie: Peace to you, St. Philomena. St. Philomena, please help me to pray well. I become so distracted sometimes during prayer.

St. Philomena: *Little sister, when this happens call upon the Holy Spirit to give you the spirit of prayer of the heart. Continue praying, and soon the distractions will leave you.*

Little sister, I have so much to share with you concerning my powerful intercession with God. To all who invoke my intercession, I am able to obtain for them the purity of spirit and of heart that leads to a perfect love of God. I desire that souls turn to me and invoke my intercession. Prayer is the great force that the world needs. I will keep a constant vigil of prayer for all who ask me to pray for their special intentions. God will grant many favors to those who trust in my help.

Little sister, I so enjoy our visits together. Please never forget that you are dear to me. Until tomorrow, farewell! I will continue to share more about me.

Janie: Farewell, St. Philomena.

Our Master Is So Sad

May 11, 1996

St. Philomena: *Greetings from Heaven, my little sister!*

Janie: Peace, St. Philomena.

St. Philomena: *Little sister, Our Master is so sad, for many who attend Holy Mass do not even acknowledge that He is truly present in the Holy Eucharist. Souls do not come prepared to receive Our Master because they do not take the time to pray.*

This is offensive to God Who gave to the world His only begotten Son to help them to draw closer to His love and mercy. Our Master is so offended. Pray, little sister, that souls will believe in prayer. Until tomorrow, farewell, little sister!

12

St. Philomena was so sad today.

All Those Who Take Our Lord's Name in Vain
May 12, 1996

St. Philomena: *Greetings from Heaven, my little sister!*

Janie: Peace to you, St. Philomena.

St. Philomena: *My little sister, continue to pray your Rosary for all those who take Our Lord's name in vain. This blasphemy is so offensive to God.*

Janie: St. Philomena, I know that people use Our Lord's name in vain. This hurts me also, but I always used profanity when I lived apart from God. I know now how much I offended our good God. I am so sorry for all the wrong I've done.

St. Philomena: *Little sister, God knows that you have repented. He has forgiven you. Pray for all souls who repeatedly offend God; please pray for all these souls. Until tomorrow, farewell, little sister!*

Janie: Farewell, St. Philomena!

After our visit, I continued to ask God to help me not to separate myself from His love. St. Philomena wished me a Happy Mother's Day and asked that I intercede for all mothers.

Pray For Those in Danger of Losing Their Virginity
May 13, 1996

St. Philomena: *Greetings from Heaven, my little sister!*

Janie: Peace, St. Philomena.

13

Conversations With St. Philomena

St. Philomena: *My little sister, today I wish to ask you to pray for all the young people who are in danger of losing their virginity. These are the young people who are searching for someone to love them. Satan does all he can to place temptations before them.*

Janie: St. Philomena, are these people girls or boys?

St. Philomena: *Little sister, these souls, which I am asking you to pray for, are both young males and females. They are so lost because their parents did not demonstrate love towards them as they were growing up.*

Janie: St. Philomena, I worked with these types of young people and they were good kids, but it was as you said. There was no love in their family. Will my prayers help these young people to remain pure?

St. Philomena: *Yes, little sister! Oh, yes! Your prayers will help them to remain strong and not to fall into temptation. Please, little sister, pray for these lost souls that have no one to turn to. Until tomorrow, farewell, little sister!*

Janie: Farewell, St. Philomena!

St. Philomena was very sad today because she loves souls so much.

For Wounded Hearts

May 14, 1996

St. Philomena: *Greetings from Heaven, my little sister!*

Janie: Peace, St. Philomena. St. Philomena, my heart is still sad because of all the young people who have no one to turn to. I recommend them all to you. I shall pray with you for these young people.

St. Philomena: *My little sister, know that prayer is the strong medi-*

14

cine needed to heal the woundedness of hearts. Prayer reaches to the ends of the world. Prayer is powerful and effective, and it helps whoever you are praying for, no matter how near or far these souls may be. Prayer is even more powerful when you fast, but Satan will discourage you from praying and fasting. Be strong, little sister, and protect all these innocent young souls through your prayers. Until tomorrow, farewell, little sister!

Janie: Farewell, St. Philomena! I will pray for all these young souls.

Pray For Priests Who Suffer for Love of Our Master
May 15, 1996

St. Philomena: *Greetings from Heaven, my little sister!*

Janie: Peace to you, St. Philomena.

St. Philomena: *Little sister, pray for all the priests who suffer for their love of Our Master. Pray for their sanctification, that they may continue responding to the call to holiness. Keep the Bride of Our Master in your constant prayers. Until tomorrow, farewell, little sister!*

Janie: Farewell, St. Philomena!

I understood that there is much suffering and persecution within the Church. We must always remember to pray for all the priests and religious.

Pray That More Souls Respond to All of His Love
May 16, 1996
The Feast of the Ascension of Our Lord

St. Philomena: *Greetings from Heaven, little sister!*

15

Conversations With St. Philomena

Janie: Peace, St. Philomena. Please pray for me. Today is the day when Our Lord comes to visit with me.

St. Philomena: *My little sister, today will be for you a day filled with much joy. Pray and prepare for your visit with Our Master. Pray that more souls will respond to all of His love. Until tomorrow, farewell, little sister!*

Janie: Thank you, St. Philomena. I will prepare.

All Who Invoke My Name Become My Special Friends
May 17, 1996

St. Philomena: *Greetings from Heaven, my little sister!*

Janie: Peace, St. Philomena. My dear little saint, could you tell me how you help those who have devotion to you? I know that you have many devotees. I know that many souls are coming to know more of you.

St. Philomena: *My little sister, it is true that I have many devotees. You have helped many souls know of me by introducing me to them. I thank you.*
Know that I help those souls who have devotion to me by leading them to understand the necessity of the salvation of the soul. I am able to help souls to respond to the call to holiness. I am able to help souls to have a hunger for purity and for love of God.
All who invoke my aid and trust in my aid become my special friends. These friends, in turn, help me to bring poor sinners to the mercy of Our Master. This is how I help my devotees. Until tomorrow, farewell!

Janie: Farewell, St. Philomena.

Pray For Marriages Everywhere

May 18, 1996

St. Philomena: *My sweet Janie, I shall not stay long, for you are most tired from working so hard in helping your husband build your home. God is pleased with your standing by your husband and being at his side when he needs you. Pray for marriages everywhere, especially for marriages that are suffering because they do not have the love of God in their lives. Farewell, little sister! Sleep now.*

Janie: Thank you, St. Philomena! Give God my gratitude and love.

I Bring You His Blessing

May 19, 1996

St. Philomena: *My sweet Janie, God knows that you are very tired. I, His humble servant, bring you His blessing. Rest and sleep well, beloved of God. Until tomorrow, farewell!*

I was very tired because I had been helping my husband build our home. St. Philomena came to bring me God's blessing. She reassured me that she was interceding for our family and our home project.

Social Justice and Poor Families

May 20, 1996

St. Philomena: *Greetings from Heaven, my sweet Janie!*

Janie: Hello, St. Philomena!

St. Philomena: *Let us pray together:*

O Father, we implore Thy help for poor sinners for their conversion. Help those who suffer from social injustice and for all the poor families that are dying of hunger. Amen.

Conversations With St. Philomena

Janie: St. Philomena, what does God think of people wasting food?

St. Philomena: *It makes God very sad when people do not recognize the blessings that He gives them. It is not good to be wasteful of food or anything else when there are so many poor people who suffer because they have no one to think of them. Sweet little sister, your country is guilty of being very wasteful. Pray for your country.*

Janie: Please pray for my special intentions.

St. Philomena: *I shall intercede for all your special intentions. Until tomorrow, farewell, sweet little sister!*

Janie: Thank you. Farewell, until tomorrow!

Reflection of the Holy Family

May 21, 1996

St. Philomena: *Good morning, my sweet little sister, Janie!*

Janie: Good morning, dear St. Philomena!

St. Philomena: *Let us implore the help of the Father for the needs of the world today:*
Dear Father, we implore Thy help for all people today. Invest people everywhere with Thy love and especially, Father, parents and children everywhere. (When St. Philomena refers to children, this includes all ages from birth to the youth.)
Shower Your blessings and graces on all hearts that lie open to Your truth. Invest parents with the fire of Thy love so that they may reflect Your spirit. Help them to love their children and to teach them about Your goodness, so that their children may learn about purity and holiness.
Protect all children who have no one to love them or to pray

18

for them. Show Thy mercy to their parents and forgive them for abandoning their responsibilities as parents. Let Thy light shine on those families walking in darkness. Amen.

Janie: St. Philomena, what is God's desire for the world?

St. Philomena: *To repent and to be truly sorry for their sins.*

Janie: What about the people who are living by God's Holy Will or trying to?

St. Philomena: *For these people, God wants them to pray for unbelievers in the world. He wants them to pray, pray unceasingly for these poor sinners.*

Janie: Does praying for unbelievers really help?

St Philomena: *Oh, most certainly! Prayers help to bring God's light to others whose hearts are closed. Your prayers are like heavenly water that helps souls blossom like heavenly flowers. Your prayers for others are so helpful, so helpful! Never forget this.*

Janie: St. Philomena, what words does God have for parents and for their children, young and old?

St. Philomena: *God wants parents, together with their children, to be a reflection of the Holy Family: to love and forgive one another, to pray together and to desire purity and holiness. God loves purity and holiness, for He is purity and holiness.*

Janie: How do parents and children obtain purity and holiness?

St. Philomena: *Through prayer and perseverance and living the holy messages that the Blessed Virgin, Thy Mother, is giving to the world.*

Janie: St. Philomena, please tell me what do we as parents do for our older children who do not believe in prayer any longer?

19

Conversations With St. Philomena

St. Philomena: *Continue to pray for them unceasingly and love them. Never stop loving souls who turn away from the love of God. Never judge, but guide them gently, being patient and loving towards them.*

Janie: Thank you, St. Philomena. Pray for the special intentions for my family.

St. Philomena: *I shall pray for these special intentions. Until tomorrow, my sweet little sister! Continue to love purity and holiness. Pray for unbelievers everywhere. Farewell!*

Janie: Farewell, St. Philomena.

Abandon This Situation into God's Hands

May 22, 1996

St. Philomena: *Greetings from Heaven! My sweet Janie, I know that you are tired and that you have suffered much. Abandon this situation into God's hands. Remember how Our Master suffered for love of us. He was persecuted and many evil things were said of Him, but nothing prevented Him from doing the Will of His Father. Be like Him, pleasing only God and be at peace. Goodnight, my sweet Janie. Farewell, until tomorrow!*

Janie: Thank you so much for knowing what was troubling me. Give the Holy Family a big kiss and hug for me. Farewell, St. Philomena.

Lack of Prayer is Destroying Many Families

May 23, 1996

St. Philomena: *Greetings from Heaven, my sweet Janie!*

Janie: Good morning, dear little friend!

We prayed for all priests.

St. Philomena: *My sweet Janie, do not be concerned for your little grandson. All will go well with him.*

Janie: St. Philomena, are there many children without parents in the world?

St. Philomena: *Oh, yes, so many! What is so sad is that most of these children have parents, but their parents do not want them.*

Janie: St. Philomena, what does God want parents to do for their children, especially the youth?

St. Philomena: *God is concerned about the lack of spirituality among the children and the youth. These precious souls are being influenced by the evils in their society. Many parents are poor examples for their precious offspring, and this drives the children and youth farther from God's love.*

Janie: St. Philomena, please tell us what to do.

St. Philomena: *Pray, asking God for mercy. Prayer is what the world is lacking. Lack of prayer is what is destroying many families and leading them on the road to perdition.*
Parents must turn to God for help and God will listen to their cry, but it must be a cry of true repentance. Parents' prayers are strong and protect their children. This is why I urge parents everywhere to pray for themselves and their offspring.

Janie: What about the children and youth who are prayerful?

St. Philomena: *These precious souls are a delight to God. I encourage these prayerful little soldiers to form an army of prayer warriors for God by being an example to their peers and teaching others about the kingdom of God.*

21

Conversations With St. Philomena

Janie: St. Philomena, how can I help?

St. Philomena: *By sharing all that I tell you with others.*

Janie: May I continue to start prayer groups of young people and little children as I travel where God calls me? May I ask these young people to name these prayer groups after you?

St. Philomena: *My sweet Janie, this is most kind of you. I am delighted and it would be most pleasing to God for you to do this. I shall be present with all who call on my intercession. Until tomorrow, my sweet Janie. Let us keep in our prayers all children in the world, praying for their purity and holiness. Farewell, until tomorrow!*

Janie: I will offer my prayers and my Mass for these petitions. Farewell, St. Philomena.

God Will Not Disappoint or Abandon You
In Your Time of Need
May 24, 1996

Janie: Thank you, St. Philomena, for coming!

St. Philomena: *Greetings from Heaven, my little sister! Let us pray.*

Her prayer was for all the unborn, the children and the youth. She loves them so much.

St. Philomena: *My dear Janie, you are suffering.*

Janie: Yes, I don't know what to do about meeting with X. I am nervous about this situation.

St. Philomena: *My sweet Janie, abandon yourself to the Most Holy Will of God. Remain confident and determined in doing the will of God by being obedient to the indwelling of the Holy Spirit within your heart. God will not disappoint or abandon you in your time of need.*

You must fast and pray for this situation. Keep your eyes on Our Master and do not allow any obstacle to come between you and Him. Our Master knows your heart and your good intentions to follow Him. Trust Him Who gave His life for love of you. My dear Janie, share with your family the suffering in your heart.

Janie: St. Philomena, I will trust Our Master, I promise. I will not allow myself to become distracted in this situation. I am grateful for the answer to my prayer about my little grandson concerning his healing. You told me that everything would go well and it did. Also, thank you for helping my older son to obtain a job. I only asked you a day ago and already you helped him. Thank you so much.

St. Philomena: *I will help all who ask me to help them. Until tomorrow, my sweet Janie. Remember, trust Our Master. Farewell!*

Janie: Farewell, St. Philomena.

Many Souls Are Blind

May 25, 1996

St. Philomena: *Greetings from Heaven, my sweet Janie!*

Janie: Thank you, St. Philomena.

St. Philomena: *Let us pray.*

We prayed for conversion in our world. We prayed for the protection of the unborn. The horror of abortion is the ultimate abuse of God's little gifts from heaven. St. Philomena refers here

23

to Holy Scripture, Jesus' words: "Let the children come to Me and do not stop them, because the kingdom of heaven belongs to such as these." (Matthew 19:14)

St. Philomena: *My little sister, you are undergoing much suffering in reparation for poor sinners. Know that God is with you as you suffer.*

Janie: I don't mind suffering. I just do not want to fall out of the grace that God gives me. It's so hard to see families not loving one another and all the division that comes from unforgiving souls.

St. Philomena: *My sweet Janie, many souls are blind, for they have fallen from the love of God. These souls are very distant from God and they are surrounded by darkness. We must pray especially for these poor souls.*

Janie: St. Philomena, I had a dream last night. Can you tell me, is there any significance to this dream?

St. Philomena: *Yes, my sweet Janie. God spoke to you through your dream. He revealed to you how it is for those souls who reject His invitation to enter into His love and mercy. In your dream the Eternal Father spoke to your soul of how offended He is by all the deaf ears that ignore His calling to His immense love. Those who reject Him will not know of His great love.*

Janie: Please pray for my soul, St. Philomena. I am in need of much prayer. I want so much to be Christ-like and to love with His love. Help me please.

St. Philomena: *My sweet Janie, do not worry. God is with you. Continue to model yourself after Our Master. I will pray for your request. Until tomorrow, farewell!*

Janie: Farewell, my dear sweet St. Philomena!

Anchor of Hope from Heaven

God is Blessing You Because of
Your Dedication to Your Grandson
May 26, 1996

St. Philomena: *Greetings from Heaven, my little sister!*

Janie: Peace to you, St. Philomena.

St. Philomena: *My little sister, how are you feeling today?*

Janie: I am feeling all right. I have been very tired. My little grandson keeps me pretty busy, so sometimes I am tired.

St. Philomena: *Little sister, God is blessing you in countless ways all because of your dedication to taking care of your grandson.*

Janie: I know that God is blessing me. I couldn't do all this without His help, but it sure helps to hear this from you.

St. Philomena: *Little sister, what you are doing for your grandson right now will serve as a blessing in his own life. He will remember you with love in his heart. Until tomorrow, farewell!*

Janie: Farewell, St. Philomena and thanks!

The Cord of St. Philomena
May 27, 1996

St. Philomena: *Greetings from Heaven, my little sister!*

Janie: Peace, St. Philomena. My dear friend, could I ask you about your cord? People believe in your cord. Forgive me for asking, but do people receive special favors by wearing your cord?

St. Philomena: *My little sister, God has granted many favors through my intercession for those who wear my cord with faith in*

25

their hearts. Those souls who wear my cord simply do it only as an observance of their devotion to me. In return, I protect all devotees who wear my cord. Through my intercession, these souls are protected from evil of body and soul.

Janie: St. Philomena, I will tell people about your cord. Please understand that I mean no disrespect. I only wanted to know more about the cord. I shall wear one myself.

St. Philomena: *Be at peace, little sister. I am happy to help you to understand more about the cord that the faithful wear as a sign of their love and devotion to me. Until tomorrow, farewell, little sister!*

Janie: Farewell, St. Philomena!

The Holy Spirit Will Direct You
On How to Spread Devotion to Me
May 28, 1996

St. Philomena: *Greetings from Heaven, my little sister!*

Janie: Peace to you, St. Philomena. Please pray for me, St. Philomena, so that I may be courageous in spreading devotion to you. I want the whole world to know you. I love you in a special way. You are a dear friend. Tell me how to spread devotion to you.

St. Philomena: *My little sister, pray to God to send you His Holy Spirit to enlighten your heart. The Holy Spirit will direct you on how to spread devotion to me. I am grateful to you, little sister, for the love and devotion that you have for me. Until tomorrow, farewell, little sister!*

Janie: Thank you, St. Philomena.

26

Spouses in Danger of Separation

May 29, 1996

St. Philomena: *Greetings from Heaven, little sister!*

Janie: Peace to you, St. Philomena.

St. Philomena: *Little sister, I ask that you join me in prayer for all spouses who are in danger of separation.*

Janie: St. Philomena, do you mean breaking up as husband and wife?

St. Philomena: *Yes, this what I mean! As I speak to you, there are thousands of spouses who are entertaining the thought of ending their relationships. These spouses will bring much sorrow to their children. Please, little sister, let us embrace these broken families through our prayers. Know for certain that our prayers will truly help these poor suffering families. Until tomorrow, farewell!*

Janie: Farewell, St. Philomena.

Encourage Youth to Turn to God During Evil Temptations
May 30, 1996

St. Philomena: *Greetings from Heaven, little sister!*

Janie: Peace to you, St. Philomena. St. Philomena, as you well know, our youth are confronted with many evil temptations throughout the day. What words do you have to help the youth in dealing with these evil temptations?

St. Philomena: *Little sister, I, St. Philomena, encourage the youth to remain strong in their faith and to turn to God for strength during these evil temptations. I encourage these young people to trust God in everything. In order to have trust in God, the youth must*

27

Conversations With St. Philomena

learn to pray more, to desire holiness and purity of heart. God will not abandon those who call out to Him in times of trouble. I encourage the youth to love God with all their hearts, for God loves them. Until tomorrow, farewell, little sister!

Janie: Farewell, St. Philomena.

Representatives of My Master

May 31, 1996

St. Philomena: *Greetings from Heaven!*

Janie: Good morning, St. Philomena! Thank you for coming.

St. Philomena: *Let us pray.*

Today, St. Philomena and I prayed for all families who do not believe in God and who turn their children against God by setting a poor example.

Janie: St. Philomena, I cannot thank God enough for you. Today, I have a very special intention concerning my X.

St. Philomena: *Little sister, do not concern yourself with anything, but abandon it into the hands of Our Master. He will see to your request. I shall intercede for all your special intentions.*
Little sister, continue to pray for all the youth that are walking in darkness. They are so lost, and if they continue to choose darkness, they will perish. So many souls go to hell because there is no one interceding for them. Never forget to pray for unbelievers, for they are in great need of prayer.
Satan keeps souls as his prisoners when they choose darkness and live by his evil ways. He especially seeks to corrupt little children and youth, so that they may grow up and become evil souls.
This is why I have come as the "Anchor of Hope" from Heaven to

28

tell parents, children and youth to choose purity and holiness, not evil.

I beg all of the representatives of my Master to teach according to God's Most Holy Will. I beg all of my Master's representatives who have abandoned His love to please return back to your Master Who loves you and weeps for you. Remember, as representatives of Jesus, you are His examples and you must follow Him Who died and rose for you.

You are called to be Christ-like and to live pure and holy lives, so that through your example you may lead many souls to Heaven. Be loving, charitable and patient with all souls, no matter who they may be. Do not scold them or reject them, but make time for them when they seek your help. Offer your assistance even when they do not ask. All must see Christ in your good example. Do not worry about anything. God will give you His grace to accomplish all things. Do not seek popularity, but rather seek holiness and purity of heart.

Until tomorrow, little sister! Thank you for being so patient in listening. Farewell!

Janie: Farewell, St. Philomena!

The Importance of Forgiveness

June 1, 1996

St. Philomena: *Greetings from Heaven, little sister!*

Janie: Peace to you, St. Philomena.

St. Philomena: *Little sister, let us pray.*

We prayed together. We both thanked God for blessing the world with Jesus, Mary and St. Joseph. St. Philomena shared with me that God valued the unity of family so much. For this reason, God chose St. Joseph and Our Lady to be the parents of His only

29

Conversations With St. Philomena

begotten Son. God wanted the world to value the role of the family. I asked St. Philomena to pray for a special intention. She responded.

St. Philomena: *My sweet Janie, do not be concerned with this matter. I will take your request to Heaven.*

Janie: St. Philomena, today you have been with me for one month. I thank God for you. Do you have anything more to share with me?

St. Philomena: *My sweet Janie, I wish to convey to you the importance of forgiveness. So many souls are so miserable because they do not believe in forgiveness. Others do not know how to forgive.*

Lack of forgiveness comes from the devil, for he knows that God's peace cannot exist in souls that do not forgive. Lack of forgiveness destroys families everywhere and destroys friendships in many cases. People do not understand that God will not forgive those souls who refuse to forgive others. This prideful attitude leads many to perdition. Pray for this special intention, little sister. Until tomorrow, farewell!

Janie: St. Philomena, please pray for my very special friend who is getting married today. Farewell, St. Philomena!

Blessing Families Through the Most Holy Trinity
June 2, 1996
Trinity Sunday

St. Philomena: *Greetings from Heaven, little sister!*

Janie: Peace, St. Philomena.

St. Philomena: *Little sister, today is a special day for all those who live by faith, doing God's Holy Will on earth. Today, God is blessing all the families throughout the world. God's blessings are being*

Anchor of Hope from Heaven

bestowed on the family through the Most Holy Trinity. The Holy Trinity is the essence of the Family of God the Father, God the Son, and God the Holy Spirit. Today is a glorious day for families everywhere. Show God your gratitude by embracing the Holy Trinity through your family. Until tomorrow, farewell, little sister!

Janie: Farewell, St. Philomena! I will embrace the glorious Trinity on this day.

Victims of Abuse
June 3, 1996

St. Philomena: *Greetings from Heaven, little sister!*

Janie: Peace to you, St. Philomena. St. Philomena, please pray for our trip to Medjugorje.

St. Philomena: *Little sister, embrace in your prayers all those children who are victims of abuse. There are millions of children who are in danger of losing their lives through the abuse inflicted upon them.*

Janie: St. Philomena, this saddens my heart. I will pray, I promise. Farewell, St. Philomena.

St. Philomena was very sad.

For Those Who Suffer Persecution and Social Injustice
June 4, 1996

St. Philomena: *Greetings from Heaven, my sweet Janie!*

31

Conversations With St. Philomena

Janie: Greetings, St. Philomena!
   Today we prayed for all who suffer persecution and social injustice because of their faith. These souls are priests, bishops, cardinals and religious. These precious souls are the ones who spend much time in prayer and believe with all their heart in the True Presence of Our Lord in the Eucharist.
   St. Philomena's visit was short due to my suffering.

Love and Pray for Children Who Have Gone Astray
June 5, 1996

St. Philomena: *Greetings from Heaven, my sweet Janie!*

Janie: Greetings, St. Philomena!
   Today we prayed for all the unbelievers in reparation for their sins.

Janie: St. Philomena, what advice do you have to give the loving parents who have been good in teaching their children all about God, but whose children have gone astray from their faith? Many parents share their pain with me and many of them blame themselves. Give us advice from Our Master.

St. Philomena: *My sweet Janie, tell parents to continue to love and pray for their children who have chosen to separate themselves from the love of God. Tell them that if they have done everything required as parents, then now is the time to place them at God's disposal. Parents need to remember that their children have free will, a gift from God. Tell them not to blame themselves, but to learn from Holy Scripture especially the parable of the two sons (Luke 15: 11-32).*
   Encourage all parents who suffer for their children to forgive them, to love them and to pray for them without passing judgment on them. When their children return, they must all give thanks to God for the return of their children. They, too, should celebrate and

32

rejoice for God's love and mercy upon their children. Until tomor-row, my sweet loving friend. Farewell!

Janie: Farewell, St. Philomena.

Continue To Pray

June 6, 1996

St. Philomena: *Greetings from Heaven, little sister.*

Janie: Peace to you, St. Philomena.

St. Philomena: *Little sister, you are suffering for your X. Continue to pray for her. God knows that you love her very much. Until to-morrow, farewell, little sister!*

Janie: Farewell, St. Philomena. Thank you for your words.

I was suffering much this day.

Accept God's Mercy and Healing in Your Life

June 7, 1996

St. Philomena: *Greetings from Heaven!*

Janie: Thank you, St. Philomena

St. Philomena: *Let us pray.*

We prayed for world peace.

St. Philomena: *My dear little sister, Janie, do not be concerned with calling your doctor to ask for details. Accept God's mercy and healing power in your life. God healed you; let this be enough for you.*

33

Conversations With St. Philomena

Janie: Please ask God to forgive me for trying to find out about my test. I wanted to have proof in writing that God had worked a miracle in my life by healing me. I want to give witness of this miracle, but I will do as you ask.

St. Philomena: *Little sister, God is always sending His healing power through His mercy to all who trust Him. You demonstrated that trust by not allowing worry to disturb you in a difficult situation. You glorified God by trusting Him.*

Janie: I am forever grateful and so is my family, especially my husband.

St. Philomena: *God hears all prayers that come from the heart. My dear sister, you are helping many souls come to know more about me. I wish to thank you. Many souls are asking for my intercession and I intercede for all who ask for my help. I am delighted, again I thank you.*

Janie: St. Philomena, thank you for everything that you have given me. What can I do for you today?

St. Philomena: *Pray with me for all families that live in darkness because they have no faith in God. Offer your suffering for all children and youth to be protected from the violence in their parents' hearts.*

Janie: What do you mean, St. Philomena?

St. Philomena: *My sweet sister, many parents cause much harm to their children through physical abuse. Many, many parents are killing their children and their unborn. Violence is destroying the entire family. Many parents need to repent for all the evil in their hearts. The most dangerous wars are the wars in the hearts of families. Pray for this request of mine. Until tomorrow, farewell, my sweet Janie!*

34

Janie: Farewell, St. Philomena!

Unite With Me In Prayer for Families

June 8, 1996

St. Philomena: *Greetings from Heaven, my little sister!*

Janie: Greetings, St. Philomena!

We prayed for special intentions for me.

St. Philomena: *My sweet Janie, do not be concerned with the information that you received regarding the messages that Our Mother gave you. Abandon everything in God's hands and leave everything at His disposal.*

Janie: St. Philomena, I will follow your advice. I trust Our Master; He knows what is best for me. Do you have anything for me to do for you?

St. Philomena: *I wish to tell you that you are doing quite well in abandoning everything to Our Master. Your yearning to follow all that He tells you is pleasing and consoling to Him. Jesus, Our Master, is pleased with your hard efforts. I encourage you to continue to unite with me in prayer for the families in the world. There are good families that lead good and simple lives. These families console Our Master and Our Lady. The families that live in darkness are the reason for the sorrow and tears of Our Master and Our Holy Mother. Pray for these families for God loves them with immense love.*

My dear sister, Heaven is so beautiful. There is only love, peace and joy. Everyone in Heaven is eternally happy for they are with God. There is no sadness or tears in heaven. The souls have no desire or longing for anything. They have everything, for they are with God.

I tell you this so that you may work and pray unceasingly for your own sanctification and the sanctification of poor sinners.

35

Conversations With St. Philomena

Through your prayers and sacrifices, many souls will convert. Until tomorrow, farewell, little sister!

Janie: Farewell, St. Philomena!

God Will Send a Warning

June 9, 1996

St. Philomena: *Greetings from Heaven!*

Janie: Greetings, my sweet little saint!

St. Philomena: *Let us pray.*

We prayed for all the coming tribulations so that God would grant us mercy.

St. Philomena: *My little sister, these are troubled times in which there is much violence in the world. Souls are not listening to the warnings that God is sending them. All the pestilence and calamities that exist in the world are the result of the sinfulness of the unbelievers who hate God and His goodness.*
Our Master is much offended. Souls must turn away from sin. Our Master cannot continue to see the brutal murder of the innocent souls being killed in their mothers' wombs. The horrible abuse of children and young people continues to pierce Our Master's heart.
God will send a warning to the world and many souls will come to know and believe that there is a Mighty God. People will realize that they will have to give God an account of all their actions. Pray that hearts will convert before it is too late. Farewell, until tomorrow!

Janie: Farewell, St. Philomena!

36

Pray For the Protection of Our

June 10, 1996

Janie: Greetings!

St. Philomena: *Let us pray.*

Today, we prayed for the Church and for her holiness and purity. We prayed for our Holy Father, Pope John Paul II. St. Philomena loves the Pope very much because he represents Our Master.

St. Philomena: *Little sister, pray with me for the protection of Our Master's Bride. Our Master loves her so much. There are many divisions and many obstacles in the Church that cause great sorrow to Our Master. Pray for His Bride and console Him. Farewell, until tomorrow!*

Janie: Farewell, St. Philomena.

Families Who Pray Together

June 11, 1996

St. Philomena: *Greetings from Heaven!*

Janie: Greetings!

St. Philomena: *Let us pray.*

We prayed for the purity of heart for all families.

St. Philomena: *Little sister, pray for all the families who pray together. These families are the ones that console the Sacred Heart of Our Master and the Immaculate Heart of Mary. The family that prays together reaps a treasure of graces for themselves. Their children grow up like healthy precious flowers. These children are protected by their parents' prayers. They seek purity and they learn to reject and flee from sin. Oh, how God blesses these families!*

Conversations With St. Philomena

Prayer is a powerful weapon for all of God's creation, but many souls do not believe this. They do not pray and they bring on themselves and their children such misery. Pray with me so hearts will desire to pray. Until tomorrow, farewell!

Janie: Farewell, St. Philomena!

This Young Generation Caught in the Web of Sin
June 12, 1996

St. Philomena: *Greetings from Heaven!*

Janie: Hello, St. Philomena! I am happy to be with you.

St. Philomena: *Let us pray.*

We prayed for all who are suffering with terminal illnesses. St. Philomena pleaded with Our Lord to send these souls someone to be with them to console them in their illness.

Janie: St. Philomena, please forgive me for meeting with you so late. I am always so busy with my family obligations and sometimes it's hard for me to hurry and free myself for our visit.

St. Philomena: *My little sister Janie, God is most pleased that you care for and love your family. You see to all their needs. Do not be concerned about all your family obligations. Know that God gives you the grace to endure and accomplish your daily tasks.*
My sweet Janie, please I beg you, continue to unite with my prayers for the family. Our Lady is so concerned about the children and the youth who are growing up without the love of God in their hearts.
All these young souls suffer so much because they do not pray. They grew up in homes where there was no one praying, for they did not believe in God. Our Lady cries with great sorrow for all those of this young generation who are caught in the web of sin. There was no one to teach these poor young souls about God. Their

38

parents were busy with their own lives, not paying attention to the existence of their children. (Here St. Philomena is referring to the young people who were raised up in homes where their parents did not believe in God.)

Pray with me so that together we may console Our Most Holy Mother. Offer all your suffering for the conversion of these young souls. Until tomorrow, farewell!

Janie: Farewell, St. Philomena!

Forgiveness Sets a Soul Free

June 13, 1996

St. Philomena: *Greetings from Heaven!*

Janie: Greetings, St. Philomena!

Today we prayed for people to respect and live by God's commandments.
Janie: St. Philomena, tell me, what does God feel about our lack of forgiveness?

St. Philomena: *My little sister, God is forgiving and merciful. He wants His people to reflect His love and mercy. People must forgive and not harbor vengeful thoughts. Recall Holy Scripture, "If anyone slaps your right cheek, let them slap the left cheek, too." You must love and forgive all who persecute you and mistreat you. You must imitate Jesus when He was treated so cruelly by those who tortured Him.*

Forgiveness sets a soul free. Sin keeps a soul in bondage. God loves a forgiving soul, because God Himself is forgiving. Pray for forgiveness in the world. Until tomorrow, farewell!

Janie: Farewell!

Conversations With St. Philomena

With My Master in Prayer

June 14, 1996

St. Philomena: Greetings from Heaven!

Janie: Greetings, St. Philomena!

St. Philomena: *Let us pray.*

St. Philomena prayed for me and my special intentions for my family.

St. Philomena: *Little sister, do not be concerned with your prayer life. If only you could realize how many poor sinners you are helping with your prayers and sacrifices. Do not allow Satan's lies to overshadow your mind. God is pleased with your love for people everywhere. Smile and rejoice.*

Janie: Oh, sweet St. Philomena! Thank you for your kind words. I get upset with myself when I feel I am distracted while in prayer. I want to give God my all and my best.

St. Philomena: *My sweet Janie, you are giving God your all and the best that you have. You give constantly of yourself to others out of love for God. You make yourself available to your family and souls whom God puts in your path. You are indeed God's humble servant. Do not forget this.*

Janie: St. Philomena, how did you spend your time when you lived with your parents? What did you do?

St. Philomena: *My little sister, I spent all my time with my Master in prayer. I had chores to do, but I always did all my chores with great joy in my heart, for I knew that once I did this for my parents, I could be with Our Master. This was my greatest delight and joy, to be in prayer with Our Master. My parents loved me very much and they were happy that I conducted myself obediently.*

40

Janie: St. Philomena, why did you vow your virginity to Our Lord? Did something happen, like a visit from Our Lord that made you do this?

St. Philomena: *My little sister, from the time that I was born to the time that I took my first step, my parents felt in their hearts that I was blessed in the eyes of God and that I would in some way help others. While I was growing up, many times I could see angels in the area where I played. They were my playmates and it was through their visits that I vowed my virginity and my all to Our Master. My playmates were lovely spirits filled with holiness and purity. I wanted to model after them.*

My little sister, this is all for today. Tomorrow, I shall continue to share with you whatever you wish to know about me. Farewell for now!

Janie: Farewell, St. Philomena!

Indeed the Mother of All

June 15, 1996

St. Philomena: *Greetings from Heaven!*

Janie: Greetings, St. Philomena!

St. Philomena: *Let us pray.*

We prayed for souls that reject Our Lady as their Most Holy and Heavenly Mother. St. Philomena prayed for God's love and mercy to penetrate the depths of their hearts.

Janie: St. Philomena, thank you for that prayer.

St. Philomena: *Little sister, it saddens God that many souls reject Mary as their Heavenly Mother, but His heart is filled with love*

41

and mercy for these souls. He gives His Mother to a world living in much sin, but She is rejected just like His Son was rejected.

The day is soon coming when the world will understand that Most Holy Mary is indeed Mother of all. Pray for souls to accept the most pure love of Mary, Thy Mother. Farewell, my sweet sister. Until tomorrow!

Janie: Farewell, St. Philomena!

Holy Mass Has Priority Over All Other Matters

June 16, 1996
Father's Day

Janie: Good morning, St. Philomena!

St. Philomena: *Greetings from Heaven, dear little sister! Let us pray.*

Today, St. Philomena prayed for all husbands and fathers in the world. We asked God to help especially those husbands and fathers who harbor unforgiveness, resentments and hate. Because there is no love in their hearts, they do not have God in their lives.

We prayed for all husbands and fathers that are following and living God's Most Holy Will. We asked God to keep them from all evil and temptation.

Janie: St. Philomena, I must get ready to go to Holy Mass. Could it be possible that we continue our visit later?

St. Philomena: *My little sister, Holy Mass has priority over all other matters. Prepare to go to be with Our Master. We shall continue our visit later on today.*

Janie: Thank you, St. Philomena.

Later that morning after Holy Mass

Janie: St. Philomena, thank you so much for being patient with me. Please pray for me and my family so that we may continue on our faith journey together. My family is sweet and supportive of me. I love them very much and they love me.

St. Philomena: *My little sister, when a family has the love of God in their hearts, there is joy in that family. There is no obstacle that a family cannot overcome together, for God is their strength. Farewell, until tomorrow!*

Janie: Farewell, St. Philomena!

When Parents Pray Together

June 17, 1996

St. Philomena: *Greetings from Heaven!*

Janie: Greetings, St. Philomena!
Today, we prayed for all parents to have a deep desire to be holy parents.

Janie: St. Philomena, how can parents be holy together? Many times only one parent prays and the other does not. Many parents do not believe in prayer. How can they become holy?

St. Philomena: *My dear Janie, prayer is the key to salvation. When parents pray together, they draw closer to God and to one another. When only one parent prays, this parent helps the other parent to convert. The prayers of parents that pray together lead to the conversion of those parents who do not pray.*

Remember that Our Blessed Mother teaches that only through prayer, one discovers God. Prayer is powerful because it is the only tool to destroy Satan. God hears all prayer, whether it is one person or thousands. Until tomorrow, farewell!

Janie: Farewell!

Conversations With St. Philomena

Charity Must Reign in Hearts

June 18, 1996

St. Philomena: *Greetings from Heaven!*

Janie: Greetings, St. Philomena!

Today we prayed, asking God to teach His people to pray from the heart so that His love may live in their hearts.

St. Philomena: *My little sister, today pray for people everywhere. Many have gone astray from the love of God. Pray also for the virtue of charity in God's people. Many are the souls that die of starvation because those who can help lack the virtue of charity in their hearts.*

Charity must reign in hearts in order to give shelter to the homeless, clothe the naked, visit the sick and those in prison, feed the hungry and provide to all who are in need. God is generous in His graces and blessings. In order to reflect Our Master, souls must be generous in their charity, for this is a great demonstration of their love for their neighbor. Until tomorrow, farewell, my little sister!

Janie: Farewell! I shall pray for everything you ask of me.

Angels Encamp in Homes Where Families Pray Together

June 19, 1996

St. Philomena: *Greetings from Heaven!*

Janie: Greetings, St. Philomena! Thank you for coming.

St. Philomena: *Let us pray.*

We prayed for God's blessings upon all hearts that believe in His goodness and for poor sinners.

44

Janie: St. Philomena, thank you so much for helping me yesterday to see all the positive things in my family. Thank you for teaching me that they, too, suffer because they have to always be ready to share me with so many people.

Thank you for telling me that God is pleased with the support that my family gives me. I was tired and I was listening to all the lies of Satan concerning my family.

St. Philomena: *My sweet Janie, God loves your family very much because of your "yes" as a family to harvest the hearts of families through the heavenly messages that you have received.*

Families are so special to God. His angels encamp in the homes where families pray together. God's blessings fall upon families that live to please Him. Showers of blessings spread like raindrops upon every member of the family, from the youngest to the oldest.

God has chosen your family to help other families learn the importance of family prayer. Many are the families that have been blessed through your charitable family love.

My sweet sister, I know how tired you are and how your hand is hurting because you have to write all that I tell you. You must rest now. Until tomorrow, farewell, little vessel of God!

Janie: Farewell, St. Philomena!

Ask For the Powerful Intercession
of St. Joseph For All Children
June 20, 1996

St. Philomena: *Greetings from Heaven!*

Janie: Greetings, St. Philomena!

Today we prayed for those souls who are most distant from God.

Conversations With St. Philomena

Janie: St. Philomena, could you please tell me more about yourself?

St. Philomena: *My sweet Janie, I will share more of myself with you during the eighth month.*
My sweet Janie, pray with me for the safety of all children. Do not forget the unborn. Ask for the powerful intercession of St. Joseph. He protected Our Master when King Herod ordered the death of all boys who were two years old or younger. St. Joseph was chosen by the Mighty God to be the protector of the Child Jesus and His Most Holy Mother.
The unborn, little children and young people are in great danger, for Satan seeks to destroy the younger generation. Pray, asking St. Joseph to watch over these precious souls who need God's love. Until tomorrow, farewell!

Janie: Farewell, St. Philomena!

The Army of Mary

June 21, 1996

St. Philomena: *Greetings from Heaven, my dear sister!*

Janie: Greetings, St. Philomena!

St. Philomena: *Let us pray.*

Today we prayed for the Bride of Christ, beginning with His Vicar and all His flock. St. Philomena prayed in a special way for the Marian Movement of Priests. She prayed for Fr. Gobbi and all the priests that will be in retreat this following week.

St. Philomena referred to the Marian Movement of Priests as the precious gold in the world, gold that is being tested and purified through much persecution and suffering. St. Philomena said in her prayers that these beloved of God are the treasures of the Immaculate Heart of Mary.

Janie: St. Philomena, thank you for this prayer. I love Fr. Gobbi and all the priests consecrated to Our Lady's Immaculate Heart.

St. Philomena: *My sweet Janie, God's blessings and graces upon these beloved sons and daughters of Most Holy Mary are without limits. These sweet and precious souls are the army of Mary, ever Virgin, Mother of All Creation. These are the souls that move through the world planting the seeds of salvation. They are saving precious souls from the abyss of perdition. Keep them always in your prayers.*

Most Holy Mary has picked this movement of her beloved ones to impregnate every soul with the love of her Son, Jesus Christ. These beloved children of Most Holy Mary are God's representatives in a world walking in darkness. They bring the light of Jesus into the dungeons of many, many who live in darkness. These beloved children of Most Holy Mary are like the sun that illuminates the day and moon by night. These beloved ones are precious to Our Lady and loved so by her. Whatever they ask of her as their Holy Mother, she immediately presents to her Son. He denies her nothing. Love and pray always for their work. Until tomorrow, farewell!

Janie: Farewell, St. Philomena.

An Act of Contrition to Our Master

June 22, 1996

St. Philomena: *Greetings from Heaven!*

Janie: Greetings, St. Philomena!

We prayed for God's peace in all hearts. St. Philomena prayed for families everywhere.

Janie: St. Philomena, I had a terrible day. I was so tired and I was cranky.

St. Philomena: *Abandon all your concerns to God, little sister. Say*

47

Conversations With St. Philomena

an Act of Contrition to Our Master and leave all your misery in His hands. He knows your heart.

Janie: St. Philomena, please thank God for your coming to me. Please help me to obtain holiness and purity of heart. I want to only serve God with my everything.

St. Philomena: *My sweet Janie, God loves you very much and all your little sacrifices are pleasing to Him. He gives you His grace to serve Him. He knows that He is your Lord and Master. Rejoice! Until tomorrow, farewell!*

Janie: Farewell, St. Philomena!

Children Are Treasures from Heaven

June 23, 1996

St. Philomena: *Greetings from Heaven!*

Janie: Good evening, St. Philomena!

Tonight, St. Philomena prayed for the special intentions of me and my family.

Janie: St. Philomena, I am sorry that I couldn't meet with you earlier, but I was babysitting my grandchildren.

St. Philomena: *My little sister, do not worry. God is pleased that you are doing this to help your husband so that he can have more help to build your home.*

Janie: St. Philomena, I was harsh when dealing with my grandchildren. I am sad about that.

St. Philomena: *My little sister, you were not harsh. You are truly trying to teach them how to love and get along together. God knows that your grandchildren need much love and guidance. You are that*

48

person who is doing this for them. Do not allow Satan to put lies in your mind.

Janie: Thank you for these kind words. I needed to hear this.

St. Philomena: *My little sister, children are treasures from heaven. No child is bad, only misguided. Children are innocent and they model what they see and hear. Their parents and caretakers should see to their spiritual well-being. Children are a joy to God. He loves them very much. Always remember this. Until tomorrow, farewell!*

Janie: Farewell, St. Philomena!

I, St. Philomena, Speak to the Young People
June 24, 1996

St. Philomena: *Greetings from Heaven, my little sister!*

Janie: Greetings, St. Philomena, my little friend!

Today we prayed for the Bride of Our Lord Jesus. St. Philomena asked Our Lord to purify the heart and soul of every priest and religious, to remove all stain of sinfulness. She asked God to heal their hearts of every painful memory and to help them to forgive others and to love everybody.

Janie: St. Philomena, thank you for this most beautiful prayer.

St. Philomena: *My little sister, Janie, I know that today is the day that you suffer and offer all your prayers for the Bride of Our Master. I know this because Our Master told me that He had made this request of you from the very beginning when He and His Mother came to you. I thought this prayer might make you happy.*

[Note: On Mondays Janie offers her suffering for the Church.]

49

Conversations With St. Philomena

Janie: Yes, it did! Thank you so much. Please give me guidance or words for the youth who are trying to live by God's Most Holy Will.

St. Philomena: *I, St. Philomena, speak to the young people. Do not be afraid of abandoning relationships that will lead you into mortal sin and separate you from God's love. Be bold in your love for Our Lord, as He was bold and loving in carrying His Cross for love of you.*

Remember, my young little friends, purity and holiness are pleasing to God. You live in a world corrupted by sinfulness, and you encounter many obstacles as you try to lead good lives. Do not fear. God is with you. Trust in Him. He will never abandon you, but you abandon Him when you choose to sin.

My little friends, you do have a choice to lead good and pure lives or to lead sinful lives. Flee from sinful and evil influences, just as you would flee from a poisonous snake whose venom would kill you. Sin kills your soul.

Abandon bad language, gossip, evil music and friends that seduce you into fornication, to drugs, to injuring or killing other young people. Respect and love yourself, for God loves and respects you. Respect and love your parents, your family and all people.

Be ready to suffer persecution from others bravely, rather than to offend and deny Almighty God. Have a true horror for sin and desire only holiness and purity. Have complete confidence in your prayers, and God will help you in all that you need to do His Most Holy Will.

I, St. Philomena, will intercede for all you ask of me. I shall present all your requests to Our Holy Mother. She will present them to her Son, Jesus. Be prayerful and be brave for God, my little friends. My sweet Janie, this will be all for today. Until tomorrow, farewell!

Janie: Thank you, St. Philomena. Farewell!

Pray for All the Division Within the Church
June 25, 1996

St. Philomena: *Greetings from Heaven, little sister!*

Janie: Greetings, St. Philomena!

We prayed for special intentions for my family.

Janie: St. Philomena, tomorrow I shall be asked questions about you concerning our visits. Is there any thing in particular I should say?

St. Philomena: *My little sister, God will speak to you through the Holy Spirit, and you will know what to say.*

Janie: Thank you, St. Philomena for helping me.

St. Philomena: *My sweet Janie, pray with me for all the division within the Church, Our Master's Bride. Our Master loves His Bride so much, and it truly hurts Him to see His Bride suffering. Pray for this special intention. Until tomorrow, farewell, little sister!*

Janie: Farewell, St. Philomena!

All Your Prayers and Sacrifices Are Important
June 26, 1996

St. Philomena: *Greetings from Heaven, my sweet Janie!*

Janie: Greetings, St. Philomena!

Today, we prayed for peace, love and purity in the world.

Janie: St. Philomena, how can we help to change hearts who do not believe in God?

St. Philomena: *My dear Janie, your prayers and sacrifices will help change the evil ways of the world.*

Janie: What kind of prayers and sacrifices are you talking about?

Conversations With St. Philomena

St. Philomena: *All your prayers and sacrifices are important. Holy Mass, Eucharistic Adoration, fasting and praying your Rosary are very powerful prayers to save thousands of souls from the abyss of perdition. Know that God accepts all forms of prayer in reparation for the salvation of souls.*

Janie: St. Philomena, please help us all through your intercession to do the Holy Will of God. Pray for us so that we may get along as a family. So many families do not love one another. Please take this request to Our Master.

St. Philomena: *I shall do this for you, little sister. Until tomorrow, farewell!*

Janie: Farewell, St. Philomena!

Souls That Suffer From Mental Illness

June 27, 1996

St. Philomena: *Greetings from Heaven!*

Janie: Greetings, St. Philomena!

We prayed for all who suffer mental illness and for those souls who are mentally handicapped. St. Philomena asked God to cover them with His love and to heal them.

Janie: St. Philomena, it is very sad to know that there are many souls that suffer from mental illness.

St. Philomena: *My little sister, always keep all these souls in your prayers. They suffer because they are very wounded. Most of their woundedness occurred early during their childhood. These souls never recover, for they have no one to love them and pray for them.*

Janie: Dear St. Philomena, why does this happen to them or how?

52

St. Philomena: *My sweet Janie, these souls are suffering because they did not have God in their lives, so they turn to other things like drugs, unhealthy relationships and many things that corrupted their lives.*

Their illness originates from not believing in God's love and mercy. These souls, because of their woundedness that was brought on by family members, developed numerous fears. They feel unloved; they do not love themselves or others. They feel paralyzed in their lives and they feel like they will never amount to anything.

Pray for these souls, little sister, and I will speak to you more on souls that suffer from mental illness. Until tomorrow, farewell!

Janie: Farewell and thank you, St. Philomena!

No Visit

June 28-29, 1996

No visit due to my schedule being very busy and traveling to Medjugorje. My guardian angel told me that St. Philomena had been praying for me so that I would accomplish all my tasks.

Prayers for the Pilgrimage

June 30, 1996

St. Philomena: *Greetings from Heaven, my little sister!*

Janie: Ave, St. Philomena.

We prayed for our pilgrimage so that we would be open to God's blessings.

That Their Hearts Will Be Open

July 1, 1996
Medjugorje

St. Philomena: *Greetings from Heaven, my little sister!*

53

Conversations With St. Philomena

Janie: Ave, St. Philomena.

We prayed in thanksgiving to God for bringing us to Medjugorje safely.

St. Philomena: *My little sister, pray for all persons who came with you on this pilgrimage, that their hearts will be open to the blessings which God wishes to give them. God cannot help them if they do not open their hearts. When they return home, they will return with sad hearts. Until tomorrow, farewell!*

Janie: Farewell, St. Philomena!

Offer Your Sacrifices for All Representatives of God
July 2, 1996
Medjugorje, Apparition Hill

St. Philomena: *Greetings from Heaven, my little sister.*

Janie: Ave, St. Philomena.

We prayed for priests to be strong in their faith.

St. Philomena: *My sweet Janie, offer your sacrifices for all the representatives of God. Many are very weak in their faith and in their love for Our Master.*
You will be privileged to have the honor of being visited by Our Master and His Most Holy Mother while you are here. They will come to you beginning today. Pray and prepare your heart.

Janie: Farewell, St. Philomena.

A Silent Visit
July 3-5, 1996
Medjugorje

St. Philomena came with Our Lord and Our Lady and she told

54

me that she would pray with me for all the intentions of Jesus and Mary. She did not share during this time, since she came to me in their company.

St. Philomena's Intercession

July 4, 1996
Medjugorje

St. Philomena again came with Our Lord and Our Lady. She was interceding for me because I was asked to pray for special intentions of Our Lord and Our Lady.

For All Pilgrims

July 5, 1996
Medjugorje

St. Philomena again came with Our Lord and Our Lady. She assured me of her intercession for me and all who are visiting Medjugorje.

For All of Medjugorje

July 6, 1996
Medjugorje

St. Philomena came tonight with Our Lord and Our Lady. She told me that she was praying for all of Medjugorje.

Trusting in My Intercession

July 7, 1996
Paris, France

St. Philomena: *Greetings from Heaven, little sister!*

Janie: Ave, St. Philomena.

Conversations With St. Philomena

We prayed for all the pilgrims on this trip and their families back home.

St. Philomena: *Little sister, I will continue to intercede for all those souls that have devotion to me. I will pray for all of them and for their special intentions. Give them my gratitude for trusting in my intercession. Until tomorrow, farewell!*

Janie: Farewell, St. Philomena!

A Little Soldier of Heaven

July 8, 1996
Paris, France

St. Philomena: *Greetings from Heaven, little sister!*

Janie: Ave, St. Philomena.

We prayed for a safe trip back home.

St. Philomena: *Little sister, you have received much during your stay in Medjugorje. Ponder everything in your heart. Know that the evil one will try to set every trap before you. He will ambush you with his temptations. Be brave during these difficulties and know that you have been clothed with the spiritual weapons to destroy him. You are a little soldier of heaven, fighting for the kingdom of God and for lost souls.*
As you journey back to your country, do not forget to pray for all the families and pilgrims who visited Medjugorje. Until tomorrow, peace and farewell!

Janie: Farewell to you, St. Philomena. I will keep in mind all that you have told me.

Thank Him For Blessings

July 9, 1996

St. Philomena: *Greetings from Heaven, little sister!*

Janie: Peace, St. Philomena.

St. Philomena: *Little sister, embrace God and thank Him for blessing you with special graces as you visited very holy places during your pilgrimage. I am interceding for you.*

Today, St. Philomena came to tell me that she is praying for me.

I Am Interceding for You

July 10, 1996

St. Philomena: *Greetings from Heaven, little sister!*

Janie: Peace, St. Philomena.

St. Philomena: *Little sister, I know that you are tired from your trip. Know that I am interceding for you. Peace, little sister, peace.*

Janie: Peace to you, St. Philomena.

For the Six Individuals Chosen in Medjugorje

July 11, 1996

St. Philomena: *Greetings from Heaven, little sister!*

Janie: Peace to you, St. Philomena.

St. Philomena: *Little sister, let us pray for the six individuals who were chosen by Our Lady in Medjugorje. These special souls give so much of themselves to others. Keep them in your daily prayers.*

Conversations With St. Philomena

Much good is coming to many souls through these special souls. Until tomorrow, farewell!

Janie: Thanks, St. Philomena.

For the Conversion of Souls Who Live in Darkness
July 12, 1996

St. Philomena: *Greetings from Heaven, little sister!*

Janie: Peace, St. Philomena.

St. Philomena: *Little sister, keep praying for the conversion of all souls who live in darkness. God will help poor sinners through your prayers. I know that you are very tired. Until tomorrow, farewell, little sister!*

Janie: Farewell, St. Philomena!

God Sent the Most Holy Mother
July 13, 1996

St. Philomena: *Greetings from Heaven, little sister!*

Janie: Ave, St. Philomena.

We prayed for souls who do not have God's love in their hearts. We prayed for God to send the flame of His love into these poor sinners.

St. Philomena: *My little sister, you have been very busy bringing the love of Thy Mother, Our Queen of Angels, into many hearts. God is pleased with your hard efforts and perseverance.*

Janie: St. Philomena, thank you for these words. I want so much for all souls, not only Catholics, to know Our Blessed Mother. I want everyone to embrace her as their Mother. This is why I asked Our Lord to help me to bring Dr. Bartholomew to our city. He is so dedicated to the work of Our Lady. He loves her very much and he refers to Our Lady as "Her Majesty," the only name most appropriate for her.

St. Philomena: *My little sister, you have done well in bringing this most humble servant of Our Holy Mother to your city. Many souls are now more aware of her great importance in the kingdom of God and in the world. Many have rejected her throughout time, but now she is being made known by the works of her humble son, Dr. Bartholomew. Many are beginning to understand her important presence in a world walking in darkness.*

God sent the Most Holy Mother to help her sinful children return back to His Son through her messages to the world. God wishes to thank you, your family and all who participated in bringing His humble son, Dr. Bartholomew, to your city. The blessing and graces received during these two days are without limit. Thank you, little sister. Until tomorrow, farewell!

Janie: Farewell, St. Philomena!

Trust God in Your Suffering

July 14, 1996

Today, I was not feeling well. I was suffering for special intentions. St. Philomena's visit was very short.

St. Philomena: *My little sister, know that I am interceding for you. Rest and trust God in your suffering. Farewell, until tomorrow!*

Janie: Farewell, St. Philomena!

Conversations With St. Philomena

Offer This Feeling of Dryness

July 15, 1996

St. Philomena: *Greetings from Heaven, little sister!*

Janie: Ave, St. Philomena.

We prayed for souls that never pray. St. Philomena asked God to allow my suffering to draw these souls closer to His love.

Janie: St. Philomena, please intercede for me so that I do not lose my spirit of prayer. I feel like I am in the desert; my soul feels dry.

St. Philomena: *Little sister, offer this feeling of dryness to Our Master and know that He is with you in a powerful way. He is calling you to a deeper relationship with Him. Trust that He is with you at all times, no matter how you feel.*

Janie: St. Philomena, I do trust Our Lord and I will keep in mind all that you tell me.

St. Philomena, please pray for my special intentions and pray for the completion of our home and our chapel.

St. Philomena: *My sweet little sister, I will pray for all your intentions.*

Janie: Today, I don't think that I can attend Holy Mass, so I have to offer this up. My little grandson is ill and I won't have a way to go to Mass. This is a great suffering for me.

St. Philomena: *Little sister, God knows your situation. Do not be distracted with this, but spend quiet time in prayer. Offer your suffering to God. Until tomorrow, farewell, little sister!*

Janie: Farewell, St. Philomena!

Private Visit from Our Lady

July 16, 1996
Feast of Our Lady of Mt. Carmel

I had my visit with Our Lady and St. Philomena came with her. She told me that she would be interceding for my special intentions.

For All the Children and Youth

July 17, 1996

St. Philomena: *Greetings from Heaven, little sister!*

Janie: Ave, St. Philomena.

We prayed for all the children and youth who are orphaned, and the children and youth who live on the streets because they have no one to love them.

St. Philomena: *Little sister, God is pleased that you have spent much time with Him in quiet prayer. He knows that you are tired, but He will refresh you. Today, continue to pray with me for all the children and youth in the world. Until tomorrow, farewell!*

Janie: Farewell, St. Philomena!

Souls That Lost Their Loved Ones

July 18, 1996

St. Philomena: *Greetings from Heaven, little sister!*

Janie: Ave, St. Philomena.

We prayed for special intentions.

St. Philomena: *Little sister, you are suffering for all the souls that lost their loved ones in the plane crash (TWA 800). These next few days will be most painful for you. I will be with you in your suffering. Until tomorrow, farewell!*

Janie: Farewell, St. Philomena.

I did not sleep at all last night. I suffered all night for these poor souls who lost their loved ones. My suffering is indescribable. I feel so much sorrow.

Suffering For the Families of the Victims

July 19, 1996

St. Philomena: *Greetings from Heaven, little sister!*

Janie: Ave, St. Philomena.

St. Philomena: *Little sister, know that I am interceding for you in your great suffering. Until tomorrow, farewell!*

Janie: Farewell, St. Philomena.

St. Philomena came to console me. I have been suffering for the tragedy that took place Wednesday (the TWA 800 plane crash). I was asked to offer my suffering for all those poor souls whose loved ones were killed in the terrible crash.

This is the second night that I did not sleep in reparation for the families of the victims of the plane crash. There are no words to describe the agony in my soul.

A Soul Is Never Tested Beyond Its Strength

July 20, 1996

St. Philomena: *Greetings from Heaven, little sister!*

Janie: Ave, St. Philomena!
Today, we prayed for all who suffer from mental illness. St.

Philomena asked Our Master to heal all souls who suffer with this terrible illness.

Janie: St. Philomena, I again ask you to please continue to intercede for me that I may stay prayerful through this dryness of my soul.

St. Philomena: *My little sister, God is utilizing this suffering that you are experiencing for the conversion of poor sinners. Recall their invitation to you when Our Master and Our Lady first came to you. They invited you to a time of prayer and suffering in reparation for poor sinners. You, with permission from your spouse, accepted this invitation.*

Our Master has made known to you that during your life you will endure much suffering. Abandon yourself to God Who knows everything. Remain prayerful and steadfast and the Holy Spirit will comfort you in your suffering. You are helping to draw many souls back to God.

Little sister, keep in mind all the destruction and the violence in the world. There is much evil in many hearts. People have forgotten their Creator. They have forgotten how to pray. There is no peace in many parts of the world because people do not believe in prayer. There is no peace without prayer. This is the very reason why you suffer for these souls. Be assured that there are other souls who suffer in reparation for poor sinners.

Remember, little sister, a soul is never tested beyond its strength. God chose you for this task and it is a great privilege to be united in suffering with Our Master. Trust Him. Until tomorrow, farewell, little humble one!

Janie: Farewell, little sweet Philomena! Thanks for everything.
Last night was the third night without sleep in reparation for the families of the victims of the plane crash. My lack of sleep and my prayers have been offered up for this intention. I feel exhausted, but God has sent me St. Gabriel to give me strength for the past three days. Praised be God forever and ever.

Conversations With St. Philomena

You Will Encounter Suffering

July 21, 1996

St. Philomena: *Greetings from Heaven, my little sister!*

Janie: Peace to you, St. Philomena. My dear heavenly little sister, please intercede for my oldest son. Today is his birthday.

St. Philomena: *My sister, I, St. Philomena, will ask Our Master to bless your son with special graces on his birthday. Little sister, your own birthday is only a few days away.*

Janie: I know, St. Philomena, and on this day the Holy Family will visit me. I am so excited.

St. Philomena: *My little sister, prepare for this glorious day with strong prayers. You will encounter suffering during the next three days. Be strong. Your suffering is for the special intentions of Our Holy Mother and her Son.*

Janie: Farewell, St. Philomena.

Embrace All the Unborn Children and Youth of the World

July 22, 1996

St. Philomena: *Greetings from Heaven, little sister!*

Janie: Ave, St. Philomena.
    We prayed for all the troubled youth in the world who do not believe in God.

St. Philomena: *Little sister, embrace all the unborn children and the youth in the world. Offer your prayers and fasting for this special intention. You shall not regret it but will experience joy as you pray and fast for this request. Farewell, little sister!*

Janie: Farewell, St. Philomena!

Do Not Be Distracted With Any Worries

July 23, 1996

St. Philomena: *Greetings from Heaven, little sister!*

Janie: Ave, St. Philomena.

Today, we prayed for families who suffer from hunger. We asked God to provide what these families need through our intercession for them.

Janie: St. Philomena, I thank you for being so patient with me. Lately I have been suffering much and I had so much to do for my family.

St. Philomena: *Little sister, know that I am interceding for you during these difficult times that you are having. Do not be distracted with any worries. Remember, God sent me to help you and to pray with you and for you during your suffering.*

Janie: St. Philomena, please ask God to give me the courage and patience to embrace my suffering.

St. Philomena: *I, St. Philomena, will intercede for you, little sister.*

Janie: Farewell, St. Philomena.

Many Are the Miracles Through My Intercessions

July 24, 1996

St. Philomena: *Greetings from Heaven, my little sister!*

Janie: Peace to you, St. Philomena.

Conversations With St. Philomena

St. Philomena, I know that you are very powerful with God, so I ask you to intercede for all the unconverted family members outside of my immediate family.

St. Philomena: *Little sister, it is true that God grants me countless favors to help bring many souls to His Beloved Son. Many are the miracles that souls have received through my intercessions. I will joyfully intercede for all souls which you recommend to me. I am honored that you place much faith in my intercession.*

Janie: St. Philomena, I don't know as much about your life as I should, but I really trust in your intercession.

St. Philomena: *My little sister, invite souls to trust in my intercession. I shall help all who ask for my assistance. Until tomorrow, farewell, little sister!*

Janie: Farewell, St. Philomena, my heavenly friend!

A Glorious Visit From the Holy Family

July 25, 1996

St. Philomena: *Greetings from Heaven, my little sister!*

Janie: Peace to you, St. Philomena.

St. Philomena: *Little sister, tomorrow is your birthday and you will receive a glorious visit from the Holy Family. I shall come with them as well. These past few days have been hard for you. Tomorrow, you will be very happy. Prepare and look for tomorrow with joy in your heart. Until tomorrow, farewell, little sister!*

Janie: Farewell, St. Philomena!

St. Philomena to Remain
July 26, 1996

Today is my birthday. St. Philomena came with the Holy Family. My gift from God today is that God has granted me a prayer request concerning St. Philomena.

About a month or so ago, I had a thought during prayer that it would be good for me if God would allow St. Philomena to remain with me and not stop her visitations in October. St. Philomena is helping me to understand my suffering and she helps me to draw closer to God. This is why I was thinking during my prayer that it would be good for St. Philomena to remain with me.

Today was a joyful day for me. Words cannot express how happy I am to have St. Philomena come to me everyday. Praised be God forever and ever. Amen.

God Is With You In Your Time of Suffering
July 27, 1996

St. Philomena: *Greetings from Heaven, little sister!*

Janie: Ave, St. Philomena.

St. Philomena prayed for me because I was ill with a virus.

St. Philomena: *Little sister, I will stay with you a very short time for you are not feeling well. Know that God is with you in your time of suffering. Abandon everything to Him. Until tomorrow, farewell!*

Janie: Thank you, my sweet St. Philomena!

Restore the Faith of Fallen Priests
July 28, 1996
Caldwell, Texas Retreat

St. Philomena: *Greetings from Heaven, little sister!*

Conversations With St. Philomena

Janie: Ave, St. Philomena.

We prayed for the first day of our prayer retreat tomorrow.

St. Philomena: *My little sister, offer to God all your prayer and supplications during the time that you are on retreat. Know that it will be a special time when God will use your prayers and sacrifices to help His Church.*

Your prayers during these next few days will help restore the faith of fallen priests. This is why Satan was so active trying to keep you from coming to spend time in prayer. He was strong in his attacks and made things difficult for you and your family.

My little sister, God is happy that you and His beloved sons and daughters responded to His call to pray for the many needs in the world. God will make known His intentions to you. Until tomorrow, farewell, little sister!

Janie: Thank you, St. Philomena.

Pray Especially For All The Fallen Priests
July 29, 1996
Caldwell, Texas Retreat: Day 1

St. Philomena: *My little sister, continue to offer your prayers and supplications for the Bride of Our Master. Pray especially for all the fallen priests who are eager to leave this vocation. Pray for the renewal of their faith, for the faith of many priests is in need of great renewal.*

God is pleased with your prayers during this time of intense prayer. Listen with your heart and do everything that Our Lady is asking of you. Our Lady needs the prayers and sacrifices of the littlest of her children to help her beloved priests.

These few little children of Our Lady will make a great difference in the conversion of many of her beloved fallen priests. Know, little sister, that it is these fallen priests that cause Our Master great sorrow, for He loves His brothers with immense love. Your prayers during this time are consoling Our Master who is in need of much consolation. Until tomorrow, farewell!

Janie: Farewell, St. Philomena.

Pray the Rosary for My Wounded Bride
July 30, 1996
Caldwell, Texas Retreat: Day 2

St. Philomena came to pray with me during my retreat. This was very personal.

Later, St. Philomena came again. She encouraged me to keep the youth in my prayers. The youth are so much under attack. This was the subject of St. Philomena's visit today. I was then visited by Our Lord.

Jesus: *My humble servant, I ask that today you pray for My wounded Bride. Offer your prayers for my intentions. I ask that you pray the Rosary for My divine peace to enter into the heart of My Bride.*

Janie: Master, you want us to pray the Rosary for Your Bride? How many decades?

Jesus: *Pray fifteen decades three times for My divine peace to return to the hearts of many of My beloved brothers.*

Janie: Very well, Master. I will convey this request to the group.

Jesus: *I am most grateful, My humble servant. My Bride is so wounded. Your prayers will help.*

Later that morning, Our Lady visited.

Our Lady: *My sweet angel, I have come to thank you for respond-*

Conversations With St. Philomena

*ing to my Son's request so quickly. You have brought joy to my Im-
maculate Heart. I shall remain with you throughout the day as you
continue to pray for my Son's intention.*

St. Philomena visited again later that day.

St. Philomena: *My little sister, I bring you Our Master's blessings
and gratitude. Know that through your prayers over two thousand
priests were converted. Until tomorrow, farewell, little sister!*

Janie: Farewell, St. Philomena.

I understood that these priests were having much difficulty
with their faith.

Sharing Pray of My Life

July 31, 1996

St. Philomena: *Greetings from Heaven, my little sister!*

Janie: Peace to you, St. Philomena. My dear St. Philomena, you
have been coming for almost three months. Now, will you ever
share with me anything about your life?

St. Philomena: *My dear Janie, I shall share with you accounts of
my life beginning in the eighth month of the year.*

Janie: I am so happy, I can hardly wait!

St. Philomena: *Little sister, I, too, am happy about sharing parts of
my life with you. Today, little sister, pray to the Holy Spirit that He
may help you to prepare for this time. Until tomorrow, farewell, little sister!*

Janie: Farewell, St. Philomena!

Prepare to Begin the Holy Journey
August 1, 1996

St. Philomena: *Greetings from Heaven, my little sister!*

Janie: Ave, St. Philomena.

St. Philomena: *Little sister, I, St. Philomena, will begin to give you accounts of my earlier life. This is God's Most Holy Will. Prepare, little sister, to write everything that I share with you.*

Janie: St. Philomena, I know that I am not worthy to receive such information on your life, for I had no devotion to you or even knew who you were.

St. Philomena: *Please, little sister, do not be sad. It was God Who chose you to receive such accounts of my life. It was God that sent me to you, to visit with you everyday. Let us both embrace God's Most Holy Will and prepare to begin the holy journey which He has provided for you through my heavenly visitations.*
One day, little sister, when you visit my little shrine in Mugnano, Italy, you will understand more about the importance of my visitations to you. There, at my little shrine, all will be confirmed. Until tomorrow, farewell, little sister!

Janie: Farewell, St. Philomena!

I understood that St. Philomena was asking something of me and that I would have a clear understanding when I visited her shrine in Italy.

The Account of My First Six Years
August 2, 1996

St. Philomena: *Greetings from Heaven, little sister!*

71

Conversations With St. Philomena

Janie: Ave, St. Philomena.

Today, St. Philomena prayed for me so that God would clothe me with His wisdom and light and that I would embrace all that St. Philomena would give me concerning her life.

St. Philomena: *My little sister, God has chosen you to receive an account of my earlier life before I was six years of age. This will help those who have devotion to me to understand how much God loved me. This is why I gave myself totally to Him. This is the account of my first six years.*

After the first year of my life, I suffered from a high fever, which affected my health. My poor parents suffered and worried so much about me. My dear father searched for the finest medical physicians to come and examine me. The physicians had no knowledge of what caused these high fevers. I had these fevers during the first five years of my life and they left me very weak.

My parents spent all their time seeing to my needs. They provided for the best of care. Every day they offered their prayers and supplications for my recovery, but I continued to suffer with these mysterious fevers that the physicians could not understand. My father never gave up in his search to find a cure, outside of their prayers, for my recovery.

I spent much time in bed, for I was very fragile and weak. My parents allowed me very few visitors.

This is enough for today, my little sister. Until tomorrow, farewell!

Janie: Farewell, St. Philomena!

I understood that these fevers that St. Philomena suffered began right after her first year and were meant to strengthen her for the greater suffering that she was to endure later in her life.

While St. Philomena shared with me, I was allowed to see bits of scenes as she suffered. Her little face was very pale and although she had a high fever, she did not cry or fuss. She had such a beauty about her. Her parents loved her very much.

72

More of My Earlier Life

August 3, 1996

St. Philomena: *Greetings from Heaven, little sister!*

Janie: Ave, St. Philomena.

Today, we prayed for my family and all families in the world.

St. Philomena: *My little sister, before we begin our visit, I want to tell you how pleased God is that you are praying the Liturgy of the Hours. You have already noticed how satisfied your soul feels as you stop from your busy schedule to pray the prayers of the Church. God is giving you special graces to feel His Presence as you join with the Church in your daily prayers.*

Janie: Thank you, St. Philomena. I am truly enjoying these prayer exercises. Please pray for me, as I still am not too familiar with the way that I should be praying the Liturgy of the Hours. The Holy Spirit is my teacher as I am learning.

St. Philomena: *Have no worry, little sister. God is pleased with your progress.*
    Little sister, today I will continue to share more of my earlier life with you. As I mentioned, because of my illness, my parents allowed very few visitors. Most were adults. No children were allowed to visit me for fear that I would get excited and exhaust myself. My parents were very careful to see to my well-being.
    My godparents came every day to visit with me. My godmother always showered me with sweet little gifts. She would always bring me little angel dolls to play with. I had many of them. Each night I chose one of these angel dolls to sleep with. My godmother started teaching me how to read at age four.
    I was three when I was first visited by the Archangel Michael. He came to inform me that I had found favor with God and that God had assigned angels to come to visit me since I could not have anyone to play with. I was ever so happy and thankful to God. My

73

sweet parents and godmother would teach me about God, heaven and the angels. I knew about God and His angels.

On my third birthday, my parents and close relatives had a small celebration. After the celebration, my parents asked me to take my afternoon nap. It was then that I was visited by three most glorious angels. They did not speak to me, but they came and knelt by my bed.

Little sister, this is all for now. Until tomorrow, farewell!

Janie: I love you, St. Philomena. Farewell! Pray for my soul mate, for today is her birthday. Ask God for special blessings upon her, also for my spiritual director. Today is our anniversary. He has been my spiritual director for four years. Ask God's blessing on him as well. Good-bye for now.

I was infused with the further knowledge that St. Philomena was about two and a half when she was not able to play with other children her age. Her father, being a king, had her quarters well protected. St. Philomena's parents began teaching her about her Christian faith in the first year of her life. Even at the age of one, St. Philomena was most clever. She learned her prayers very quickly, that is to say, making the Sign of the Cross and bowing her little head during prayer.

Her parents brought her up in a strong Christian environment. Of the three angels that visited her, one was St. Gabriel, the Archangel. The other two were special angels assigned to play with her.

Her godparents were very close friends with her parents. They adored St. Philomena. Her godparents were devout Christian people who loved God very much but had no children of their own.

I was inspired as St. Philomena spoke to me about her life.

God Loves You For Your Perseverance During Suffering
August 4, 1996

St. Philomena: *Greetings from Heaven, little sister!*

Janie: Ave, St. Philomena.

St. Philomena prayed for me, for God to protect me by His love and power in my times of suffering.

St. Philomena: *Little sister, you have had a difficult day and your suffering was hard. Know that it was the Holy Spirit who protected you in your weakness. You asked God to help you in your confusion and He came to your aid immediately.*

Janie: St. Philomena, I almost made a terrible mistake. I am forever grateful for God's love and mercy.

St. Philomena: *Yes, God's love is immense and beyond any human comprehension. Little sister, God loves you for your perseverance during suffering and your trust in Him. Continue to trust Him in everything. I will not speak of my life tonight, for you need to rest. Your day was filled with much suffering. Until tomorrow, farewell, dear Janie!*

Janie: Farewell, little St. Philomena!

The Angels Were Constantly With Me

August 5, 1996

St. Philomena: *Greetings from Heaven, little sister!*

Janie: Ave, St. Philomena.

We prayed in thanksgiving to the Father for bringing spiritual healing in our family.

St. Philomena: *Little sister, it brings joy to my heart that through your devotion to me many are beginning to know about me. There are many souls that you helped foster devotion to me. I am deeply grateful.*

Janie: St. Philomena, I, myself, have begun to love you. That is why I am always talking about how powerful your intercession is to those who trust you.

St. Philomena: *Little sister, I will intercede for all who turn to me for help. Now I will continue to share my childhood life with you.*

Recall that I was visited by three glorious angels right before I took my nap. These heavenly spirits remained with me while I took my nap. As time went by, these glorious angels would come and play with me during my free time. I spent much time indoors, but once a day, if the weather permitted, I was taken outdoors to sit in our garden. The angels were constantly with me and we played together. They helped me with my prayers.

St. Michael would also keep vigil while the angels visited with me. Many times my mother would come to where I was, to see why I was carrying on a conversation with myself. She tried to explain to me why I could not have young visitors due to my illness. I was three-and-a -half.

Once I told her that I did have young visitors to play with. She looked surprised and asked, "And who are these young visitors who come and play with you?" I said, "They are angels from Heaven, mother. They are with me all the time, and we have such a good time together." My poor mother had a worried look on her face. Later that evening she told my father that she thought that I had invented some imaginary friends to keep me from being lonely.

My little sister, we will continue our conversation tomorrow. You have to finish your night prayers. Until tomorrow, farewell!

Janie: Farewell, St. Philomena!

I understood that St. Philomena's parents suffered from worry about their little princess. They wanted to give her the best of everything, but they had to follow the doctor's orders and not allow St. Philomena to exhaust herself. The little princess was quite content playing with her heavenly visitors. St. Philomena never complained. She was always obedient in allowing her parents to care for her.

As I write all this, I feel as though I have lost my mind, but in

God I trust. I am quite aware that when it is time for these accounts of St. Philomena's life to be shared, I will suffer. God knows that I write in obedience, and He knows that if it were up to me I wouldn't write these accounts but only ponder them in my heart.

Distracted By What Others Think

August 6, 1996

St. Philomena: *Greetings from Heaven, little sister!*

Janie: Ave, St. Philomena. I am so happy to be with you. I am concerned about the accounts of your life that you are sharing with me. They seem so strange, and do I share this with others? They will think that I am out of my mind.

St. Philomena: *Do not worry, little sister. God will take care of everything for you. Do not allow yourself to be distracted by what others think of you. Remember, your first responsibility and duty is to God. To Him alone you must surrender your all. It was God Who chose that I, St. Philomena, come to you and share accounts of my life. He has allowed me to share with a few other souls the accounts of my life.*

Janie: St. Philomena, please understand. I want to do only what pleases God, but there is much weakness in me, which causes me to doubt your visits with me. I only see you with the eyes of my soul, but I hear clearly all that you tell me. Still, I doubt. I will be obedient and record everything you tell me.

St. Philomena: *My little sister, you have acted wisely. Remember, obedience brings victory to those souls who surrender their all to God. You shall not regret anything. Until tomorrow, little sister! Farewell! We will talk more about my earlier years. Be at peace, all will go well for you.*

Janie: Thank you, St. Philomena.

Conversations With St. Philomena

I saw a vision that St. Philomena showed me before I visited her shrine. I was kneeling down and then I saw my spiritual director kneeling by me. St. Philomena has shared with me that when I go to her shrine in Italy, something very special will happen there. In this I trust.

Angels Visited Me to Give Me Strength

August 7, 1996

St. Philomena: *Greetings from Heaven, little sister!*

Janie: Ave, St. Philomena. Thank you for coming.

St. Philomena: *Little sister, recall our last conversation when I told you that my poor parents were concerned about me. They thought that I had invented imaginary friends!*
My parents kept an eye on me as I played in our garden. It was a beautiful garden surrounded by every kind of flower that one could imagine. My dear mother was very fond of flowers. Our gardener took such good care of all the green plants and flowers.
The angels continued to visit me and played with me until I was to turn five years old.

Janie: St. Philomena, did your parents continue to keep an eye on you?

St. Philomena: *Yes, little sister, but I soon learned to keep the visits of the angels quiet. I did not want my parents to worry about me. They were so protective of me since I was their only child, and they loved me so much.*
I played with the angels all the time. The angels stayed with me almost all day. During these times that I was visited by the angels, they showed me visions of Heaven. The angels told me that I would soon be in Heaven. Of course, being so young, I was very happy to hear this. I did not understand that in a matter of years I would undergo severe suffering under the hands of the evil em-

78

peror, Diocletian.

It was for this very reason that the angels visited me, to give me strength and to increase my love for my Spouse and Master. These heavenly visitations were to help me be strong during the cruel suffering I was to undergo in the years to come.

My little sister, I know that you are tired. Until tomorrow, farewell! I love you, my dear little sister.

Janie: I love you, St. Philomena.

I saw a vision of St. Philomena in a dark room. She had blood all over her body. The angels were attending to her. It made me very sad.

Ceased Suffering With Fever

August 8, 1996

St. Philomena: *Greetings from Heaven, my little sister!*

Janie: Ave, St. Philomena. Thank you for coming. St. Philomena, when did you recover from your illness?

St. Philomena: *My little sister, it was just before I reached my fifth birthday that I ceased suffering with fever episodes. One morning, I woke up feeling quite well and strong. My nurse, who lived in the palace in the service of my father, was preparing my morning bath. She was so surprised to see the color on my cheeks. She said in a loud voice, "Why sweet little Philomena, you are radiant with color! How are you feeling this morning?" I responded, "I am feeling quite well! I am so hungry." My nurse called to the other servants to call my parents to come to my quarters.*

Janie: St. Philomena, what was the name of the nurse who took care of you? Are you allowed to tell me?

St. Philomena: *Oh, yes! I am glad to tell you. Her name was X.,*

79

Conversations With St. Philomena

probably of Italian descent. (I did not write the name of St. Philo-mena's nurse, but kept it to myself.) She was a very holy soul who loved God with all her heart. Her husband was taken by God a few years before she was employed by my father. She was most loyal in seeing to all of my medical needs, but most importantly, she loved me and helped me to pray to God for strength during my illness.

Janie: What happened to her after you recovered from your illness?

St. Philomena: *She stayed on being my nurse for a while, and then she accepted an assignment with another family who had a son who couldn't walk. She always wrote to my family and came to see me whenever she could.*
     Now, my little sister, this is all for now. Until tomorrow, fare-well, little sister!

Janie: Farewell, St. Philomena!

     I was so excited to see St. Philomena's recovery from her ill-ness. She looked radiantly beautiful. I saw this in a vision. Praised be God forever and ever. Amen.

Private Visits
August 9-12, 1996

Janie: The visits of St. Philomena during August 9-12, 1996 took place while I was in a Divine Mercy Symposium in Flagstaff, Ari-zona. These were private conversations for some people from Flag-staff, Arizona. I gave the first class relic of St. Philomena to a pre-cious 12-year-old who had a great love for St. Philomena. This pre-cious soul was also suffering with a serious illness. I knew that St. Philomena would help her.

Now I Could Attend Holy Mass
August 13, 1996

St. Philomena: *Greetings from Heaven, my little sister!*

Janie: Ave, St. Philomena. Today, I ask if you can share your parents' reaction to the recovery of your illness. (I was so excited; I wanted to know everything about St. Philomena's life.)

St. Philomena: *My parents were delighted and filled with great joy and gratitude to God. They had offered numerous Masses and prayers for my recovery. I suffered four years with these fevers.*

My parents summoned my doctor, who was also a dear friend of the family. He examined me, he asked me to walk back and forth in front of him. I did this several times. He examined my hands; my grip was strong, my breathing was strong, and my heart and lungs were strong.

Not quite convinced that my fevers would not reoccur, he thought that it would be wise if I remained in bed for another month, following the same close care as before. My parents, wanting only the best for me, agreed to all that he said. I was obedient to all that was asked of me.

Janie: Were you excited, St. Philomena, about not suffering from these fevers? I am so happy just knowing that your illness came to an end.

St. Philomena: *I was quite excited, my little sister, for now I could attend Holy Mass without feeling so tired and weak. This is what excited me the most. My parents had been giving me Christian instructions and I was quite aware of Our Master in the Most Holy Eucharist. I longed to receive Him but I could not, for I had not yet made my First Communion.*

My little sister, I know that you are tired. We will continue this conversation tomorrow. Until then, my little sister, farewell!

Janie: Farewell, St. Philomena.

Today, I was so excited to know that St. Philomena had recovered from her illness. For me, this has been a journey into her young life.

81

Conversations With St. Philomena

Our Lady Will Come to All Her Children

August 14, 1996

St. Philomena: *Greetings from Heaven, my little sister!*

Janie: Ave, St. Philomena. I am so excited, for tomorrow is the feast of Our Lady's Assumption. She will be with us.

St. Philomena: *Tomorrow will indeed be a joyful day for you. Our Lady will come to all her children. She will bless all her children through her presence. Prepare with much prayer for her visit.*
Until tomorrow, farewell! We will continue the accounts of my life after the glorious feast of Our Lady's Assumption.

Janie: Thank you, St. Philomena.

Our Mother's Most Holy Visit

August 15, 1996

St. Philomena: *Greetings from Heaven, my little sister!*

Janie: Peace to you, St. Philomena.

St. Philomena: *My little sister, you have been so patient in writing everything which I have been sharing with you. I know that you wonder and have doubts in your heart about all that I tell you.*

Janie: St. Philomena, what you say about my doubts is true, but I guess that it's my nature to have doubts. You see, I never thought that anything like this happened to people on earth. However, no matter how much I doubt, I will remain committed to writing everything which you give me.

I am very excited, for Our Lady will be coming today. Her visit will occur on our land.

St. Philomena: *Little sister, I shall not share anything with you today, for you have much to do to prepare for Our Most Holy Mother's visit. I shall be interceding for you. Until tomorrow, farewell, little sister!*

Janie: Farewell, St. Philomena!

My Complete Recovery

August 16, 1996

St. Philomena: *Greetings from Heaven, my little sister!*

Janie: Peace to you, St. Philomena.

St. Philomena: *Little sister, today I shall continue to share with you the success of my complete recovery.*
Recall in our last conversation in which I shared with you that my doctor was not completely convinced that I was truly cured of the fevers which had affected the first four years of my life. He had insisted to my parents that I remain in bed under close observation for a month. My parents, of course, agreed to his medical advice.
I remained in bed for yet another month, but during this month not once did I suffer with fever. There were no recurrences of this terrible fever. Finally convinced that I was cured, but not so sure that these fevers would not come back, I remained under my doctor's care. He examined me once a week. I was not allowed to engage in daily activities too much. My poor parents guided me in the things I could do. I was ever so happy to cooperate with everything that they asked of me.
My little sister, we shall continue. I know that it is hard on your hands when you write. Until tomorrow, farewell!

Janie: Farewell, St. Philomena!

I was suffering the Passion of Our Lord, so I couldn't write very well.

Conversations With St. Philomena

Allow Yourself to Be Guided by the Holy Spirit

August 17, 1996

St. Philomena: *Greetings from Heaven, little sister!*

Janie: Peace to you, St. Philomena. I want to thank you, St. Philomena, for sharing all this with me. You know that I am not a very good writer.

St. Philomena: *Little sister, the Holy Spirit is the one who is helping you to listen with your heart. Do not be concerned about your writing. God knows everything about you. He could have chosen an excellent writer to write all that I am giving you, but instead He chose you. Rejoice and allow yourself to be guided by the Holy Spirit. You shall not regret it.*
Little sister, tomorrow we shall continue sharing the accounts of my life. Until tomorrow, farewell, little sister!

Janie: Farewell, St. Philomena!

I wasn't feeling well today. I suffer often for Our Lord and Our Lady's special intentions. These intentions are revealed to me by my guardian angel.

A Good Catholic Foundation

August 18, 1996

St. Philomena: *Greetings from Heaven, little sister!*

Janie: Peace to you, St. Philomena.

St. Philomena: *My dear Janie, you have not been doing well these past few days. Know that your suffering helps bring the conversion of others.*

Janie: St. Philomena, I don't mind suffering, but sometimes I get so weak and I am not able to do anything.

St. Philomena: *Do not worry, little sister. I am always interceding for you. Are you strong enough to write today?*

Janie: Yes, St. Philomena. I am feeling better today.

St. Philomena: *Very well then, we will continue sharing some of the accounts of the first years of my life.*
Recall that in our last conversation concerning my recovery, I explained that my doctor wanted me to be very careful with any activity. My parents and I followed all that my doctor asked of us.
During the time in which I was under my doctor's continuous care, I told my parents that I wanted to make my First Communion. During my illness, whenever I had good days, my mother or my godmother would teach me the prayers I needed for my First Communion. My father was too busy with his royal duties as king, but he read Holy Scripture to me once a day.

Janie: St. Philomena, what kind of preparation did you need to make your First Holy Communion?

St. Philomena: *Little sister, I was given lessons on the catechism and was taught the importance of Holy Mass. I was taught all the prayers which I needed to learn as a good Catholic. My parents educated me with a good Catholic foundation. I learned to pray before meals and to say my night prayers at an early age. Once a day, my parents would come to my room and my father would read Holy Scripture from the Bible. My parents attended Mass quite frequently.*

Janie: St. Philomena, you must have been very smart!

St. Philomena: *Little sister, God blessed me with two good loving and prayerful parents. The honor goes to my dear parents for working so hard to teach me everything about my Christian faith. It was the grace of God and my early Christian formation which kept me*

85

strong when I was tortured by the cruel emperor, Diocletian. Little sister, I have shared enough about my life. Tomorrow, we will continue. Farewell, little sister!

Janie: Farewell, St. Philomena and thank you for everything!

During the time in which St. Philomena shared with me, I could see her with her parents. I could sense the love that St. Philomena's parents had for her.

Truly Healed

August 19, 1996

St. Philomena: *Greetings from Heaven, my little sister!*

Janie: Peace to you, St. Philomena.

St. Philomena: *My little sister, again I wish to thank you for your patience in recording all that I, St. Philomena, share with you.*

Janie: St. Philomena, what you share with me is so precious and dear to my heart.

St. Philomena: *Little sister, recall our last conversation a few days ago in which I shared with you my desire to make my First Communion. Today, I wish to continue the accounts of my childhood.*
The day came when my doctor finally was convinced that I had been healed through the many Masses and prayers which everyone had offered for me. On this day when my doctor announced that I was truly healed, my father and mother prepared a great celebration.
During this time both my parents had met with the priest asking him for special permission to allow me to make my First Communion. I was already five years old. The priest told my parents that he, himself, would examine my knowledge to see if I understood my catechism well enough to make my First Communion.
The priest gave me a verbal examination to see how much I knew

86

and understood about my catechism. He was quite impressed with my knowledge concerning my Christian faith. My parents and my god-mother taught me well, and the angels also had helped me to know the importance of loving and serving God.

My little sister, tomorrow we shall continue to share the accounts of my early childhood. I know that you have commitments to your family. Until tomorrow, farewell, little sister!

Janie: Thank you so much, St. Philomena.

In a vision I saw St. Philomena as the priest was asking her questions about her catechism. She was so young and filled with love for God. She wasn't nervous at all. She saw the priest as Jesus. She answered each question with wisdom and she was most humble in her manner towards the priest. For example, when the priest first entered St. Philomena's room, St. Philomena quickly stood up and kissed the priest's hand and then bowed her head as if thanking God to be in the presence of the priest. I was so touched by this vision.

Up All Night Suffering

August 20, 1996

St. Philomena: *Greetings from Heaven, little sister.*

Janie: Peace, St. Philomena.

St. Philomena: *Little sister, I know that you have been up all night suffering. I am praying for you. Until tomorrow, farewell, little sister!*

Janie: Farewell, St. Philomena.

The Bread of Angels

August 21, 1996

St. Philomena: *Greetings from Heaven, my little sister!*

Conversations With St. Philomena

Janie: Peace to you, St. Philomena. Dear St. Philomena, I am so excited to be receiving visitations from you. I am so grateful to God.

St. Philomena: *Little sister, God chose you through all eternity to receive these heavenly visitations. God delights in blessing you with such gifts.*

Janie: I know that God loves me, St. Philomena. His love is my daily strength.

St. Philomena: *Little sister, today I shall continue to share the accounts of my childhood. Recall in our last conversation that my parents prepared a feast in thanksgiving to God for my recovery from my illness. It was during this time that the priest visited our palace to give me a verbal examination of how much I knew about my catechism. My parents had planned all this ahead of time with the priest. They wanted to present me with a surprise.*

My parents understood how much I wanted to make my First Communion. It was on this day, when my doctor released me from his care, that my parents prepared a big celebration. It was at this time that my parents announced to me that I would make my First Communion. I burst into tears and my parents thought that they had said something to offend me. My mother said, "Our dear little princess, what have we said to cause you to cry?" I responded, "Mother, my tears are tears of joy. I am so happy to know that I will receive Jesus Who is dear to my heart. My dear parents, thank you very much. This is the greatest gift a soul can ever receive."

Our celebration began with Holy Mass, which was to be my First Communion Mass. When I received the Bread of Angels, I felt as if I was in heaven. There were so many angels on the altar and all over the church. I thought that everybody present was aware of their presence.

After the celebration of Holy Mass, everyone went to our palace to continue with the celebration. I was so consumed with the love of Our Master that I wanted to be alone, but I had to be part of the celebration. This was a day filled with the presence of Heaven. I

knew that I would look forward everyday to receiving the Bread of Angels. From this moment I began to live Heaven on earth.
Little sister, we will continue tomorrow. Farewell, little sister!

Janie: Farewell, St. Philomena, farewell!

I saw in a vision of St. Philomena's First Communion. She looked like a little bride, so innocent, so pure and so filled with love for God.

My Best and Truest Friend

August 22, 1996
Queenship of Mary

St. Philomena: *Greetings from Heaven, my little sister!*

Janie: Peace to you, St. Philomena.

St. Philomena: *My dear little sister, today you will be blessed with a visit from Our Lady. This will be a joyful day for you and your family.*

Janie: Dear St. Philomena, I am excited about today. This is indeed a joyful day. I am so looking forward to seeing Our Lady.

St. Philomena: *Little sister, let us continue with our conversation of yesterday. After my recovery, I was able to live a normal life. My parents continued to educate me in my Catholic faith. The visitations of the angels also ceased, but I could see their presence during Holy Mass. St. Michael the Archangel informed me that later in my life the angels would visit me again.*
This was to be the time of my great suffering under the hands of Diocletian. I was not aware that I was to undergo a most horrible suffering, but I prayed everyday to God to bless me with a strong love for Him and a sound faith. I wanted to do only the will of God so I could spend much time in quiet meditation.

Conversations With St. Philomena

Janie: St. Philomena, did you have close friends?

St. Philomena: *Little sister, I had a few friends as I lived a very normal life, but my best and truest Friend was Our Master. My goal was to earn Heaven by living a pure and holy life. I was aware at a young age that God loved purity and that He rewarded all my good intentions. I spent my life trying to please God in everything that I did.*

Janie: St. Philomena, I wish I could have lived in your time, just so I could have met you.

St. Philomena: *My dear Janie, you have met me and you do know me.*

Janie: I know this, St. Philomena, but I mean in the human sense.

St. Philomena: *Little sister, this is the way that God wanted things to happen in your life and in mine.*

Janie: You are right, St. Philomena. Thank you for reminding me to keep my focus on God.

St. Philomena: *Little sister, tomorrow we shall continue our conversation. Until tomorrow, farewell, little sister!*

Janie: Farewell, St. Philomena!
   I knew in my heart that St. Philomena was a very prayerful little person. She was so young, and yet so full of love for God!
   O Lord, help me to imitate the life and example of St. Philomena.

Vowed My Virginity to Him

August 23, 1996

St. Philomena: *Greetings from Heaven, little sister!*

Janie: Peace, St. Philomena. St. Philomena, please continue to

90

share with me more about your life.

St. Philomena: *Little sister, after I recovered from my illness, my life was normal, as I mentioned yesterday. I spent the rest of my eight years living a good life. I did this by honoring my parents, being obedient to them, and being of service to others through my good deeds. Of course, I put God first in my life and my duties to Him came first.*

I continued my studies through the education which my parents provided for me. My parents continued to educate me, so I continued to learn all about my faith.

Janie: Did you miss your visits with the angels?

St. Philomena: *Oh, yes, but I knew for certain that they were always with me. My greatest joy was that I could receive Our Master in Holy Communion. My sweet Jesus was my everything. The more I received Him in Holy Communion, the more I wanted to be totally united with Him. He was my love and it was during these later years of my life that I vowed my virginity to Him.*

My dear parents thought that I would grow out of this promise to Him. My desire to be completely His grew deeper and deeper everyday.

Janie: St. Philomena, I, too, wanted to belong totally to Jesus, but my parents would not give me permission to go to the convent. This made me suffer greatly.

St. Philomena: *Little sister, I am aware of your own suffering. Although your mother never gave you instructions as you were growing up, you, too, loved Our Master very much. Your own heart was being formed by Our Master. He knew that during your life you would suffer much for poor sinners.*

Your own suffering began right after your first year of life, just as my own suffering did. You suffered for five years just as I did. You suffered humiliation; you were rejected by your own mother. You were denied many things, including your mother's love. My lit-

91

Conversations With St. Philomena

*tle sister, as a young child, you suffered alone. I was blessed to
have my parents' love and prayers. Your path of suffering came to
you at a very young age.*

Janie: St. Philomena, all these things you say are true. My poor
mother was so wounded as a child. I loved her very much.

St. Philomena: *Little sister, your mother loved you, but she did not
know how to demonstrate her love.*

Janie: St. Philomena, thank you for talking to me about my childhood and my suffering. I am so blessed to have you as my little
heavenly sister.

St. Philomena: *Little sister, I am delighted to share my suffering
and my life with you. Until tomorrow, farewell, little sister!*

Janie: Farewell, St. Philomena!

I Was Not Afraid

August 24, 1996

St. Philomena: *Greetings from Heaven, my little sister!*

Janie: Peace, St. Philomena and thank you again for sharing so
much yesterday. Tell me, did your parents object to your desire to
vow your virginity to Our Master?

St. Philomena: *Little sister, my parents were delighted with how
much I loved Our Master, but they were unaware of how Our Master's love had affected my heart and soul.*

Janie: St. Philomena, when did you vow your virginity to Our Master? Were your parents aware of this?

St. Philomena: *Little sister, I had shared with my parents that I had*

92

a deep desire to belong totally to Our Master. They did not object, but thought that as time passed I would grow out of this desire.

Janie: St. Philomena, did this desire increase?

St. Philomena: *Oh, yes, little sister. I looked to the day when I would fulfill my desire to have Our Master as my Spouse.*

Janie: St. Philomena, you are so brave to have died for love of Our Master. Pray that I may be brave as you. St. Philomena, were you afraid of the evil emperor who wanted your hand in marriage?

St. Philomena: *Little sister, I was not afraid. The grace of God gave me strength. I suffered because my parents wanted me to submit to their request to marry the evil Diocletian. I was never afraid, for I knew that my kingdom was Heaven and nothing could change this. My virginity, which I had vowed to Our Master, came before everything. No threats by the evil emperor would change my mind.*

Janie: St. Philomena, you were a brave little girl. I thank God for you.

St. Philomena: *Little sister, you, too, are very brave. You have endured much suffering for love of Our Master. Until tomorrow, farewell, little sister!*

St. Philomena: Farewell, St. Philomena!

Always Keep Your Promises to God
August 25, 1996

St. Philomena: *Greetings from Heaven, little sister!*

Janie: Peace, St. Philomena.

St. Philomena: *Little sister, you have been so patient in listening to*

93

Conversations With St. Philomena

all that I share with you.

Janie: St. Philomena, I am honored to know all this about you. I must admit, I feel as though this is all a dream. I know that I will get criticized for what you are sharing with me; but like you, I want to please God.

St. Philomena: *Little sister, you will be criticized and persecuted for what you will write about me. Pay no mind when this happens, but know that Our Master will render you the grace to endure everything.*

All that I did in my life, I did for love of God. With the grace which God rendered me, I lived a pure and holy life. I did all that I could to keep myself pure for my Divine Spouse. Purity, little sister, leads one to holiness, and holiness was what I longed for. For this very reason, I suffered by the hands of Diocletian. All his threats, his violent rage, his allurements could not induce me to yield to his wishes. My parents were also most disappointed and heartbroken at my refusal to submit to their own demands to marry the evil emperor.

My father threatened me and commanded me to accept the hand of Diocletian. I continued to refuse. God was first in my life. He came before my parents and everything else. This commitment to God led to my death, but I remained true to my God. All suffering which I endured by the hands of Diocletian only made my love stronger for God. Nothing would make me break my promise which I had made to God. Nothing!

Little sister, always keep your promises to God and you will have victory in all your suffering. Until tomorrow, farewell, little sister!

Janie: Farewell, St. Philomena!

Heaven is Your Kingdom

August 26, 1996

St. Philomena: *Greetings from Heaven, my little sister!*

94

Janie: Peace to you, St. Philomena. St. Philomena, I have been pondering all that you have shared with me. All that you have told me is helping me to remain peaceful in my own suffering.

St. Philomena: *Little sister, I have revealed parts of my life to help you in your own path to holiness. You have been given the task to pray and to suffer for poor sinners. Your vocation as a wife, mother and grandmother has helped you to understand family life.*

Heaven is your kingdom and you have embraced this journey. Our Master and His Mother have invited you to offer yourself as a victim soul to suffer for the conversion of others. You accepted this invitation. Our Master has invited you to share in His Passion, to suffer His wounds. You accepted. The suffering of His Passion on your body - hands, feet, side and head - will last as long as you live on earth. You endure this suffering quietly and patiently.

Little sister, God has given you all the graces which you need to follow the path that His Son has traced out for you. Always trust God in everything, no matter what kind of storms come your way.

Janie: St. Philomena, thank you for all your guidance. God knows that all I want is to do His Holy Will. This is what I live for.

St. Philomena: *Little sister, remain in this attitude always and you will obtain eternal life. Until tomorrow, farewell, little sister!*

Janie: Farewell, St. Philomena!

You Will Bring Me Many More Devotees

August 27, 1996

St. Philomena: *Greetings from Heaven, my little sister!*

Janie: Peace to you, St. Philomena.

St. Philomena: *Little sister, during these past several days I have been sharing a little bit about my earlier life. Although you have*

95

had to write all of this while your hands are hurting, you have been very obedient and patient. Little sister, through your own love and devotion you will bring me many more devotees.

Janie: St. Philomena, I feel bad. I really haven't read too much about you, yet I am called to foster devotion to you. Please help me and educate me so that I may do you justice.

St. Philomena: *Little sister, again I say one day you will visit my shrine in Mugnano, Italy. There you will receive guidance on how to spread devotion to me. A very special soul dedicated to taking care of my shrine will help you. Have no worry.*

Janie: St. Philomena, I trust all you say to me.

St. Philomena: *Thank you, little sister, for your cooperation. Until tomorrow, farewell, little sister!*

Janie: Farewell, St. Philomena!

Permission For The Archangels To Visit

August 28, 1996

St. Philomena: *Greetings from Heaven, little sister!*

Janie: Peace, St. Philomena. Thank you so much for everything. I know that God loves you very much and I love you, but I could never love Him as you do.

St. Philomena: *Little sister, God loves all souls, but those who hunger to do His will glorify Him. Always put God first in your life and set a good example for your family and for others. God will protect you from the hands of the evil one.*
    The Queen of Heaven will encourage you to live for God alone. She will intercede for you and help you in your suffering, as she helped me. St. Joseph will also encourage you to remain obedient to God when your spirit lags. He will protect you as he pro-

tected Our Master.

Little sister, you have been blessed with many heavenly visitations. The Queen of Heaven has asked God permission for the Archangels to visit. This permission was granted. You have the glorious St. Michael to defend you in your battles with the evil one. St. Gabriel, whose name expresses force, will strengthen your faith and St. Raphael, the healing angel, will pour the balm of healing in your heart, body and soul. Little sister, remember God loves you. Embrace His love by living a pure, simple and good life. Until tomorrow, farewell, little sister!

Janie: Farewell, St. Philomena!

God Delight's In the Little Ways

August 29, 1996

St. Philomena: *Greetings from Heaven, my little sister!*

Janie: Peace, St. Philomena. St. Philomena, I am so grateful to God for you. I want to do something special for you. I am going to ask my husband if we can build you a small shrine next to the Infant of Prague Chapel. If he agrees, I will do this for you. I will make it very beautiful, but I need you to help me obtain a life-size statue.

St. Philomena: *Little sister, I am honored that you would even consider such a task. I will assist you.*

Janie: St. Philomena, remember first my husband has to agree. I will be obedient to any response he gives although I pray that he will say "yes." Can I cheat a little bit and ask you to intercede so that he may say "yes?" I hope this is not a selfish request.

St. Philomena: *Little sister, you are not cheating but merely asking God to help you through my intercession. Your request is not a selfish one. You want to demonstrate your love for me and bring more*

97

devotees to me. God delights in the little ways in which you ask for special favors. Until tomorrow, farewell, little sister!

Janie: Farewell, St. Philomena!

Many Will Be the Blessings and Graces
August 30, 1996

St. Philomena: *Greetings from Heaven, my little sister!*

Janie: Peace to you, St. Philomena. St. Philomena, I have good news! My husband agreed right away to build you a little shrine. I was so happy. He didn't even hesitate to answer. He is happy that you are helping us.

St. Philomena: *Little sister, I am greatly honored by your husband's response. Many will be the blessings and graces rendered to him by God for his generous heart.*

Janie: St. Philomena, I am excited about this. I will share this with my spiritual director. He will be happy as well.

St. Philomena: *Little sister, I am grateful to you for everything. Until tomorrow, farewell, little sister!*

Janie: Farewell, St. Philomena!

She knew that I was ill.

The Grace to Do Everything
August 31, 1996

St. Philomena: *Greetings from Heaven, little sister!*

Janie: Peace to you, St. Philomena. St. Philomena, please pray for me that I can write all that you tell me. Sometimes my hands hurt so much. They become numb with the pain. I feel as though I have no hands. They hurt so much that at times I cannot do any housework or write. Please intercede for me.

St. Philomena: *Little sister, I know that you suffer much as you write down all that I share with you. Do not be concerned with this. I will intercede for you and God will render you the grace to do everything. I know that you are suffering as we visit. I will pray for you. Until tomorrow, farewell, little sister!*

Janie: Farewell, St. Philomena!

No Work Is As Important

September 1, 1996

St. Philomena: *Greetings from Heaven, my sweet sister!*

Janie: Greetings, St. Philomena.

St. Philomena: *My little sister, this is a very special time for you. Our Master is helping you to grow more in holiness. Your soul is indeed being prepared for the work that Our Master is blessing you with.*

My little sister, know that no work is as important as the work to save souls. Your mission is to pray for the Bride of Our Master and the family. Our Master has entrusted you with this important mission. Much prayer and fasting is required to continue this holy work of bringing souls to Our Master. Your weapons are: the Eucharist, Adoration, reading Holy Scripture, the Rosary, prayer and fasting. Every day, you must ask the Holy Spirit to guide your path to only do the Holy Will of God.

Little sister, you have Heaven at your side to help you to win souls for Our Master. Work with holy joy in your heart. Until tomorrow, farewell!

99

Conversations With St. Philomena

Janie: Farewell, St. Philomena!

Pray for These Precious Souls

September 2, 1996

St. Philomena: *Greetings from Heaven, little sister!*

Janie: Greetings, St. Philomena! St. Philomena, please pray for my son's studies, especially where he is having a difficult time.

St. Philomena: *Little sister, I will intercede for him. Continue praying for him and show him how much you love him. There is much goodness in his heart.*

Janie: Thank you, St. Philomena.

St. Philomena: *Little sister, young people are so loved by Our Master. They have a difficult time in their journey of life. They are trying to mature at a rapid pace. They are in need of much prayer, especially those who do not have a relationship with God. Pray for these precious souls. Until tomorrow, farewell!*

Janie: Farewell, St. Philomena! I will keep these souls in my prayers.

Pray for the Pope

September 3, 1996

St. Philomena: *Greetings from Heaven, little sister!*

Janie: Greetings, St. Philomena!

St. Philomena: *My little sister, today keep in your prayers the Bride of Our Master. She is in the midst of much agony. There is, as you know, much division and tribulation within the Church. Pray for the Pope. He suffers for all of his flock.*

100

Janie: St. Philomena, I hear many stories of how the Church will be persecuted to the point where the Church will go underground. I don't exactly know what this means. Do you know anything about this?

St. Philomena: *Little sister, many things will happen as it is written in Holy Scripture. Do not be distracted by these thoughts. Concentrate on offering all your prayers and sacrifices so that God in His mercy will show mercy on the things to come.*

The Bride of Our Master will suffer much, but if many offer their sacrifices for these intentions, the Church will see the mercy of God.

Pray much, little sister, for all the world. Until tomorrow, farewell, little sister!

Janie: Farewell, St. Philomena. I love you.

Oh, How They Suffer!

September 4, 1996

St. Philomena: *Greetings from Heaven, little sister!*

Janie: Greetings, St. Philomena!

St. Philomena: *My sweet Janie, you have been suffering much for the conversion of your loved ones and of the world. You are especially suffering for young people who are distant from God. Many of these troubled souls are committing much evil. Many have no one to guide them. Many are victims of family violence themselves. Oh, how they suffer!*

Janie: St. Philomena, there is much destruction among the youth. I know that many come from broken homes, but what makes them so hateful?

St. Philomena: *My sweet Janie, it is lack of love, lack of prayer in*

101

Conversations With St. Philomena

the years while they were growing up. Many of their parents were absent when these young people needed love, warmth, comfort and guidance.

Janie: St. Philomena, this is true. I remember my own childhood. Let us pray very much for all these young, troubled people.

St. Philomena: *Yes, my little sister, we must pray. Through our prayers, many of these young souls will find God in their broken lives. I shall join my prayers with yours. Until tomorrow, farewell, my dear Janie!*

Janie: Farewell, St. Philomena!

Help All the Youth

September 5, 1996

St. Philomena: *Greetings from Heaven, little sister!*

Janie: Greetings, St. Philomena!

St. Philomena: *My dear friend, today let us continue to pray for all the troubled youth who have no families. These precious souls are lost and are in confusion. Satan has seduced them with his lies. He puts much temptation in their path and they fall into his web of perdition.*

My little sister, help all the youth that God puts in your path. Speak to them about the love and mercy of Our Master. Speak to them about Satan who only seeks to destroy them. He uses drugs, violence, fornication, prostitution, homosexuality, witchcraft, lies, pornography and profanity. He employs many other means to seduce the youth.

Little sister, these are troubled youth. Pray for them and keep vigil for them through your prayers. Your love and prayers for these precious souls will disarm Satan, and he will flee from the lives of these young souls.

Janie: St. Philomena, I understand. I will pray and fast for these intentions with love in my heart.

St. Philomena: *Thank you, little sister. With your prayers and the prayers of others for the youth, there is hope for their salvation. Only prayer, fasting and love will help them. Until tomorrow, farewell, little sister!*

Janie: Farewell, St. Philomena!

Celebrating Our Lady's Birthday
September 6, 1996

St. Philomena: *Greetings from Heaven, little sister!*

Janie: Greetings, St. Philomena!

St. Philomena: *My little sister, you are excited about celebrating Our Lady's birthday. God is pleased that you would care so much to give your Heavenly Mother such a warm celebration.*

Janie: St. Philomena, Our Lady has taught me so much and has given me much motherly love. She deserves my best.

St. Philomena: *All will go well with the celebration. Continue praying for the conversion of souls. Until tomorrow, farewell, little sister!*

Janie: Farewell, St. Philomena!

The Horrible Sin of Homosexuality
September 7, 1996

St. Philomena: *Greetings from Heaven, little sister!*

103

Conversations With St. Philomena

Janie: Greetings, St. Philomena!

St. Philomena: *My dear Janie, today let us pray for those trapped in the horrible sin of homosexuality. This way of life is most offensive to God. This way of life is against the teaching of God's commandments.*

Homosexuality is one of the many evil movements that is destroying many families. The leader of this sinful movement is Satan. He has perverted souls to rebel against the commandments of God. In doing this he is destroying many souls.

Little sister, pray to dissolve this evil that is growing with each moment that goes by. Although many people in the world accept this way of life, many others know that this is against God's teaching. Little sister, pray, pray to help stop this evil movement. Until tomorrow, farewell!

Janie: Farewell, St. Philomena! I will pray.

Our Lady Was Most Pleased

September 8, 1996

St. Philomena: *Greetings from Heaven, my little sister!*

Janie: Greetings, St. Philomena!

St. Philomena: *My little sister, today was a joyful day for you. Our Lady was most pleased with the prayers and the celebration that her children offered her. You made her very happy.*

Janie: St. Philomena, I really enjoyed this day. Everything went well, as you told me. Thank you for everything.

St. Philomena: *My little sister, you have had a busy day. Rest now. Until tomorrow, farewell!*

Janie: Farewell, St. Philomena!

For All the Youth Who Live in Darkness

September 9, 1996

St. Philomena: *Greetings from Heaven, my little sister!*

Janie: Peace, St. Philomena.

St. Philomena: *Little sister, today let us pray together for all the youth who live in darkness. These young people suffer so much, for they do not have God in their lives. Let us pray for these precious lost souls. Until tomorrow, farewell, little sister!*

Janie: St. Philomena, I will spend my day praying for all the youth in the world!

God Is Using Your Prayers

September 10, 1996

St. Philomena: *Greetings from Heaven, little sister!*

Janie: Greetings to you, St. Philomena!

St. Philomena: *Little sister, I wish to thank you for offering all your prayers and sacrifices for young people. God is using your prayers to help these young souls.*

Janie: St. Philomena, I am doing the best that I can to bring other souls to you, especially young people. I want young people to embrace your spirituality, to love purity and holiness as you do. I talk about your spirituality every chance that I get. Please keep me in your prayers as I go about planting the seeds of your spirituality.

St. Philomena: *Little sister, you are doing me much justice in the way in which you promote my spirituality. I am always interceding for you and those souls whom you recommend to me. Until tomorrow, farewell, little sister!*

105

The Family Is in Need of Conversion

September 11, 1996

St. Philomena: *Greetings from Heaven, little sister!*

Janie: Greetings, St. Philomena! Dear St. Philomena, today I need your prayers to help me prepare for my trip to New Orleans. I always have trouble leaving my little grandson. He is so special to me. I entrust him to your intercession, St. Philomena.

St. Philomena: *Little sister, do not be sad. Your little grandson is in God's hands. Your husband and your sons will take good care of your little grandson. Have no worry. God is calling you to go out to others who need to hear the heavenly guidance which you have received from the Holy Family.*
The family is in need of conversion. Go in peace, little sister, and bring many souls to God through the witness of your own conversion. I shall intercede for you. Until tomorrow, farewell, little sister!

Janie: Farewell, St. Philomena! Thank you for your encouraging words.

Prepare With Prayer

September 12, 1996
New Orleans, Louisiana

St. Philomena: *Greetings from Heaven, my little sister!*

Janie: Peace to you, St. Philomena. Sweet St. Philomena, I recommend to you all who will attend my talk tonight. Ask God to bless everyone, especially this family who invited me. They are dear to me.

St. Philomena: *Little sister, I shall intercede for all your special*

106

intentions and for those who invoke my intercession. You have a busy schedule ahead of you. Prepare with prayer. Until tomorrow, farewell, little sister!

Janie: Farewell, St. Philomena!

St. Philomena said that many would be the blessings that God would give His people.

Souls Alight with the Fire of His Love
September 13, 1996
New Orleans, Louisiana

A morning prayer, an inspired prayer to the Eternal Father:

Eternal Father, restore us to Your friendship. Look upon our hearts and afflicted spirits. Heal our troubled consciences so that in the joy and strength of the Holy Spirit, we may reflect Your heavenly love. Amen.

A night prayer to the Eternal Father:

Heavenly Father, illumine the night. Bring the dawn to scatter the darkness. Let us pass this night in safety, free from Satan's power, and rise when morning comes to give thanks and praise. Let Your holy angels keep watch over us and grant us holy dreams. Amen.

Prayer for daily guidance:

Eternal Father, today guide our feet in the way of Your peace. Restrain us from every evil impulse. Guard our thoughts, words and actions. May everything we do this day be pleasing in Your sight. Through the Cross and Resurrection of Your Son, fill our day with the consolation of the Holy Spirit. Amen.

107

Conversations With St. Philomena

Work Together in Peace for the Glory of God

September 13, 1996

St. Philomena: *Greetings from Heaven, little sister!*

Janie: Greetings, St. Philomena! Please pray for all who are here present. (I recommended everyone by name.)

St. Philomena: *Little sister, know that God is pleased with all the holy work that is being offered here for the salvation of souls. God wants to set all souls on fire with His love, but this can only be done when hearts are open to His love.*

Janie: St. Philomena, please intercede for the people in this area and their special intentions.

St. Philomena: *Little sister, I am interceding for this area, for there are many souls that have devotion to me. Share with the people that God is blessing this area. It is important that everyone work together in peace for the glory of God. Until tomorrow, farewell, little sister!*

Janie: Farewell, St. Philomena!

Our Master Will Refresh You

September 14, 1996

St. Philomena: *Greetings from Heaven, little sister!*

Janie: Peace to you, St. Philomena.

St. Philomena: *Little sister, you have done well in your sharing with the people. God is pleased with your efforts. Your obedience to go, leaving your loved ones behind, has brought victory to many souls who heard you speak.*
  Today, Our Master will visit with you. You will be blessed and

you will rejoice. You are tired now from all the holy work you did, but soon Our Master will refresh you. Prepare with joy for His visit. Until tomorrow, farewell, little sister!

Janie: Farewell, St. Philomena!

Listen to All That She Tells You

September 15, 1996
The Feast of Our Lady of Sorrows

St. Philomena: *Greetings from Heaven, little sister!*

Janie: Peace, St. Philomena.

St. Philomena: *Little sister, today God will bless you with the visit of Our Heavenly Queen and Mother. Your heart will rejoice with love for the Heavenly Queen. Although she will share with you some of her sorrows, your heart will embrace her with love.*
Little sister, Our Heavenly Queen loves you very much. Listen to all that she tells you. Until tomorrow, farewell, little sister!

Janie: Farewell, St. Philomena!

Sufferings For Our Master's Vicar on Earth

September 16, 1996

St. Philomena: *Greetings from Heaven, little sister!*

Janie: Peace to you, St. Philomena.

St. Philomena: *Little sister, today is the day in which you offer all your sufferings for Our Master's vicar on earth. Our Master has designated that each first day of the week you suffer for His Bride. These days are hard for you, but your obedience to embrace this suffering for the conversion of His Bride pleases Him.*

109

Conversations With St. Philomena

Janie: St. Philomena, I am honored to accept this invitation from Jesus to suffer for the Holy Father and for all of the Church. I try to fast on this day, but my spiritual director has advised me to eat small meals since I already fast on Wednesdays and Fridays. He does not want me to do too much fasting because he knows that I also suffer the Passion of Our Lord, especially on these three days.

St. Philomena: *Little sister, it is wise to listen to the guidance of your spiritual director for he is God's voice on earth; he is God's representative. I will intercede for you, little sister, as you offer your prayers and sacrifices for Our Master's Bride. Until tomorrow, little sister, farewell!*

Janie: Farewell, St. Philomena!

Pray to the Holy Spirit for Guidance

September 17, 1996

St. Philomena: *Greetings from Heaven, little sister!*

Janie: Peace, St. Philomena.

St. Philomena: *Little sister, abandon all concerns for your family to the Holy Spirit. God will hear all your prayers. Know that God is blessing your family through your prayers and sufferings. Pray to the Holy Spirit for guidance. You shall not regret it. Until tomorrow, farewell!*

Janie: Farewell, St. Philomena!

Today, I was suffering for a particular situation in our family.

Two Angels Who Visited Me

September 18, 1996

St. Philomena: *Greetings from Heaven, little sister!*

110

Janie: Peace to you, St. Philomena. St. Philomena, please pray for me. Today my suffering is immense. My hands and my feet feel like someone is burning a hole through them. My head feels like it will crack from the piercing of the thorns. My side pain is not as intense. Please help me to endure this suffering for the love of Jesus, my Love and my All.

St. Philomena: *Little sister, do not be concerned. You are doing well in enduring your suffering for the conversion of poor sinners. I will intercede for you. I will ask Our Master to send you the two angels who visited me in the dungeon after I had been lashed and dragged by the prison guards at the order of Diocletian.*

These two angels will pour a soothing balm over your own wounds to help you to endure Our Master's Passion. Know that your suffering is saving many souls. Until tomorrow, farewell, little sister!

Janie: Farewell, St. Philomena!

Rest Little Sister

September 19, 1996

St. Philomena: *Greetings from Heaven, my little sister!*
Janie: Peace to you, St. Philomena. St. Philomena, I am doing much better today, thanks to your intercession. I am still very tired.

St. Philomena: *Little sister, enjoy this day and thank God for everything. Rest, little sister, rest. Until tomorrow, farewell!*

Janie: Thank you, St. Philomena. I will rest.

These Poor Young People

September 20, 1996

St. Philomena: *Greetings from Heaven, little sister!*

111

Conversations With St. Philomena

Janie: Peace to you, St. Philomena. St. Philomena, the suffering of the unconverted youth is so strong in my heart. I don't understand why, but I will offer my fasting for them.

St. Philomena: *Little sister, Our Master places these thoughts in your heart so that you may pray for the youth. These poor young people have lost their virginity, the purity of their hearts. Satan has seduced them through his many temptations. You, little sister, must pray and fast to help these poor souls to repent. Our Lord impressed these young people on your heart because they need your prayers. I will pray with you. Until tomorrow, farewell, little sister!*

Janie: Farewell, St. Philomena!

Continue Battling Satan for the Salvation of Souls
September 21, 1996

St. Philomena: *Greetings from Heaven, little sister!*

Janie: Peace, St. Philomena.

St. Philomena: *My little sister, I want you to know that I have been praying for you. Your suffering has been intense and at times you feel all alone and unloved. God is allowing you to experience the Passion of Our Master. Know that the evil one is working hard to discourage you from carrying out God's plan for your family and families everywhere.*

My little sister, if you only knew how many families are being helped through your prayers and sacrifices. Many marriages are being reconciled because of your perseverance in carrying out God's plan for all His children. Your prayers for the Church are helping the vicar of Our Master and many priests and religious. Your prayers for the youth are helping to detach many from Satan's web of sin. Your prayers for the unborn are helping to protect many innocent souls from being murdered in their mothers' wombs.

Your prayers and sacrifices for protection over the world are

112

serving to protect so many souls. Satan is very angry with you because he knows that God has given you special graces and discernment to recognize his evil traps.

The Holy Spirit is always at your side to help you to see clearly with the eyes of your soul the works of Satan. God has assigned special angels to protect you, for you are in the midst of much spiritual warfare. You are in need of protection; this is why God gives you angels to help you.

My little sister, I share all this with you to encourage you to continue battling Satan for the salvation of souls. Until tomorrow, farewell, little sister! God is with you.

Janie: Farewell, St. Philomena!

Keep Your Eyes on Our Master

September 22, 1996

St. Philomena: *Greetings from Heaven, little sister!*

Janie: Greetings, St. Philomena!

St. Philomena: *My little sister, be patient with your family. God is listening to your prayers for them. Keep your eyes on Our Master and all His glory. I know that things are hard for you right now, but God is your strength. Never forget this.*

Janie: St. Philomena, I am not very strong in my love these days. I am trying, but sometimes it seems the more that I try, the worse things become. My main concern is to do God's Most Holy Will above all things. He is the One that I serve.

St. Philomena: *Little sister, keep this attitude always, and God will send His angels to help you in any difficulty. Until tomorrow, farewell, little sister!*

Janie: Farewell, St. Philomena! Thank you for your prayers.

Conversations With St. Philomena

Three Months of Prayer and Fasting

September 23, 1996

St. Philomena: *Greetings from Heaven, my little sister!*

Janie: Ave, St. Philomena.

St. Philomena: *My little sister, prepare yourself and your family through much prayer, for the next three months are crucial to your country. Know that the sinfulness of the leaders in your country and their decisions are responsible for the annihilation of the unborn.*

Already, God is greatly offended by the slaughter of the unborn. Oh, so offended! My little sister, God yearns for the reconciliation of His people so that the horror of slaughtering precious souls may cease.

Pray for your president and all who support the evil he wants to endorse which will allow the annihilation of the unborn. Pray and fast in reparation for the leaders in your country and do not forget to include all world leaders whose hearts are filled with evil. Offer to the Father all your prayers and sacrifices.

Little sister, next month is recognized by the Church as the month of the Rosary. Offer this whole month for the intentions of the Immaculate Heart of Mary to stop the slaughter of the unborn. Offer the following month to the Holy Spirit so that people in your country will choose God-sent leaders to lead your country. Continue your prayers and fasting for this effort. In the third month, continue with prayer and fasting in preparation for the birth of Our Master. These three months of prayer and fasting will purify your own heart. Know that God will bless your country and much evil will cease.

My little sister, know that God has given me, St. Philomena, this request to guide you to share with others. Do not be concerned with anything but know that God will send His Holy Spirit to guide all who respond to this request.

Janie: St. Philomena, what kinds of prayers and sacrifices should we offer?

Anchor of Hope from Heaven

St. Philomena: *My sister, you may offer daily Mass, reading Holy Scripture, your daily Rosary, spending time with Our Master in Adoration and other daily devotions. Deny yourself eating you favorite foods. Do not quarrel, but be kind, offering works of mercy. Refrain from watching television programs; instead, spend this time with your family or quiet time with God. The Holy Spirit will guide you, be open to Him. Until tomorrow, little sister, farewell!*

Janie: Farewell, St. Philomena!

I heard these words in my soul: *A country that kills their children is a country without hope.*

Restore Devotion to Me

September 24, 1996

St. Philomena: *Greetings from Heaven, little sister!*

Janie: Greetings, St. Philomena!

St. Philomena: *My little sister, I know that you wish deep in your heart to restore devotion to me. There are many souls who have great devotion to me. Please do not be sad about what you heard concerning my sainthood.*

Speak to your spiritual director and God will guide you through him. As your twenty-four hours of fasting comes to an end, know that your prayers and fasting on the Eucharist are helping to save souls.

Janie: Oh, St. Philomena, I yearn so much to go to Mugnano, Italy to visit your shrine.

St. Philomena: *My little sister, you will visit my shrine. Do not be anxious. Pray today for your oldest son. Talk to him about God's love for him. Until tomorrow, farewell, little sister!*

Conversations With St. Philomena

Janie: Farewell, St. Philomena!

Youth on Their Way to Perdition

September 25, 1996

St. Philomena: *Greetings from Heaven, little sister!*

Janie: Greetings, St. Philomena!

St. Philomena: *My little sister, continue to pray for all the youth who are on their way to perdition. These young people have chosen destructive lifestyles. They have no one who really cares for them. Their own parents have turned their backs on these poor souls.*
Little sister, there is very little purity in the world of the youth. Drugs and fornication are the biggest weapons that Satan uses to trap the youth. He uses drugs to get these poor souls to alter their thinking. He knows that drugs inhibit their morals and values. Once they are under the influence of drugs, fornication follows.
Many young boys and girls lose their virginity when they are under the influence of drugs. Many times pregnancy follows, and these young people become frightened. This leads to abortion. Please, little sister, pray and fast for the youth. They need God's love to help them. Only His love can free them of all their misery.

Janie: I will pray for all the youth, my sweet St. Philomena.

St. Philomena: *Thank you so much, little sister. Until tomorrow, farewell!*

Janie: Farewell, St. Philomena!

Unbelievers Who Have Leadership Positions

September 26, 1996

St. Philomena: *Greetings from Heaven, little sister!*

Anchor of Hope from Heaven

Janie: Greetings, St. Philomena!

St. Philomena: *Little sister, today continue to pray in preparation for the next three months.*

Keep in mind especially your president who is in need of much prayer. He continues making decisions that are affecting many souls, believers and unbelievers.

Pray for the conversion of all unbelievers who have leadership positions. Always offer especially your daily Masses and your daily Rosary for these intentions. Until tomorrow, my little sister, farewell!

Janie: Farewell, St. Philomena!

When Families Pray Together

September 27, 1996

St. Philomena: *Greetings from Heaven, my little sister!*

Janie: Greetings, St. Philomena! St. Philomena, please pray for my family that we may carry out God's plan together. We are constantly under Satan's attacks. My family supports me and they do their best to live Our Lady's messages.

St. Philomena: *Little sister, God's love and protection are upon you and your family. He knows that you are doing your best and that is all He asks of His children.*

These are times when destruction of the family continues to increase. This happens because families do not pray so they are without protection. This is why Our Holy Mother asks that her children intercede for the conversion of poor sinners. Your prayers help others to convert.

Little sister, when families pray together, their prayers dissolve the attacks of Satan. Remain strong in prayer and Satan will flee from you. Until tomorrow, little sister, farewell!

117

Conversations With St. Philomena

Janie: Farewell, St. Philomena! Thank you.

For Priests and Religious Gone Astray

September 28-29, 1996

I spent my visit with St. Philomena praying for priests and religious who have gone astray.

For the Pope and the Church

September 30, 1996

Today, St. Philomena and I prayed for the Pope. During the past three days, St. Philomena has shared with me the many reasons why the Church needs prayers. All she revealed is personal, which I only share with my spiritual director.

Sharing My Spirituality

October 1, 1996

St. Philomena: *Greetings from Heaven, little sister.*

Janie: Peace to you, St. Philomena.

St. Philomena: *Little sister, continue to foster devotion to me by sharing my spirituality with people whom you meet. I will help all who ask for my assistance.*

Janie: St. Philomena, I will do as you say.

St. Philomena: *Thank you, little sister. Until tomorrow, farewell.*

Janie: Farewell, St. Philomena.

Spread Devotion to God's Holy Messengers

October 2, 1996

St. Philomena: *Greetings from Heaven, little sister.*

Janie: Greetings, St. Philomena.

St. Philomena: *Little sister, today is a glorious day for all who have love and devotion to their guardian angels. These holy heavenly messengers are helping many souls who love their guardian angels to live like children of God.*

Little sister, show God your gratitude by spreading devotion to God's holy messengers. Always remember that your guardian angels love you very much. Trust in their intercession. Know that these heavenly messengers helped me, St. Philomena, when I was being tortured under the orders of Diocletian. He inflicted on me, St. Philomena, a cruel suffering. He imprisoned me in a dark and filthy dungeon. This evil emperor was accustomed to getting his way and was very angry with me when I refused to marry him.

My little sister, know that during this horrible suffering, God sent His angels, Our Lady and the Christ Child to give me strength. It was the angels who came to my rescue when I was thrown into the Tiber River with a heavy anchor around my neck. The angels again kept me from harm when I was shot with arrows. These arrows never touched my body.

Throughout time, God has sent his holy messengers to help His people. In Holy Scripture you read that God sent His angel to St. Peter when he was put in jail (Acts 5:17-20). It was the angel who freed St. Peter from his chains and opened the door to his cell (Acts 12:7).

Little sister, throughout Holy Scripture you will find passages that describe how these heavenly messengers have been sent by God to help His children. Never fear in the midst of your suffering, but remain calm. Know that your angel is at your side. No harm will befall you. Your guardian angel will see to that. Trust these holy messengers. Until tomorrow, little sister, farewell.

119

Conversations With St. Philomena

Janie: St. Philomena, thank you from the bottom of my heart for sharing all this with me. I do love and trust my guardian angel, and I thank God for him.

Open Your Heart and Abandon All to God

October 3, 1996

St. Philomena: *Greetings from Heaven, little sister.*

Janie: Peace to you, St. Philomena.

St. Philomena: *Little sister, I am here to help you in your many concerns. You have much on your mind. Open your heart and abandon all your concerns to God.*

Janie: St. Philomena, having the responsibility of my little grandson sometimes worries me. I want to do the best that I can for him. He has suffered by not being raised by his natural mother. I want to provide him with everything.

St. Philomena: *Little sister, you are providing your grandson with everything that he needs. You have been teaching him, first of all, about God. You have taught him how to pray before meal time and at night time. Do not worry, little sister. God is pleased with your duty as a grandmother. Until tomorrow, have peace, little sister.*

Janie: Thanks, St. Philomena.

St. Francis Will Help You

October 4, 1996

St. Philomena: *Greetings from Heaven, little sister.*

Janie: Peace, St. Philomena. St. Philomena, I am joyful today because today is First Friday and also the feast of St. Francis of Assisi. He is my spiritual father. Today, I will fast in honor of the Sacred Heart of Jesus and for the love of my spiritual father, St. Francis.

St. Philomena: *Little sister, today is a special day for you and for all who have devotion to the Sacred Heart of Jesus. Many blessings are rendered to those who embrace this devotion.*
    St. Francis lived a most holy life of suffering for the love of Our Master. St. Francis will help you to embrace the spirit of prayer and fasting. Little sister, your little ways are pleasing to God. Trust in Him always. Until tomorrow, farewell, little sister.

Janie: Farewell, St. Philomena.

Hunger for the Bread of Angels

October 5, 1996

St. Philomena: *Greetings from Heaven, little sister.*

Janie: Ave, St. Philomena.

St. Philomena: *Little sister, you are very joyful this morning. Truly, St. Francis interceded for you to receive holy joy when you asked him to pray for you.*

Janie: Oh, yes, St. Philomena! Yesterday was a day filled with the spirit of my spiritual father, St. Francis. I was so unhappy at first, because my pastor was ill and unable to celebrate Holy Mass. It was too late to go to any other church. I prayed and received spiritual communion and accepted this with a sad spirit.

    Later on that day, a dear priest friend came to give a retreat in our town. He came by our home and he celebrated Holy Mass at our home. I was amazed at the great love that God showed me especially on the feast of St. Francis. Praise be to God, forever and ever.

St. Philomena: *Little sister, God will always come to the aid of*

121

Conversations With St. Philomena

those who hunger to be nourished on the Bread of Angels. In your hunger, you reached out to Him and He, Himself, came to you through His priest. Recall Holy Scripture, "Draw closer to God and He will draw closer to you." (James 4:8)

Little sister, tomorrow we will visit again. I know that your hand is hurting you and that you are suffering. Until tomorrow, farewell, little sister.

Janie: Farewell, St. Philomena.

Consecrate Yourself to the Two Hearts Every Day
October 6, 1996

St. Philomena: *Greetings from Heaven, little sister.*

Janie: Peace to you, St. Philomena. St. Philomena, again I am joyful, for today is First Saturday. I went to confession yesterday. Today I will attend Holy Mass in honor of Our Blessed Mother in response to her request in Fatima.

St. Philomena: *Little sister, in honoring the Queen of Heaven you glorify God. You also make our heavenly Father very happy. Always remember, little sister, that in honoring the devotion of the Two Hearts, you are embracing the Holy Will of the Eternal Father. Consecrate yourself to the Sacred Heart of Jesus and the Immaculate Heart of Mary every day, and you will obtain purity and holiness in your faith journey. Until tomorrow, farewell, little sister.*

Janie: Thank you, St. Philomena.

Today the Heavenly Queen Will Visit
October 7, 1996

St. Philomena: *Greetings from Heaven, little sister.*

Janie: Peace to you, St. Philomena.

St. Philomena: *Little sister, today the Heavenly Queen will visit you. Prepare your heart to embrace your Heavenly Mother who loves you so very much. Prepare, little sister, and be ready for your Heavenly Mother. Until tomorrow, farewell, little sister.*

Janie: St. Philomena, I will prepare. I love you. Thank you.

Prayer Helps a Soul to Grow in Love and Faith
October 8, 1996

St. Philomena: *Greetings from Heaven, little sister.*

Janie: Peace to you, St. Philomena. St. Philomena, please help me to be as brave as you when persecution comes my way. I believe that God sent you to me to help me to have a strong faith and to learn to love God the way you did. You were so young and yet so strong in your love and faith. Tell me how to obtain strong faith and how to love God as you do.

St. Philomena: *Little sister, prayer is what helps a soul to grow in love and in faith. I spent my days in prayer. My mind was always occupied in doing the work of God. I knew in my heart that I could never do enough for Our Master, He who gave His life for all of humanity with such love and obedience to His Father.*
I prayed and thus I was able to grow in faith and in love for God. I abandoned my own will and embraced His will. I prayed very hard, so that I could die to myself and be able to live only for God.
Through prayer I learned perseverance, I learned to trust God and to abandon myself totally to Him. Through prayer I was able to die to myself more and more every day. Prayer helped me to embrace the virtue of obedience. Holy obedience is the virtue which I lived for everyday of my life. Through prayer I learned to put God first in my life.

Conversations With St. Philomena

This was my reason for living; to live and to die for the love of God. This is how you must live, little sister. Until tomorrow, farewell.

Janie: Farewell and thank you for your heavenly guidance.

You Are a Pillar of Strength

October 9, 1996

St. Philomena: *Greetings from Heaven, little sister.*

Janie: Peace to you, St. Philomena. I am learning so much about your spirituality and I am impressed by your love for God. I want so much to imitate you. I want to be strong for God, but I have many obstacles. Sometimes I don't know if I am pleasing God. Being a wife, mother and grandmother is a big responsibility. I am always in spiritual warfare with Satan for the conversion of my loved ones.

St. Philomena: *Little sister, you are a mighty prayer warrior. You stand strong against the attacks of Satan. You help your family to keep their focus on heaven in times of crisis. You are a pillar of strength for your family and all who seek your help. You are courageous in your love for God.*
Do not allow Satan to deceive you by placing these thoughts in your mind. Continue to pray and trust God. This is your path; embrace it. Until tomorrow, farewell, little sister.

Through Our Prayers, Families May Convert

October 10, 1996

St. Philomena: *Greetings from Heaven, little sister.*

Janie: Peace, St. Philomena.

St. Philomena: *Little sister, offer your prayers for all the families*

124

who suffer because they do not have God in their lives. There are many broken marriages that end up in violence. This destroys the spirit of the children. So many children are suffering due to the sinfulness of their parents. These children are innocent; they do not deserve this kind of suffering brought on by their parents. Pray with me, little sister, so that through our prayers families may convert. Until tomorrow, farewell, little sister.

I saw in a vision the suffering in the families. I was very sad after this visit. I prayed for this intention.

A Good Teacher

October 11, 1996

St. Philomena: *Greetings from Heaven, little sister.*

Janie: Peace, St. Philomena. St. Philomena, today I wish to recommend to you all my grandchildren. They love you very much and they have good intentions to live pure and holy lives. They love for me to speak of Heaven to them. They are so precious and dear to me. Keep them close to your own heart. I recommend all children and the youth, especially those who have no one to teach them about God.

St. Philomena: *Little sister, you are a good teacher for your grandchildren. I will intercede for your special intentions. Until tomorrow, farewell, little sister.*

Janie: Thank you, St. Philomena.

You Will Overcome These Doubts

October 12,1996

St. Philomena: *Greetings from Heaven, my little sister.*

Janie: Peace to you, St. Philomena. St. Philomena, pray for me,

125

Conversations With St. Philomena

today especially, for I am feeling sad. I don't wish to be ungrateful to God, but writing everything which you share with me seems so crazy to me. This is the 20th century. Who would believe that a saint who died in the 3rd or 4th century after Christ would come to me -- and why? I know that you came to a few other souls, but why to me? Please help me, St. Philomena, please, I need your prayers.

St. Philomena: *Little sister, I know that you suffer from doubts, but this is also a cross for you. Be obedient and continue to write our conversations and abandon all your concerns into God's hands. Know that there are many souls who have devotion to me and that God could have sent me to visit one of these many souls. He sent me to you, instead, one who did not know anything about me. I am most happy that God chose you.*

Rejoice! Do not be concerned with what others think. Remember your responsibility is to be obedient to God's most Holy Will. This is your duty. You will overcome these doubts. Until tomorrow, farewell, little sister.

Janie: Thank you, St. Philomena. You're good for me.

Prepare For Holy Mass

October 13, 1996

St. Philomena: *Greetings from Heaven, little sister.*

Janie: Peace to you, St. Philomena. St. Philomena, today I recommend to your special intentions my friend in Florida whom I will be visiting in a few days. Pray for him; he is so giving and has done much for me and many others. I recommend to you all his family.

St. Philomena: *Little sister, I will intercede for your special intentions for your dear friend and family. Prepare for Holy Mass and to receive Our Master. Until tomorrow, farewell, little sister.*

Janie: Thank you, St. Philomena.

Suffering From Family Problems

October 14, 1996

St. Philomena: *Greetings from Heaven, little sister.*

Janie: Peace to you, St. Philomena.

St. Philomena: *Little sister, you are preparing for your visit to Florida. Know that you will help many souls who are suffering with family problems. During your stay you will have an opportunity to spend much time before the Blessed Sacrament with Our Lord. He will give you guidance on how to spend your time with Him. Until tomorrow, farewell, little sister.*

Janie: Farewell, St. Philomena. Thank you.

Personal Messages

October 15-18, 1996

During October 15 - 18, I was in Florida for a retreat. During these times St. Philomena came, but her guidance was personal for the people with me at this time.

Keep Your Eyes on God

October 19, 1996

St. Philomena: *Greetings from Heaven, little sister.*

Janie: Peace to you, St. Philomena.

St. Philomena: *Little sister, you are suffering today, and you are having a difficult time with prayer. Know that I will intercede for you. Keep your eyes on God who loves you. He will help you. Until tomorrow, farewell, little sister.*

I was suffering for some difficulties. St. Philomena carried me

127

through with her prayers.

The Suffering of Mothers

October 20, 1996

St. Philomena: *Greetings from Heaven, little sister.*

Janie: Peace to you, St. Philomena. St. Philomena, thank you for yesterday. Your prayers helped me so much. Today my spirit is joyful.

St. Philomena: *Little sister, I am your heavenly companion. I will help you in your journey towards holiness.*

Janie: St. Philomena, the path towards holiness is hard, but this is all I hunger for. This is why I try my best to trust God in times of my suffering. St. Philomena, today, I don't know why, but I recommend all mothers to your powerful intercession.

St. Philomena: *Little sister, you are experiencing the suffering of mothers for their husbands and their children. These mothers want the best for their families spiritually. You are experiencing their anguish. I will intercede for them. Until tomorrow, farewell, little sister.*

For All Priests Persecuted

October 21, 1996

St. Philomena: *Greetings from Heaven, little sister.*

Janie: Peace to you, St. Philomena.

St. Philomena: *Little sister, offer your suffering for all priests who are being persecuted for the love they have for Our Master. These are good and obedient priests whose only desire is to do God's will.*

Pray for them. They suffer so much at the hands of others. Until tomorrow, farewell, little sister.

[I understood that these priests suffered persecution from other priests.]

The Chaplet of St. Philomena

October 22, 1996

St. Philomena: *Greetings from Heaven, little sister.*

Janie: Peace to you, St. Philomena. St. Philomena, I want to teach others how to demonstrate devotion to you. Can you show me? I know that some of the many ways of expressing love for you is by reciting your chaplet, wearing your cord, saying the novena honoring you, using the holy oil which burns before your statue, and visiting your shrine. Today, I wish to know about your chaplet. What will it do for your devotees?

St. Philomena: *Little sister, by the recitation of my chaplet, a soul is better able to imitate my spirituality. Many blessings and answers to their prayers are received by those souls who recite my chaplet with faith in their hearts. Those who recite the chaplet in my honor receive many favors as well.*

Tomorrow, little sister, we shall speak about other devotions to me. Until tomorrow, farewell, little sister.

Janie: Thank you, St. Philomena.

[Note: The Chaplet is found in the Appendix.]

Encourage My Devotees To Wear The Cord

October 23, 1996

Janie: Peace, St. Philomena.

Conversations With St. Philomena

St. Philomena: *Little sister, today I would like to continue to teach ways of promoting devotion to me. Another way is wearing the cord in my honor. The Church has approved it and blesses it.*

Many are the privileges and favors granted to those who wear the cord. Many souls who are experiencing illness of mind, body and spirit have recovered. The cord has been worn by many of my devotees. Those wearing the cord are protected from many evils of soul and body. I help those wearing the cord to desire perfect chastity. Little sister, the favors granted to those wearing the cord are numerous. Encourage my devotees to wear the cord and remind them of their duty to pray the daily prayer.

Tomorrow I will speak of other devotions to me. Until tomorrow, farewell, little sister.

Janie: Thank you, St. Philomena.

[Note: The daily prayer to be said by those who wear the cord is found in the Appendix.]

Use This Oil

October 24, 1996

St. Philomena: *Greetings from Heaven, little sister.*

Janie: Peace to you, St. Philomena.

St. Philomena: *Today, little sister, I wish to speak to you about another devotion to me, which is the use of the oil from the lamp that burns perpetually before my statue.*

Many souls have received healing through their faith in using this oil. The different types of healing are too numerous to mention. Please encourage those souls who have devotion to me to use this oil.

Those using this oil should pray according to the perfect will of the Father to obtain healing. It is God the Father who grants all

130

those favors to those who have faith. Until tomorrow, farewell, little sister.

Janie: Farewell, St. Philomena.

[Note: An explanation of the oil of St. Philomena and how to obtain it is contained in the Appendix.]

Numerous Favors For My Devotees

October 25, 1996

St. Philomena: *Greetings from Heaven, little sister.*

Janie: Peace to you, St. Philomena. St. Philomena, I am deeply grateful to you for teaching me how to bring others to devotion to you.

St. Philomena: *Little sister, I will help you in your call to foster devotion to me. Many are my devotees and to them many favors are granted. My intercession before God is powerful; therefore, I am able to obtain numerous favors for my devotees.*
 Continue, little sister, fostering devotion to me; this is your task. I shall assist in all your needs. Until tomorrow, farewell, little sister.

Janie: Thank you, St. Philomena.

St. Philomena Prayed

October 26, 1996

Due to illness, St. Philomena 's visit was very short. She prayed for me.

Conversations With St. Philomena

Trust In What I Say to You

October 27, 1996

St. Philomena: Greetings from Heaven, little sister.

Janie: Peace to you, St. Philomena. St. Philomena, yesterday you told me that my task is to spread devotion to you. I trust that you will guide me in how to do this.

St. Philomena: *Little sister, I am paving the way for you, for your task comes with immense grace. All that you do for me will be in harmony with my shrine in Italy. Trust in what I say to you. I know how much you love the virtue of obedience, and this is the virtue which you must have to respond to my call.*

Janie: St. Philomena, I love you very much. I will do anything to help you, and I will be obedient even unto my death. I mean this with all my heart.

St. Philomena: *I know you do, little sister. That is why you were chosen for this task. I am grateful for your love and devotion. Until tomorrow, farewell, little sister.*

Janie: Farewell, St. Philomena.

In Harmony With My Shrine in Italy

October 28, 1996

St. Philomena: *Greetings from Heaven, little sister.*

Janie: Peace to you, St. Philomena. St. Philomena, I am so excited to have you helping me. I trust totally in your assistance.

St. Philomena: *Little sister, each day in which we visit I am helping to pave your way with what is to come for you.*

Janie: St. Philomena, what do you mean?

132

Anchor of Hope from Heaven

St. Philomena: *Little sister, through your love and devotion you will make me even more known, but everything must be in harmony with the guidance of my shrine in Italy. You don't understand this now. Don't worry; soon you will visit my shrine in Italy, then you will understand. Until tomorrow, farewell, little sister.*

Janie: Thank you, St. Philomena.

You Will Visit My Shrine

October 29, 1996

St. Philomena: *Greetings from Heaven, little sister.*

Janie: Peace to you, St. Philomena. St. Philomena, I feel your presence in a powerful way, even after your visits are over. I am so grateful to God for you. I am excited about going to visit your shrine. I don't know how, since it's an expensive trip. My family does not have that kind of money. I trust in you.

St. Philomena: *Little sister, I am always at your side. This is why you feel my presence with you.*
You will visit my shrine; remember, with God all things are possible. You will receive many blessings and graces when you visit my shrine. This is another favor granted to my devotees who visit my shrine. Until tomorrow, farewell, little sister.

Janie: Peace to you, St. Philomena.

Foster Devotion to Me

October 30, 1996

St. Philomena: *Greetings from Heaven, little sister.*

Janie: Peace, St. Philomena. St. Philomena, you have been sharing so much with me about yourself. Thank you with all my heart.

Conversations With St. Philomena

St. Philomena: *Little sister, your heart is open to everything which I share with you. You will be strong in your love and devotion to me. Through my intercession God will grant you many favors, many favors. I am deeply grateful to you, little sister, for your "yes" to foster devotion to me. Until tomorrow, farewell, little sister.*

Janie: Farewell, St. Philomena.

Children Who Will Celebrate Halloween

October 31, 1996

St. Philomena: *Greetings from Heaven, little sister.*

Janie: Peace to you, St. Philomena.

St. Philomena: *Little sister, offer your prayers and suffering for all the children who will celebrate Halloween. Much evil comes out of this celebration, and many innocent people will suffer. I will unite my prayers with yours. Until tomorrow, keep vigil over souls through your prayers.*

Janie: I will pray, St. Philomena.

The Intercession of the Saints

November 1, 1996
All Saints' Day

St. Philomena: *Greetings from Heaven, little sister.*

Janie: Peace to you, St. Philomena. Today I am very happy, for we are honoring all saints, so I wish to congratulate you on this special day. God is so good to us to bless us with the intercession of all the saints. I am so grateful to Him, and I salute all the saints in heaven, beginning with Our Heavenly Queen, St. Joseph, and all my patron saints. I am so happy, for it is also First Friday.

134

St. Philomena: *Little sister, today is a special day for all who believe in the intercession of the saints. Oh! how blessed are those souls who have love and devotion to the saints. It is through the intercession of the saints that God grants many favors to those who have faith in them. Rejoice on this day, little sister; rejoice, for the saints rejoice with you!*

Until tomorrow, farewell, little sister. Spend time with Our Master. Tell Him how much you love Him.

Janie: I will. Farewell, St. Philomena.

Today Many Souls in Purgatory Will Enter Heaven
November 2, 1996
First Saturday

St. Philomena: *Greetings from Heaven, little sister.*

Janie: Peace to you, St. Philomena. St. Philomena, I am happy again today. Today is First Saturday and All Souls' Day. I will go to Mass to fulfill my First Saturday obligation and offer my prayers for the holy souls.

St. Philomena: *Little sister, today is another special day for those who are dedicated to First Saturday and who pray for the holy souls. All who have a devotion to First Saturday help to console the sorrowful heart of their Heavenly Queen and Mother, who cries copious tears for the offenses committed against her beloved Son, Jesus.*

Little sister, God is pleased with you and your family for your own devotion to First Saturday. Know that this devotion will help you and your family's sanctification.

Today many souls in Purgatory will enter heaven. You have a devotion and special love for the souls in Purgatory, and your prayers have helped these holy souls enter heaven. Continue to embrace this special devotion, for it is marked with the approval of the Church. Until tomorrow, farewell, little sister.

135

Conversations With St. Philomena

Janie: Thank you, St. Philomena, for everything.

Spend Time With Him In The Most Blessed Sacrament
November 3, 1996

St. Philomena: *Greetings from Heaven, little sister.*

Janie: Peace to you, St. Philomena.

St. Philomena: *Little sister, spend time with Our Master today in the Most Blessed Sacrament. Console Him, for He has been abandoned by so many of His representatives on earth. Spend time with Him, telling Him how much you love Him and how grateful you are for all that He has done for you.*
Little sister, never before has Our Master been so rejected by His own representatives as He is in these present times. Your visit with Him will mean so much to Him. Your time spent adoring Him in the Blessed Sacrament will bring much healing to all His representatives whose faith is weak.

Janie: St. Philomena, I will go and spend time with Our Lord in the Blessed Sacrament. I will console Him. I am sad for the pain that Our Lord suffers for us. I will console Him.

St. Philomena: *Thank you, little sister. You shall not regret it. Farewell, little sister.*

Holy Mass Is the Greatest Prayer
November 4, 1996

St. Philomena: *Greetings from Heaven, little sister.*

Janie: Peace to you, St. Philomena. St. Philomena, please pray for my family, so that they will embrace prayer more. I want them to truly understand the importance of prayer. I especially want them to understand the importance of Holy Mass as a form of prayer.

St. Philomena: *Little sister, you have a good and loving family. Your love for them is great. This is why you desire that they grow more towards Our Master through prayer. You are correct in understanding that Holy Mass is the greatest prayer to God. When families attend Holy Mass frequently, these families grow closer to one another, and together they overcome all obstacles which the evil one puts in their path.*

Little sister, share with your family and families whom you meet, that Holy Mass is the highest form of prayer. Our Master is sad because families do not celebrate the Eucharist as they should. If families would understand the grace and the gifts they receive, they would prepare before attending Holy Mass. Share all this, little sister, with your loved ones, and they will believe you. Until tomorrow, farewell, little sister.

Janie: Thank you, St. Philomena.

Spiritually Adopt All the Young

November 5, 1996

St. Philomena: *Greetings from Heaven, little sister.*

Janie: Peace to you, St. Philomena. St. Philomena, today I am suffering for all the youth who are living in darkness of drugs, violence, abortions, fornication, and everything that separates them from God. My heart is very sad. What do the youth need to do? They are so confused and lost.

St. Philomena: *Little sister, the young people live in darkness because they do not pray. Those souls who do not pray, do not know God. The parents of the young people have the responsibility of seeing to the spiritual needs of their children. Many of the young people who are walking in darkness are following the path of their parents. Parents who do not believe in God pave the road to perdition for their children. Parents who are walking in darkness will have*

137

Conversations With St. Philomena

children who will also live in darkness.

Little sister, prayer is what is needed in the lives of the lost young people. Your prayers will help these poor lost souls. As a mother, you can spiritually adopt all the young people in the world who have no one to pray for them. God will take your own prayers and sacrifices to help these young people. Pray always for all the young people and children who do not know how to love. Pray. They are so lost and wounded. I shall pray with you. Until tomorrow, farewell, little sister.

Janie: Thank you, St. Philomena. I will love the children and the youth through my own prayers.

Copious Tears for All Souls in Darkness

November 6, 1996

St. Philomena: *Greetings from Heaven, little sister.*

Janie: Peace to you, St. Philomena. St. Philomena, I have been praying for all the children and youth in the world. I am especially praying for their parents. At times, while I am praying, I feel such sorrow in my soul.

St. Philomena: *Little sister, Our Master is allowing you to experience the sorrow in His own heart for the children and the young people who suffer so much. Our Master, together with His Most Holy Mother, cry copious tears for all souls who live in darkness.*

Little sister, offer Holy Mass, Adoration and the Rosary for all these poor little precious souls. I assure you, that as you offer these prayers, many of these souls will find their way back to Our Master's love. Until tomorrow, farewell, little sister.

Janie: Thank you, St. Philomena.

138

No Message Given

November 7, 1996

I was sick, so St. Philomena came for a private visit.

For Offenses Against Our Master

November 8, 1996

St. Philomena: *Greetings from Heaven, little sister.*

Janie: Peace to you, St. Philomena.

St. Philomena: *Little sister, today you are suffering for the offenses committed against Our Master. This suffering is most difficult for you as you unite in the pain of Our Master. Little sister, draw your strength from Our Master. Although you are experiencing dryness in your soul, Our Master is very close to you. Trust Him. Until tomorrow, farewell, little sister.*

Janie: St. Philomena, pray for me, please.

His Love Is Greater Than Your Suffering

November 9, 1996

St. Philomena: *Greetings from Heaven, little sister.*
Janie: Peace to you, St. Philomena. St. Philomena, again, I need your prayers to help me embrace the suffering which I undergo each day in reparation for poor sinners. Please pray that I am strong enough to attend Holy Mass, so that I may offer this great form of love for all who have abandoned Our Lord. Please pray for me. I need your help.

St. Philomena: *Little sister, I understand your great suffering, for I, too, suffered much for the sake of my love for Our Master. I suffered to the end, keeping my eyes on Our Master and not allowing all the cruel tortures to distract me from breaking the promise*

139

which I made to Our Master. You, too, must keep your eyes focused on Our Master, for His love is greater than your suffering. He will strengthen you and refresh you. Trust Him. Until tomorrow, farewell. I shall pray for you; do not worry.

Janie: Thank you, St. Philomena. Your words are courage for me.

Yearning for the Eucharist

November 10, 1996

St. Philomena: *Greetings from Heaven, little sister.*

Janie: Peace to you, St. Philomena. St. Philomena, today is a good day for me. Holy Mass was beautiful. Receiving Our Lord in the Holy Eucharist brought so much joy to my heart. I live for the Holy Eucharist.

St. Philomena: *Little sister, God has given you special graces to embrace Our Master in the Holy Eucharist. The more you attend daily Mass, the closer you are united to Our Master's divine love. To live daily, yearning for Our Master, is a great gift of love which Our Master has bestowed on you. Rejoice, little sister, and share this hunger which you have to receive Our Master in the Eucharist with others! Let this yearning for the Eucharist be a testimony of your reason for living. Until tomorrow, little sister, farewell.*

Janie: St. Philomena, I love you.

Gifts of Love From Heaven

November 11, 1996

St. Philomena: *Greetings from Heaven, little sister.*

Janie: Peace to you, St. Philomena. St. Philomena, today I have been thinking about what you told me when you first came to me. You said that you came as "the Anchor of Hope from heaven to help the family and the youth in these troubled times."

Today, I wish to thank you for being obedient by coming to help us. You also said that you came to help me in my suffering. You have most certainly done that. I am so grateful to God for you. I pray that people embrace all that you've shared with me.

I know that you have great love for the youth and children. Tell me, why do you love the children and the youth so much?

St. Philomena: *Little sister, I love children, because they are gifts of love from Heaven. All children, by nature, are good, because God created them, but it is the teachings of their parents which corrupt their sweet innocent hearts and minds.*

I always desired to have brothers and sisters. I loved children when I lived on earth, and now that I am in Heaven, my love for children is greater.

The young people are also dear to my heart, for I, too, was a young person before my death. I yearned to have young friends, but my parents were very protective of me. I spent most of my time with my family and my educators.

I yearned to have young friends so that I could share with them all the importance of praying, my love for Our Master and His love for all of humanity. I did not have the privilege of doing this while I lived on earth.

Our loving God has rendered me special favors now that I'm in heaven to help all children and young people through my prayers. I especially pray for the purity and holiness of all children before they are born. I especially hold dear to my heart all those young souls who suffer from physical, sexual and emotional abuse. Little sister, like yourself, I too, have much love for all these precious souls. Until tomorrow, farewell, little sister.

Janie: Thank you, St. Philomena. You are sweet.

141

Conversations With St. Philomena

Forgive the Mistakes of Their Children

November 12, 1996

St. Philomena: *Greetings from Heaven, little sister.*

Janie: Peace to you, St. Philomena. St. Philomena, today I am praying for all the families who are suffering because they have no control over the lives of their youth. Many of these parents have repented and have changed their way of living, but their children are consumed by the ways of the world. What guidance can you give to these poor suffering parents?

St. Philomena: *Little sister, God wants all parents to forgive the mistakes of their children and to love them with unconditional love. God wants parents to pray for their children and to have peace with them. Parents must be patient with their children as God is patient with their own actions as parents. God wants parents to teach their children about His love for them. Parents must also invite their children to pray together with them. In short, parents must do everything to bring their children back to God. Parents should pray for the conversion of their children without hesitation.*

Parents who belong to the Catholic faith should make Holy Mass a daily prayer which they offer for the conversion of their children. The prayer of the Rosary is powerful to help convert loved ones. For parents who belong to a different faith, their prayers are also strong for the conversion of their children.

In prayer, parents discover the power of God's love, His mercy and His healing power. Prayer is the remedy for families to help heal the woundedness of unforgiveness in their hearts. Little sister, share this with parents. Until tomorrow, farewell, little sister.

Janie: Farewell, St. Philomena.

Distractions in Prayer

November 13, 1996

St. Philomena: *Greetings from Heaven, little sister.*

142

Janie: Peace to you, St. Philomena. St. Philomena, today I am having a difficult time remaining in the spirit of prayer. I am so distracted. How can I remain in the spirit of prayer with so much distraction?

St. Philomena: *Little sister, do not stop praying because you are distracted but continue to pray, and soon you will experience peace of mind. The evil one does not like it when you pray. He knows that your prayers are strong, because you pray with love in your heart. He places distractions in your mind so that you may think that you should not pray when you are in this state of mind.*

Remember, prayer does not originate in the mind but in the heart. Do not listen to your thoughts, listen to your heart, for God speaks to the heart. Be at peace; God is listening to all yours prayers, no matter how poorly you are praying. Until tomorrow, farewell, little sister.

Janie: Thank you, St. Philomena.

Pray for Our Master's Vicar on Earth
November 14, 1996

St. Philomena: *Greetings from Heaven, little sister.*

Janie: Peace to you, St. Philomena.

St. Philomena: *Little sister, spend quiet time before the Blessed Sacrament, praying for Our Master's Vicar on earth. He is suffering much for all the disobedience within Our Master's Bride. Today, you will suffer much for the sinfulness of fallen away priests. Until tomorrow, farewell, little sister.*

Janie: Pray for me, St. Philomena, so that I may remain in prayer all day.

Conversations With St. Philomena

Pray for the Bride of Our Master

November 15, 1996

St. Philomena: *Greetings from Heaven, little sister.*

Janie: Peace to you, St. Philomena.

St. Philomena: *Little sister, continue to pray for the Bride of Our Master. Many priests are living such wicked lives. Many priests have allowed themselves to be consumed by the ways of the world. Many are being led astray because they have not worshipped the true Christ who lives among them. Oh! how sad is Our Master's heart for these fallen-away souls. Pray, little sister, pray. Until tomorrow, farewell, little sister.*

Janie: I will pray, St. Philomena, I will pray.

Suffering Among the Children and Youth

November 16, 1996

St. Philomena: *Greetings from Heaven, little sister.*

Janie: Peace to you, St. Philomena.

St. Philomena: *Little sister, please remember all the children and the young people in your prayers today. Little sister, you could never imagine how much suffering there is among the children and the youth in the world.*

I saw a vision as St. Philomena was speaking. I saw thousands of children and young people suffering. Many children were victims of prostitution. (These children were as young as 11 years old and older.) Many were addicted to drugs, many were homeless, many were suffering from the AIDS virus, many were homosexuals, many were pregnant and many had abortions. There was such sadness and pain in their eyes. This vision made me so sad.

144

St. Philomena: *Little sister, know that all these children and youth suffer due to the neglect of their parents. Many are from broken homes; many are from very wealthy parents. These families do not have God in their lives; therefore, their children become victims of abuse and neglect.*

Pray for them; there is much suffering in these children and young people. Many take their own lives, for there is no one to love them or to help them. Our Most Holy Mother weeps copious tears for all these precious souls.

Janie: Oh, St. Philomena, I will pray much for these special intentions. I promise!

St. Philomena: *Little sister, I will be praying with you. Until tomorrow, farewell, little sister.*

Janie: Thanks, St. Philomena.

He is at Your Side When You Suffer

November 17, 1996

St. Philomena: *Greetings from Heaven, little sister.*

Janie: Peace to you, St. Philomena. St. Philomena, please pray for me so that I can have courage when I am suffering for Our Lord. I so want to please Him.

St. Philomena: *Little sister, it is your faith which gives you courage to remain steadfast under suffering. Faith will give you courage to remain true to Our Master in whatever He may ask of you.*

During my own suffering, it was my faith and love for Our Master that gave me great courage. No matter what the cruel emperor did to me, he did not break my spirit, for my faith was strong. I know that Our Master was by my side during my own suffering. He is at your side when you suffer. Trust in this and have faith. Un-

til tomorrow, farewell, little sister.

Janie: Farewell, St. Philomena, and thank you so kindly. You've been a great help.

Prayers and Sacrifices Will Help These Priests
                                        November 18, 1996

St. Philomena: *Greetings from Heaven, little sister.*

Janie: Peace to you, St. Philomena.

St. Philomena: *Little sister, today as you offer your prayers and sufferings for the Bride of Our Master, especially keep in mind all the priests who no longer respect or honor their priestly vows. Their hearts are in great danger for these priests have fallen into all the traps that the devil sets before their path.*

Janie: St. Philomena, excuse me for asking, but can my prayers really help these priests?

St. Philomena: *Oh, yes, little sister! The power of prayer is so strong, especially when you offer it with love in your heart. Your prayers and sacrifices will help these priests to see the wrong that they are doing against Our Master. Always trust and have faith in the power of prayer for any difficulties. Until tomorrow, farewell, little sister.*

Janie: Farewell, St. Philomena.

Share What You Have
                                        November 19, 1996

St. Philomena: *Greetings from Heaven, little sister.*

Janie: Peace to you, St. Philomena. St. Philomena, please help us as a family, through your intercession, so that we may prepare for Thanksgiving. I wish to gather some food so that we can help all the poor people around us. There is so much poverty and I want to brighten up poor people's lives by helping them.

St. Philomena: *Little sister, your desires are pleasing to God. Sharing what you have with the poor around you brings about great joy to their hearts. Always pray, asking God to give you the spirit of charity. In this way you will lessen the suffering of those who are victims of poverty. Sharing with others also brings about much peace and joy. I will intercede for your special intentions. Until tomorrow, farewell, little sister.*

Janie: Farewell to you, St. Philomena.

The Youth in Such Darkness

November 20, 1996

St. Philomena: *Greetings from Heaven, little sister.*

Janie: Peace to you, St. Philomena. St. Philomena, please keep me in your prayers. Tomorrow is the feast of the Presentation of Mary and Our Lady will come to me. I am excited about her visit. I miss her.

St. Philomena: *Little sister, tomorrow will be a joyful day for you. Our Holy Mother will help you in your suffering. Her visit will bring you much guidance. Prepare today for this heavenly visit. You shall not regret it.*

Little sister, please continue to pray for all the youth who are lost and who live in such darkness. Already your prayers and sacrifices have helped many, many young people and suffering children, as well.

Rejoice, little sister, for Our Master looks to your prayers and sacrifices to draw poor sinners closer to His love and mercy. Until

147

tomorrow, farewell, little sister.

Janie: Farewell, St. Philomena. Thank you for everything.

Ponder Everything in Your Heart
November 21, 1996

St. Philomena: *Greetings from Heaven, little sister.*

Janie: Peace to you, St. Philomena. Oh! I am so happy after my visit with Our Lady. She brought much joy to my heart. We had a wonderful visit. Thank you for your prayers.

St. Philomena: *Little sister, Our Holy Mother loves you very much, for you have a generous and obedient heart. You respond to all the instructions which Our Master and Our Most Holy Mother give you. You are a loving and loyal servant and Heaven is at your disposal. Embrace all that Our Holy Mother shares with you; ponder everything in your humble heart. Until tomorrow, little sister, farewell.*

Janie: Farewell, St. Philomena. You are so kind.

I Have Come to Help You Carry Your Cross
November 22, 1996

St. Philomena: *Greetings from Heaven, little sister.*

Janie: Peace to you, St. Philomena. St. Philomena, I am so grateful to God for sending you to me. I am so happy to be your little sister. You know I really knew nothing of you and never heard of you before. I don't remember if I've asked you this, but why did God allow you to come to me?

148

St. Philomena: *Little sister, your path has been a difficult one with much suffering. You had a painful childhood and you had no one to truly love you. I had wonderful and loving parents, but my path was a difficult one as well for I also suffered much. I suffered much to the point of death. You have suffered much humiliation, persecution and abandonment by your parents.*

Our lives have many similarities. I was sent by God to help you in your suffering, to give you courage and to share my own suffering with you. I have shared parts of my life which no one else has any knowledge of. We have shared such heavenly moments that bring much joy to my heart.

Little sister, I am your heavenly sister. I have come to help you to carry your cross by sharing many heavenly things with you. We have become such close friends that I really look with great joy to our time together. You have a good and loving heart and your only desire is to do the Holy Will of God. I have come to help you to do this. I have come to pray with you for poor sinners and I so enjoy praying with you. Your prayers come from your heart for you pray with love for humanity. I am happy to spend this time with you.

Janie: St. Philomena, all that you say is true. When will our time together end?

St. Philomena: *Little sister, Our Master will let us know. Let us enjoy our time together. Until tomorrow, farewell, little sister.*

Janie: I love you, St. Philomena.

The Devil Is Trying to Steal Your Peace
November 23, 1996

St. Philomena: *Greetings from Heaven, little sister.*

Janie: Peace to you, St. Philomena. St. Philomena, please pray for me that I may be a loving wife, mother and grandmother. Sometimes, it is so hard to remain patient and at peace during family trials. Sometimes, my faith is weak and I give in to the spirit of anger.

St. Philomena: *My little sister, be at peace. God knows how very hard you try to be a loving wife, mother and grandmother. Your only desire is to draw your family to God. The devil is trying hard to steal your peace but your prayers will dissolve all his attempts.*

Remember, little sister, that all families have disagreements, but what is important is how the family handles their disagreements. If the family prays together, they will overcome all the attacks of the devil. Your family is a prayerful and loving family. Trust in their love for you. Until tomorrow, little sister, farewell and be at peace.

Janie: Thank you, St. Philomena.

Great Blessings for All Your Family
November 24, 1996

St. Philomena: *Greetings from Heaven, little sister.*

Janie: Peace to you, St. Philomena. St. Philomena, I am very happy for today Our Lord will come and visit with me. I always look forward to these heavenly visitations.

St. Philomena: *Little sister, Our Master loves you very much and today He will bring great blessings for all your family and relatives, especially those of your relatives who are far from Our Master's heart. Your prayers and sufferings, little sister, have been most helpful to all your loved ones.*

This is why Our Master will bless all your relatives. He remembers all your supplications for your loved ones. Always pray for the conversion of your entire family and relatives. I love you, little sister, and I rejoice in the blessings which you will receive on this day. Until tomorrow, farewell, little sister.

Janie: Farewell, St. Philomena. I love you.

Unite Together as God's Family

November 25, 1996

St. Philomena: *Greetings from Heaven, little sister.*

Janie: Peace to you, St. Philomena. St. Philomena, please pray for me. Today I am baking pumpkin pies which are family favorites. I am trying to also prepare the corn bread dressing and homemade cranberry sauce. I enjoy cooking and I learned all this from my mother. She was a professional cook.

St. Philomena: *Little sister, have no worry. Everything you prepare for your Thanksgiving meal has God's blessing for you prepare everything with such love. You also provided a Thanksgiving meal for the poor and God is pleased with your charitable heart.*

My parents had servants who prepared all our meals, however once in a great while my mother and I would sneak into the cooking quarters. My mother would prepare a special treat for me and for herself. Oh, these were our secret golden moments! I found so much joy in doing this. I always enjoyed special days with special meals, when we met with relatives and friends. These were also special times.

Little sister, anytime a family unites together as God's family is pleasing to God, and He blesses this union. I will intercede for you as you prepare your Thanksgiving family meal. Until tomorrow, farewell, little sister.

Janie: Peace to you, St. Philomena.

To Our Master Through Our Lady

November 26, 1996

St. Philomena: *Greetings from Heaven, little sister.*

Janie: Ave, St. Philomena. Thank you for being here with me.

151

Conversations With St. Philomena

St. Philomena: *My little sister, know that I have been interceding for you during your suffering. I am always with you in prayer. I take all your petitions to Our Master through Our Lady. I ask Our Lady to intercede for you and your family. I speak to Our Lady about your concerns, then I tell her all your petitions. She gladly presents them to her Son.*

Janie: St. Philomena, I am most grateful for all your help. Please tell Our Lady to help X. This soul is truly distant from the Lord. I love this soul very much.

St. Philomena: *My little sister, I will present all your concerns to Our Lady, so that she may take your prayers to her Son.*

Pray, my little sister, that the world may accept Our Lady as their Mother. God, Himself, has sent Our Lady to the world to help all His children. This is why she is appearing and speaking to God's children.

There is so much sin in the world, and the spirit of paganism lives in many souls. Many souls have forgotten that God exists and this is the message that Our Lady is conveying to the world. Many souls read her messages, but very few live the messages. They are too busy and consumed with materialism. Many souls have no time for God.

Pray, little sister, for Our Lady suffers much for her unconverted children. Until tomorrow, farewell, little sister.

Janie: St. Philomena, thank you for sharing Our Lady's pain. I will pray for all her special intentions.

All The Homeless and Hungry

November 27, 1996

St. Philomena: *Greetings from Heaven, little sister.*

Janie: Ave, St. Philomena.

152

Anchor of Hope from Heaven

St. Philomena: *Little sister, pray for all the homeless and the hungry who suffer so much. These poor souls are lost and need much prayer and love. Always keep them in your prayers.*

Little sister, continue to offer your prayers for the Vicar of Our Master. He suffers so much. Keep in mind dear Mother Teresa for she is totally committed to living the gospel message to feed the hungry and clothe the naked through her works of mercy and charity. I know that you love Mother Teresa very much, and that you pray for her every day.

Little sister, share with your dear friends that God always listens to their prayers. I will intercede for all your special intentions. Until tomorrow, farewell, little sister.

Janie: Farewell, St. Philomena.

I Will Intercede For You

November 28, 1996
Thanksgiving Day

St. Philomena: *Greetings from Heaven, little sister.*

Janie: Peace to you, St. Philomena. St. Philomena, we are preparing to go to Thanksgiving Mass, and then we will eat our Thanksgiving dinner. We will pray and give thanks to God for everything. Today is special for our family. Pray for us.

St. Philomena: *Little sister, I will intercede for you and your family. Until tomorrow, farewell, little sister.*

Janie: Thank you, St. Philomena. Good bye!

God Is Helping Your Husband

November 29, 1996

St. Philomena: *Greetings from Heaven, little sister.*

Conversations With St. Philomena

Janie: Peace, St. Philomena.

St. Philomena: *Little sister, do not be concerned about your husband. He will be all right; abandon him to God. God is helping your husband to build your new home. It will all be done. Trust God with this project. Until tomorrow, farewell, little sister.*

Janie: Peace to you, St. Philomena.

Recognize Your Weakness

November 30, 1996

St. Philomena: *Greetings from Heaven, little sister.*

Janie: Ave, St. Philomena. Thank you for coming.

St. Philomena: *My little sister, I am happy to be with you. This morning Our Master wants me, St. Philomena, to convey to you how pleased He is with all your prayers and sacrifices. He wants you to persevere in your continuous suffering for poor sinners and for His Bride.*
My little sister, Our Master sees all your good efforts and He blesses your perseverance.

Janie: St. Philomena, all I want is to be good and to please Our Master, but sometimes I feel like a failure. Please pray for my weakness.

St. Philomena: *Little sister, Our Master is pleased that your recognize your weakness and that you yearn to grow strong in these areas. Know, my little sister, that it takes God's grace to recognize your sinfulness. These graces are obtained through your constant prayers. Prayer is important for the soul to grow in spiritual maturity. Prayer is the medicine that the soul needs to recover from all the woundedness that has accumulated from living a sinful life. Prayer changes the soul and perfumes the soul with heavenly fra-*

154

grance.

My little sister, pray unceasingly, offering all your supplications to God Who will not ignore your cry for divine intervention.

Janie: St. Philomena, I will continue to pray for all souls beginning with my own soul. Will you please intercede for this little boy who will be coming for prayer?

St. Philomena: *Know, for certain, that I will intercede for your special request. Until tomorrow, farewell, my little sister.*

Janie: Farewell, St. Philomena.

She Suffers Much

December 1, 1996

St. Philomena: *Greetings from Heaven, my little sister.*

Janie: Ave, St. Philomena. Thank you for coming.

St. Philomena: *My little sister, I know that you are not feeling well. Offer your suffering for the special intentions of Our Lady. She suffers much for the sins of poor sinners. She especially suffers when souls reject her as their Mother. She is always interceding for all her children; she brings all her own petitions before her Son. Through her love and prayers for her children, God is pouring His mercy upon the world as never before. Pray, my little sister, for your prayers help to draw souls closer to God.*

Janie: St. Philomena, sometimes I feel like I am not helping others when I become distracted by my suffering. Please pray for me, so that I may suffer well with joy in my heart.

St. Philomena: *My little sister, your suffering is intense, but you are not distracted by your suffering. Abandon yourself completely to God in your suffering and trust Him. He is always with you. Your*

155

Conversations With St. Philomena

suffering helps others to convert, and it purifies your own soul. Little sister, remember what Our Lady said to you about your suffering: "My child, while you live in the world your suffering will be great. God has called you to a life of prayer and suffering. Know, my angel, that your reward is great in heaven." Embrace these words from Our Lady, little sister. Allow her words to penetrate your heart. Until tomorrow, farewell, little sister.

Janie: Farewell, St. Philomena. Thank you for everything.

Prayers For Mother Teresa

December 2, 1996

St. Philomena: *Greetings from Heaven, little sister.*

Janie: Ave, St. Philomena.

St. Philomena: *Little sister, continue to offer your prayers for Mother Teresa; she is suffering. Keep in mind Our Lady's special intentions. Until tomorrow, farewell, little sister.*

Janie: Farewell, St. Philomena.

Never Grow Tired of Praying

December 3, 1996

St. Philomena: *Greetings from Heaven, my little sister.*

Janie: Ave, St. Philomena. Thank you for coming.

St. Philomena: *My little sister, you are tired and you have been suffering for poor sinners. Rejoice and embrace your suffering for there is no greater suffering than to suffer for the salvation of poor sinners.*
    Pray with your family for all the families that suffer because

they do not have God in their lives. Little sister, never grow tired of praying; prayer is what the world needs.

Prepare your heart for the birth of Our Master. Allow Him to live in your heart so that your heart will be filled with His love. Allow your heart to be the little manger that He seeks. In this way He will live in you and you in Him.

My little sister, do not worry about X. I will intercede for her.

Janie: St. Philomena, this poor soul does not know God and has no one who really loves her.

St. Philomena: *God loves her. No matter whether or not she knows God, He knows her. Be at peace and continue to pray for her. Until tomorrow, little sister, farewell.*

Janie: St. Philomena, I have a question. I almost forgot. What should I say to her about her question?

St. Philomena: *Reassure her that God is taking care of all that she needs. Encourage her to put all her trust in God and not to worry.*

Janie: Thank you, St. Philomena and farewell.

Scarred By The Rejection of Parents

December 4, 1996

St. Philomena: *Greetings from Heaven, my little sister.*

Janie: Ave, St. Philomena.

St. Philomena: *My little sister, your heart continues to suffer for that poor little lost soul for whom you have been praying. The world is filled with poor little lost souls such as this one, who is so heavy in your heart.*

Pray, little sister, for God's blessings on the family, and pray

Conversations With St. Philomena

especially that the parents love and accept their children with love in their hearts. So many parents have no relationship with God and this lack of relationship with God brings much suffering to their children.

The world is full of young children and young people who are without parents. These poor precious souls suffer immensely because their hearts are scarred by the rejection of their parents. They are afraid to trust anyone for fear of rejection.

Little sister, God knows that your heart understands the suffering of all young children and young people. This is the very reason that you were chosen to be blessed with the visitations of the Holy Family. God chose you and your family to spend your days praying for families everywhere.

Little sister, you have a loving and charitable heart. Your heart is full of compassion for those who suffer because they do not have God's love in their hearts. Continue to pray for all these families.

My little sister, I, St. Philomena will continue to intercede for all your petitions. Do not worry about X. He will be employed soon. Your prayers have been answered. Until tomorrow, farewell, little sister.

Janie: Farewell, St. Philomena.

Our Most Holy Mother and St. Joseph
December 5, 1996

St. Philomena: Greetings from Heaven, my little sister.

Janie: Peace, St. Philomena.

St. Philomena: *Little sister, pray, asking the powerful intercession of Our Most Holy Mother and of St. Joseph to help prepare you and your family for the birth of Our Master. Through the intercession of Our Holy Mother and St. Joseph, you and your family will embrace*

158

the blessings of this holy season.
Little sister, there is no greater intercession than that of Our
Holy Mother and St. Joseph to help prepare you for the birth of Our
Master. Our Most Holy Mother and St. Joseph are the heavenly ex-
amples to help prepare souls to receive the birth of the Christ
Child. Trust in their intercession all the time, but most especially
during this holy season. Until tomorrow, farewell, little sister.

Janie: Thank you, St. Philomena.

For All of God's Children

December 6, 1996

St. Philomena: *Greetings from Heaven, little sister.*

Janie: Peace to you, St. Philomena.

St. Philomena: *Little sister, today spend quiet time with Our Mas-*
ter in the Most Blessed Sacrament. Do this after Holy Mass. Pray
your Rosary for all of God's children so that through your prayers
more souls will love Our Master. There are so many souls who re-
ject Our Master. This rejection is painful for Our Master for He
cannot help those who reject His love and mercy. Until tomorrow,
farewell, little sister.

Janie: I will visit Our Lord in the Most Blessed Sacrament.

For Parents Who Abandon Their Responsibility

December 7, 1996

St. Philomena: *Greetings from Heaven, little sister.*

Janie: Peace to you, St. Philomena.

St. Philomena: *Little sister, today let us entrust all the children and*
young people to the Immaculate Heart of Mary. Let us, together,

159

Conversations With St. Philomena

pray in reparation for all the parents who have abandoned their responsibility as parents. Let us pray for all parents who have had abortions for these parents are in need of repentance. Our prayers will help everyone, especially when we pray together with Our Most Holy Mother who loves all her little children. Until tomorrow, farewell, little sister.

Janie: I will unite in prayer with you. I will entrust everyone to the Immaculate Heart of Mary.

Many of Her Children Present
December 8, 1996

St. Philomena: *Greetings from Heaven, little sister.*

Janie: Peace to you, St. Philomena.

St. Philomena: *Little sister, offer your Mass today so that tomorrow Our Holy Mother will have many of her children present when she visits with you. Rejoice, for God will grant you special favors tomorrow to help you in your faith journey. Until tomorrow, farewell, little sister.*

Janie: Farewell, St. Philomena. I will offer my Mass for this intention.

[Note: December 8 fell on a Sunday. The Church celebrated the feast of the Immaculate Conception on Monday, December 9.]

Ponder All That Our Lady Said
December 9, 1996
Solemnity of the Immaculate Conception

St. Philomena: *Greetings from Heaven, little sister.*

160

Janie: Peace to you, St. Philomena. Oh, St. Philomena! I was so happy to be with Our Lady today. Her message was so beautiful and so helpful. Everybody was so happy to have this heavenly visit. Thank you for your prayers.

St. Philomena: *Little sister, ponder all that Our Lady said to you. Share her message with everyone. Until tomorrow, farewell, little sister.*

Janie: Farewell, St. Philomena.

For All the Suffering and Abused Children
December 10, 1996

St. Philomena: Greetings from Heaven, little sister.

Janie: Peace to you, St. Philomena.

St. Philomena: *Little sister, today I invite you to pray with me for all the suffering and abused children in the world. Little sister, the children and the young people are so dear to Our Master. He is greatly offended by those souls who are responsible for the suffering of any child or young person. Your prayers console Our Master for He knows how much you love children and young people.*

Pray for these intentions, please, little sister, for my heart, too, is sad! Remember Our Master's words in Holy Scripture: "Let the little children come to me and do not prevent them, for the Kingdom of God belongs to such as these (Mt 19:14)." Little sister, pray for the suffering families in the world who do not have God in their lives. Until tomorrow, farewell, little sister.

Janie: Farewell, St. Philomena.

Conversations With St. Philomena

Our Holy Mother Knows How Much You Love Her
December 11, 1996

St. Philomena: *Greetings from Heaven, little sister.*

Janie: Peace, St. Philomena. St. Philomena, I am so happy for tomorrow I will have another visit with Our Lady. This is one of my favorite titles, "Our Lady of Guadalupe." I did not know too much about Our Lady, but as a child I knew the name of "Nuestra Senora de Guadalupe." She is well-known in the Hispanic culture and everybody loves her under this title, but Our Lady knows that I love her, no matter what title she has. She is dear to me and I love her with all my heart.

St. Philomena: *Little sister, you are indeed happy this morning. Our Holy Mother knows how much you love her and how dear she is to your heart. Little sister, I will pray for you to help you prepare for tomorrow. Farewell, my sweet little sister.*

Janie: Farewell, St. Philomena. Yes, my heart is very happy.

The Heavenly Queen
December 12, 1996
Feast of Our Lady of Guadalupe

St. Philomena: *Greetings from Heaven, little sister.*

Janie: Peace to you, St. Philomena. Oh, what a great day this is, St. Philomena! Our Lady's visit brought so much joy to my heart. Again, she helped all of the people present. Thanks be to God for Our Lady.

St. Philomena: *Little sister, always praise God for all the heavenly blessings which He bestows upon the world through the Heavenly Queen. Continue throughout this day sharing the blessings of God. Until tomorrow, farewell, little sister.*

Janie: Thank you so much, St. Philomena.

The Holiness of This Time

December 13, 1996

St. Philomena: *Greetings from Heaven, little sister.*

Janie: Peace to you, St. Philomena. St. Philomena, please pray for my family and for me so that we will not be distracted from the true meaning of Christmas. Sometimes it is hard to remain focused on the spirit of Christmas when everybody is focused on spending lots of money and on buying expensive gifts. Christmas is a holy time and there are many good things that people do during this time, but the spirit of commercialism is alive in many hearts. St. Philomena, I don't know if I am making myself clear. Do you understand what I am trying to say?

St. Philomena: *Little sister, I understand what is in your heart. Pray, asking St. Joseph and Our Holy Mother to intercede for all who no longer understand the holiness of this time. Unite your prayers with the parents of Our Master who were chosen by God. Together, your prayers united with theirs will help to open many hearts. I will also unite my prayers with your prayers. Until tomorrow, farewell, little sister.*

Janie: Thank you, St. Philomena. You give such good heavenly advice.

She Is Helping You

December 14, 1996

St. Philomena: *Greetings from Heaven, little sister.*

Janie: Peace to you, St. Philomena. St. Philomena, please pray for my special intentions for my family. We are trying hard to remain prayerful during this time. Today, I am not feeling too well.

163

Conversations With St. Philomena

St. Philomena: *Little sister, I will intercede for your special intentions. Do not worry; you and your family are in the Immaculate Heart of Mary. She is helping you. Until tomorrow, farewell, little sister.*

Janie: Farewell, St. Philomena.

Doubt Is the Devil's Work

December 15, 1996

St. Philomena: *Greetings from Heaven, little sister.*

Janie: Peace to you, St. Philomena. St. Philomena, today I am suffering with the spirit of doubt. Did your ever doubt during your suffering when the emperor was doing all kinds of evil things to you? Did you know that God would protect you? This sounds dumb, but I am in a strange place, or my soul is in a strange place. I cannot explain it; I do not understand it myself!

St. Philomena: *Little sister, do not listen to the lies of the devil. Your soul is experiencing a dryness, nothing that prayer of the heart cannot fix.*
I, myself, remained prayerful, hopeful and faithful to God's saving, loving power during my suffering. What I did, I did for the love of my Master, for I had given myself and my love to Him, and nothing would make me break my vow which I had made to Him.
Have no worry, but trust. Remember that Our Master's love is mightier than all the lies of the devil. Keep in mind that doubt is the devil's work; trust is the fruit of God's love. Be at peace. Until tomorrow, farewell, little sister.

Janie: Thank you, St. Philomena.

The Holy Spirit Will Illumine Your Heart

December 16, 1996

St. Philomena: *Greetings from Heaven, little sister.*

Anchor of Hope from Heaven

Janie: Peace to you, St. Philomena.

St. Philomena: *Little sister, prepare with strong prayer for the next few days you will suffer for all those poor souls who do not love Our Master. During your suffering the Holy Spirit will illumine your heart. During this time you will see many souls who hate Our Master. Pray and fast for these poor unbelieving souls. Until to-morrow, farewell, little sister.*

Janie: St. Philomena, I will pray and do as you request of me. I love you.

St. Philomena: *I love you dearly, little sister.*

You Are Consoling Our Master

December 17, 1996

St. Philomena: *Greetings from Heaven, little sister.*

Janie: Peace to you, St. Philomena. St. Philomena, the Holy Spirit has helped me to pray for all those souls who hate Our Lord and who say evil things about Him.

St. Philomena: *Little sister, you are consoling Our Master. Until tomorrow, farewell, little sister.*

I was suffering very much on this day. In a vision I saw many ways in which people who hate Our Lord desecrate His Holy Name.

Your Suffering Will Soften the Hearts of Unbelievers
December 18, 1996

St. Philomena: *Greetings from Heaven, little sister.*

165

Conversations With St. Philomena

Janie: Peace to you, St. Philomena. St. Philomena, my suffering continues. As you know, it is so difficult for me to write; my hand is in great pain.

St. Philomena: *Little sister, you are suffering for all the unbelievers who have rejected Our Master. Your suffering will help to soften the hearts of the unbelievers. Many of the souls for whom you are suffering will convert during this holy season. Until tomorrow, farewell, little sister. I am praying with you.*

Janie: I love you, St. Philomena.

All of Heaven Is at Your Disposal

December 19, 1996

St. Philomena: *Greetings from Heaven, little sister.*

Janie: Peace to you, St. Philomena.

St. Philomena: *Little sister, I will be very brief in my visit, for I know that your suffering is intense. Know that all of heaven is at your disposal. I love you, little sister. Peace!*

Janie: Peace, St. Philomena, and thank you.

In Reparation for Poor Sinners

December 20, 1996

St. Philomena: *Greetings from Heaven, little sister.*

Janie: Peace to you, St. Philomena.

St. Philomena: *Little sister, you have embraced your suffering in reparation for poor sinners in a most courageous way. Remain faithful and continue to bring many unconverted souls to Our Master. Until tomorrow, farewell, little sister.*

Janie: Thank you, St. Philomena.

Our Master Wants You to Rest

December 21, 1996

St. Philomena: *Greetings from Heaven, little sister.*

Janie: Peace to you, St. Philomena.

St. Philomena: *Little sister, today Our Master wants you to rest. He will fill you with His peace. He is grateful for your "yes" to embrace your cross with an obedient heart. Peace, little sister, peace.*

Janie: St. Philomena, I will rest today. I am very tired. Give my love to Our Lord for me and tell Him, "Thank you."

Prayers Always Help

December 22, 1996

St. Philomena: *Greetings from Heaven, little sister.*

Janie: Peace to you, St. Philomena. St. Philomena, today I am doing much better and I went out for a little while. I was a little disappointed at how many people were behaving badly towards one another. Children were angry with their parents because they couldn't have many expensive gifts. There was so much arguing among many people that I had to come home. Maybe I just went to the wrong shopping center!

St. Philomena: *Little sister, continue to pray for all that you see. Prayers always help, always. Until tomorrow, farewell, little sister.*

Janie: I am sorry, St. Philomena, I know that my focus must be on Our Lord. I'll try to do better. I guess the suffering has made me a bit grouchy.

Conversations With St. Philomena

The True Meaning of Christmas

December 23, 1996

St. Philomena: *Greetings from heaven, little sister. I, St. Philomena greet you with God's peace.*

Janie: Oh, St. Philomena! I greet you with my love. Thank you so much for your prayers.

St. Philomena: *My little sister, rejoice, for Our Master has responded to your cry to fill your heart with His peace.*

Janie: Indeed! He did, and I am rejoicing with great peace in my heart. St. Philomena, I cannot help myself. I get upset with the attitude of people in regard to Our Master. It seems to me that so many people are busy shopping for Christmas rather than focusing on Our Master.

St. Philomena: *Little sister, you and I must pray that the attitude of people will change and that people will understand more clearly the true meaning of Christmas.*
Many souls have forgotten the great gift of love that God gave to His people through the birth of His only begotten Son. The great gift of love came into the world through the birth of the Divine Savior, a Savior born in a humble stable, born to a humble Virgin and an upright humble man.
This Most Holy Virgin was chosen throughout eternity to be the Mother of the King of Kings. A humble carpenter was chosen to be the spouse and foster-father of this great Savior, of Whom many of the prophets spoke in Scripture. God chose these two humble servants to care for His Son. Most Holy Mary and St. Joseph suffered much, but they persevered and remained faithful to their "yes."
Many have forgotten this wonderful miracle that took place in a little town in Bethlehem. This miracle continues to occur every year, but many look on this as a time to receive gifts and to buy gifts for those souls close to them. Very few think of this as the time of the birth of Our Master.
Little sister, God loves all His children, and He calls His chil-

168

dren to reflect the spirit of Our Blessed Mother and St. Joseph. Our Blessed Mother and St. Joseph were obedient to God in all that He asked of them. They, too, had many struggles and great sufferings that have never been recorded by mankind.

St. Joseph suffered very much as he cared for Our Master and His Most Holy Mother. Our Blessed Mother did everything she could to help St. Joseph carry out everything that God had asked of them.

As they prepared for the birth of Our Master, they encountered many obstacles. They had no family close by to ask for assistance. St. Joseph and Our Most Holy Mother were exhausted from trying to find a place for the birth of Our Master. They were rejected time and time again, but they remained charitable, at peace and trusting in God throughout their great struggle. They both prayed for those who rejected them and refused them help.

Little sister, I, St. Philomena share all this with you so that you may share with others the struggles of the Holy Family and how they never abandoned God's plan for the salvation of the world. God gave Our Most Holy Mother and St. Joseph all that they needed to carry out His divine plan for the salvation of the world. He will do the same with all those souls who trust in His divine assistance.

Pray for all souls, asking the powerful intercession of Our Most Holy Mother and St. Joseph to help prepare their hearts. This most holy couple, chosen by God to love and care for His only beloved Son, will respond quickly to all who invoke their powerful intercession.

Little sister, Our Master has requested that I, St. Philomena, share all this with you. He invites the world to invoke the intercession of Our Most Holy Mother and St. Joseph to help prepare hearts for His birth. On Christmas Day, the miracle of His love will be born in the hearts of those who respond to His request. Until tomorrow, farewell, little sister.

I looked to the sky and saw the Holy Family gazing upon the world. Then St. Joseph picked up the Babe in the manger and the Child Jesus blessed the whole world. Great light poured forth

169

Conversations With St. Philomena

upon the world. They smiled at me and St. Joseph said to me, "My little one, this is how it will be on Christmas Day. Rejoice and share this blessing that will come into many hearts through the birth of this humble Babe."

The Birth of His Only Begotten Son
December 24, 1996

St. Philomena: *Greetings from Heaven, little sister.*

Janie: Peace to you, St. Philomena. St. Philomena, I am very happy for tonight we will all go to Midnight Mass. I so look forward to this time of the year. We did well, as a family, in keeping our focus on Our Lord. As a family, we shared our blessings with the poor families. We will all exchange humble gifts. Our greatest gift is the love that we have for one another through Our Lord.

St. Philomena: *Little sister, God is blessing the world in a mighty way through all whose hearts are open to receive the birth of His only begotten Son. Tomorrow Our Master's visit with you will bring much joy. I will come with Our Master. Until tomorrow, rejoice, rejoice!*

Heavenly Beautiful
December 25, 1996

St. Philomena came with Our Lord. There was no conversation. St. Philomena was very happy and looked beautiful with a heavenly beauty.

Great Love for Family Life
December 26, 1996

St. Philomena: *Greetings from Heaven, little sister.*

Janie: Peace to you, St. Philomena. I am so happy with Our Lord's visit yesterday. I am so grateful to God. Thank you, St. Philomena, for everything. I look forward to our conversations for you help me so much. I hope I have helped bring devotion to you in a small way. I do talk to everybody about your powerful intercession.

St. Philomena: *Little sister, I am most grateful to all that you do to help foster devotion to me. Know that I have many new devotees because of your love for me. Little sister, I, too, enjoy our conversations. Your heart is full of love for your own family and families everywhere. I, too, have great love for family life. Until tomorrow, farewell, little sister.*

Janie: Thank you, St. Philomena.

For All Families Who Have Abandoned God
December 27, 1996

St. Philomena: *Greetings from Heaven, little sister.*

Janie: Peace, St. Philomena.

St. Philomena: *Little sister, for these next two days offer your prayers and sacrifices for all families who have abandoned God. In two days you will receive your heavenly visit from the Holy Family.*

All who make the sacrifice to be present during your heavenly visit will receive an abundance of special graces and blessings. Ask families to prepare for this special day with prayer as a family. God will bless all their efforts through the intercession of the Holy Family. Until tomorrow, farewell, little sister. I shall also come with the Holy Family. Until tomorrow, farewell, little sister.

Janie: Farewell, St. Philomena.

Conversations With St. Philomena

God Will Bless All Your Hard Efforts

December 28, 1996

St. Philomena: *Greetings from Heaven, little sister.*

Janie: Peace, St. Philomena. St. Philomena, today we are preparing for the visit of the Holy Family. All are very happy.

St. Philomena: *Little sister, remember, God will bless all your hard efforts as your pray and prepare as a family. Until tomorrow, farewell, little sister.*

Janie: Thank you, St. Philomena.

Feast of the Holy Family

December 29, 1996

St. Philomena came with the Holy Family. I can tell how much the Holy Family loves her. Praise be God, forever and ever.

Continue to Pray and Prepare

December 30, 1996

St. Philomena: *Greetings from Heaven, little sister.*

Janie: Peace, St. Philomena.

St. Philomena: *Little sister, during this month you and your family have been blessed with heavenly visitations. Be very grateful to God. I encourage you to continue to pray and prepare as a family for Our Most Holy Mother will come to you once more.*

Janie: St. Philomena, we are truly blessed. I am very happy because the visit of the Holy Family has helped us to bring this year to a close. The visit of Our Lady will help us to begin the new year. Praise be God for His infinite goodness.

St. Philomena: *Little sister, God is indeed good. Always remember this and always trust in Him in everything. Until tomorrow, farewell, little sister.*

Janie: Farewell, St. Philomena. I won't forget anything you share with me.

Our Holy Mother Will Help You To Prepare
December 31, 1996

St. Philomena: *Greetings from Heaven, little sister.*

Janie: Peace, St. Philomena. St. Philomena, today we are praying as a family to prepare for the visit of Our Lady tomorrow.

St. Philomena: *Little sister, many things will take place in the new year: much suffering in the world, much evil. Our Holy Mother will help you to prepare for the new year. Until tomorrow, farewell, little sister.*

Janie: Farewell, St. Philomena.

173

1997

Listen With Your Heart

January 1, 1997
Solemnity of Mary, the Mother of God

St. Philomena: *Greetings from Heaven, little sister.*

Janie: Peace to you, St. Philomena.

St. Philomena: *Little sister, you are in a very joyful spirit and I know that you are truly ready for the visit of Our Heavenly Mother. Listen with your heart for all that she tells you.*

Janie: Oh, St. Philomena! I will listen to everything. I promise, and I will live her messages, together with my family.

St. Philomena: *Little sister, I will come to you again today during your heavenly visit with Our Holy Mother. Until then, farewell, little sister.*

This is a prayer inspired by the Holy Spirit.

Prayer to Our Heavenly Mother

O Mary, Mother of God and Our Heavenly Mother! Today, I praise God for having given you to all of humanity. Your invitation to all your children is a call to purity and holiness, to love and conversion, to turn away from sin and to embrace Our Heavenly Father.

You invite your children to pray, pray, pray, so that we may discover God in our daily lives. Help us to open our hearts to the call to purity and holiness, so that someday we may be in Heaven with you. I love you, Mary, my Heavenly Mother. Pray for us, so that we may love your Son, Jesus with your heart. Amen.

Pray, Pray, Pray

January 2, 1997

St. Philomena: *Greetings from Heaven, little sister.*

Janie: Peace, St. Philomena.

St. Philomena: *Little sister, you received a great blessing from God the Father through the visit of Our Heavenly Mother. Today, the three Archangels will bring important guidance from Heaven. Embrace everything that the Archangels give you, and remember always, always to turn to St. Michael for protection and support. God has greatly blessed you through the visitation of the three Archangels and all who embrace their heavenly guidance are greatly blessed as well.*

Janie: St. Philomena, you are full of God's love. Please, pray for us so that we, too, may have God's love in our hearts.

St. Philomena: *Little sister, the key to God's love is prayer. This is why Our Heavenly Mother invites all her children to pray, pray, pray. Listen to this powerful message which many souls consider repetitious. They do not understand, because they do not pray. Pray always! Until tomorrow, farewell, little sister.*

Janie: Farewell, St. Philomena.

The True Presence of Our Master in the Holy Eucharist
January 3, 1997

St. Philomena: *Greetings from Heaven, little sister.*

Janie: Peace to you, St. Philomena. St. Philomena, I am so happy for today is First Friday. I will offer all my prayers today in honor of the Sacred Heart of Jesus. I will attend Holy Mass after I have gone to Confession. I will spend my day praying for the whole world to love the Sacred Heart of Our Lord and Master.

St. Philomena: *Little sister, all that you offer God in honor of His Son's most Sacred Heart is pleasing to God, for God so loved the world that He gave His only-begotten Son. The more that the world honors the Sacred Heart of Our Master, the more God blesses the world.*

Pray, little sister, so that the world may come to believe in the True Presence of Our Master in the Holy Eucharist. Know that the true way to honor and to adore God is to believe in the True Presence of Jesus in the Eucharist. Indeed, the message of the Sacred Heart of Jesus to all of humanity is that the Eucharist is Our Master Himself. His yearning and longing is to have a personal relationship with each soul and to set every heart on fire with His divine love.

Little sister, try very hard to attend daily Mass and to take one hour of Adoration with Our Master. If you do this, great will be the blessings bestowed on you and your prayers will help those souls who entrust their petitions to you. Until tomorrow, little sister, farewell.

Janie: Farewell to you, St. Philomena.

Devotion to First Fridays and First Saturdays
January 4, 1997

St. Philomena: *Greetings from Heaven, little sister.*

177

Conversations With St. Philomena

Janie: Peace, St. Philomena. St. Philomena, today I recommend my sister to you for tomorrow is her birthday. It's a very special day for me because tomorrow is also the Solemnity of the Epiphany. Our Lord will visit me tomorrow. I am joyful about this, but I would be most grateful if you intercede for my sister on her birthday.

Today is First Saturday and I will be going to Confession and to Mass to honor the request of Our Lady for First Saturdays.

St. Philomena: *Little sister, I will intercede for your special petition for your sister. I am very happy that you have such devotion to First Fridays and First Saturdays. You are demonstrating the great love that you have for Our Master and His dear Mother. Until tomorrow, farewell, little sister.*

Janie: Farewell, St. Philomena.

I Will Pray for You

January 5, 1997

St. Philomena: *Greetings from Heaven, little sister.*

Janie: Peace, St. Philomena.

St. Philomena: *Little sister, I know that you are preparing for Holy Mass. I am here to tell you that I am praying for your sister. I know you care about her. After Holy Mass, you will have your heavenly visit with Our Master. I will pray for you. Until tomorrow, farewell, little sister.*

Janie: Thank you, St. Philomena for responding to my prayer request.

God Will Never Abandon Those Who Trust

January 6, 1997

St. Philomena: *Greetings from Heaven, my little sister.*

Janie: Greetings, St. Philomena! I am so happy that you are with me.

St. Philomena, I know that God knows the outcome of every situation, therefore I choose to put all my trust in Him, no matter how painful my suffering may be.

St. Philomena: *Little sister, God will never abandon those who trust in Him. He will reward your effort in trusting Him by giving you all the grace that you need in your suffering.*

Janie: St. Philomena, please continue to intercede for my X. Tell Our Master to help me to remain strong in everything.

St. Philomena: *Little sister, He will help you. Remain steadfast, placing all your trust in God and His Most Holy Mother. Until tomorrow, farewell, little sister.*

Janie: Farewell, little sister.

He Will Not Give You Suffering Beyond Your Strength
January 7, 1997

St. Philomena: *Greetings from Heaven, little sister.*

Janie: Ave, St. Philomena.

St. Philomena: *My little sister, do not grow weary of your constant suffering. Remember that Our Lady is asking you to suffer for all the unbelievers whose sins corrupt the world.*

God knows that your suffering is intense; know that He will not give you suffering beyond your strength. Little sister, there are millions of unbelievers who hate God and do evil against those who believe in God. Our Master has already won the great victory of salvation for the world, but those souls who reject God have chosen darkness instead of light.

Your prayers and fasting will help to draw these poor sinners

179

closer to God. Your sacrifices are helping poor sinners to repent. Millions of souls live in darkness. Through your suffering, you are bringing light to their hearts. Persevere in your prayers and rejoice for all the poor sinners who you are helping.

Do not worry, little sister. God will help you with your personal intention. Until tomorrow, farewell, little sister. Continue praying, especially today for little children who are victims of child abuse.

For Victims of Calamities

January 8, 1997

St. Philomena: Greetings from Heaven, little sister.

Janie: Greetings, St. Philomena.

St. Philomena: *Peace, little sister.*

Janie: Peace, St. Philomena.

St. Philomena: *My little sister, pray for all those souls who are the victims of the calamities that are spreading throughout the world. Many people are suffering as we visit. Let us offer our prayers to Our Master that He may protect them through His love and mercy.*

Janie: St. Philomena, I know that there is much suffering in our world. I also know that it is our suffering that distracts us from praying more.

St. Philomena: *Little sister, turn to Our Lady in your suffering and have courage. Until tomorrow, farewell, little sister.*

Celebration of Mass With Great Joy

January 9, 1997

St. Philomena: *Greetings from Heaven, little sister.*

Janie: Peace to you, St. Philomena.

St. Philomena: *Little sister, today, let us continue to pray for Our Master's Bride. Especially, keep in mind Our Master's Vicar who suffers so much. The devil works very hard to corrupt the hearts of good priests and the priests whose faith is very weak. The devil confuses their hearts.*

Pray, little sister, that every priest looks to the celebration of Holy Mass with great joy, for it is in Holy Mass that they will meet our precious and loving Master. Pray, that the Bride of Our Master will believe in the True Presence of Our Master in the Holy Eucharist. Little sister, let us together pray for these intentions, so that we may console Our Master. Until tomorrow, little sister, farewell.

Janie: St. Philomena, I will pray with you for these special intentions.

I Am Rejoicing With You

January 10, 1997

St. Philomena: *Greetings from Heaven, little sister.*

Janie: Peace, St. Philomena. St. Philomena, today I am so happy for today is our youngest son's birthday. This is the day when Our Lord called my mother home and it's your birthday as well. Happy and blessed feast day to you, my heavenly sister! I thank God for you and my son is blessed to be born on the same day as you. This is a great joy!

We are going to Mass. Then tonight, after our son is out of school, we will have a family celebration. You, of course, are included in our celebration. What a great day this is! Praise be God, forever and ever. Amen.

St. Philomena: *Little sister, you know that I am rejoicing with you and with your family. I am honored to be included in your family's celebration. I will intercede in a special way for you and your family and your son. Until tomorrow, farewell, little sister.*

181

Conversations With St. Philomena

Janie: Thank you, St. Philomena. Give a kiss to my mother.

Embrace Your Husband in His Suffering
January 11, 1997

St. Philomena: *Greetings from Heaven, little sister.*

Janie: Peace, St. Philomena. St. Philomena, today I ask that you pray for my husband. He worries so much about the completion of our home. We have little money and my husband sometimes gets anxious about how we will finish the house. I always reassure him that we will complete our house because God will provide everything that we need to finish our home. I believe this with all my heart, but it hurts to see my husband worried. Pray for us, please.

St. Philomena: *Little sister, embrace your husband in his suffering. Continue to encourage him to have faith in God with this project. God will most certainly provide for all your needs. The devil enjoys filling God's children with all his lies, especially when the devil knows that God's children are worried about something. Pray together, and God will give you His strength to continue. Until tomorrow, farewell, little sister.*

Janie: Farewell and thank you, St. Philomena.

Joy Beyond Your Understanding
January 12, 1997

St. Philomena: *Greetings from Heaven, little sister.*

Janie: Peace to you, St. Philomena.

St. Philomena: *Little sister, today Our Master will bless you with His visit. Listen to everything that He tells you, and you will know joy beyond your understanding Prepare then for His visit. I love*

182

you, little sister, and I am rejoicing with you. Until tomorrow, fare-well, little sister.

Janie: St. Philomena, I love you. I love you, my dear heavenly sister. Farewell.

Prayer Is the Language of Love

January 13, 1997

St. Philomena: *Greetings from Heaven, little sister.*

Janie: Peace to you, St. Philomena. St. Philomena, please help me to pray for all the parents who ask for my prayers because their children have abandoned their faith. These poor parents suffer so much for their children and they fear for their children's spiritual and physical safety. Many parents are wounded by their children's disrespect. Many parents wonder if their prayers really help their children. I reassure them that prayers always help. Please help me.

St. Philomena: *Little sister, encourage all parents to always love and pray for their children and never to give up on them. Prayer is the language of love. God is love, and He loves all His children un-conditionally. When parents pray with faith and love in their hearts for their prodigal children, God will bring their children to their spiritual senses.*

I will pray for all troubled parents everywhere and for their children. Until tomorrow, farewell, little sister.

Janie: Thank you, St. Philomena.

You Suffer to Bring Many Souls to Faith

January 14, 1997

St. Philomena: Greetings from Heaven, little sister.

Conversations With St. Philomena

Janie: Peace to you, St. Philomena.

St. Philomena: *Little sister, I know that you are suffering in reparation for poor sinners. I will pray for you as you suffer to bring many souls to faith. Until tomorrow, farewell, little sister.*

Janie: Thank you, St. Philomena.

Do Not Lose Courage

January 15, 1997

St. Philomena: *Greetings from Heaven, little sister.*

Janie: Peace to you, St. Philomena.

St. Philomena: *Little sister, know that Our Master is with you in your intense suffering. Do not lose courage. Until tomorrow, farewell, little sister.*

Janie: Farewell, St. Philomena.

Be At Peace in Your Suffering

January 16, 1997

St. Philomena: *Greetings from Heaven, little sister.*

Janie: Peace to you, St. Philomena.

St. Philomena: *Little sister, your suffering continues to intensify. Know that you are helping to save many who live in darkness. Be at peace in your suffering. Until tomorrow, farewell, little sister.*

Janie: Farewell, St. Philomena.

A Vision of Times to Come

January 17, 1997

St. Philomena: *Greetings from Heaven, little sister.*

Janie: Peace, St. Philomena.

St. Philomena: *Little sister, I am here to console you in your suffering. Recall Our Holy Mother's words about your suffering.*

Then I saw a vision of the times to come: 1998-2000. The year 1998 will be filled with much division, confusion, lack of faith in Marian apparitions and Eucharistic miracles. Satan will bring about confusion with many of the Marian apostolates. Where the Church condemns Marian apparitions and other miracles, the people will suffer, for this will confuse them and weaken their faith. It will be a most intense time of great suffering as many of the faithful will not know what to believe. There will be much persecution for apparition sites, such as Medjugorje, and for other true visionaries. The Church will suffer with the spirit of apostasy. Within the Church there will be turmoil as many of the clergy will persecute one another. The devil will be most active in bringing about this confusion.

For Future Calamities and Pestilence

January 18, 1997

St. Philomena: *Greetings from Heaven, little sister.*

Janie: Peace to you, St. Philomena.

St. Philomena: *Little sister, you will continue to suffer for many future calamities and pestilence. Your suffering and prayers will help to reduce the troubled times. As of today, I will continue to pray with you everyday for all the intentions that Our Holy Mother asked you to pray for. It will not be necessary to write down any-*

185

Conversations With St. Philomena

thing. It will be difficult for you to write for your suffering will be intense. Until tomorrow, farewell, little sister.

Janie: Thank you, St. Philomena.

Visits and Prayer, No Messages

January 19-31, 1997

From Jan. 19, 1997 to Jan. 31, 19997, St. Philomena came everyday and we prayed for all special intentions entrusted to me by Our Lady.

Devotion to First Saturdays

February 1, 1997

St. Philomena: *Greetings from Heaven, little sister.*

Janie: Ave, St. Philomena, my heavenly little friend and helper.

St. Philomena: *My little sister, today offer all your prayers to Our Lady, that she may take your prayers to her Son. It pleases Our Master that you have devotion to First Saturdays. All who have devotion to First Saturdays bring much joy to Our Lady's Sorrowful and Immaculate Heart. Remain true to this devotion, and you will assist Our Lady to help unconverted souls.*

Janie: I will do as you say, St. Philomena. Remaining faithful to First Saturdays is important to me.

St. Philomena: *Little sister, know that First Saturdays are dear and important to Our Lady also. Those souls who have devotion to First Saturdays receive an abundance of blessings from Heaven. Until tomorrow, farewell, little sister. Pray for all sinners.*

The Presentation of Our Master

February 2, 1997

St. Philomena: *Greetings from Heaven, little sister.*

Janie: Ave, St. Philomena.

St. Philomena: *Little sister, today is a joyful day for you. You will be visited by the Holy Family, for today is the Presentation of Our Master. Spend this day in prayer. Present your family and all families in the world to God the Father. Until tomorrow, farewell, little sister.*

Janie: Farewell, St. Philomena.

Much Healing of Mind and Body

February 3, 1997

St. Philomena: *Greetings from Heaven, little sister.*

Janie: Greetings, St. Philomena. Please intercede for all the prayer group that we may get everything ready for our anniversary with Our Lady.

St. Philomena: *My little sister, do not be concerned. Our Lady will see to it that all plans go according to her wishes and desires. Trust in her intercession. She will bless all her children present with her Motherly blessing. There will be much healing of mind and body and much conversion. Our Lady will help all her children.*

Janie: St. Philomena, thank you for helping me in redirecting me to Our Lady's intercession. I will rely on her help.

St. Philomena: *Until tomorrow, farewell, little sister. Pray to avert the attacks of the evil one on the priests who will be coming to your anniversary.*

187

Conversations With St. Philomena

Janie: I will do as you say, St. Philomena.

Hunger for Holiness and Purity of Heart

February 4, 1997

St. Philomena: *Greetings from Heaven, little sister.*

Janie: Ave, St. Philomena. Please help me to hunger more for holiness and purity of heart. I know that this desire pleases God.

St. Philomena: *Little sister, to hunger for holiness and purity of heart means to desire to be one with Our Master. Prayer is the key which stimulates this hunger. This is why Our Lady invites all her children to pray, pray, pray. In prayer one discovers God.*
Prayer, little sister, prayer is what leads to holiness and purity of heart. Therefore, pray unceasingly. Remember, the closer you draw to Our Master, the closer He draws to you. Share with others the importance of unceasing prayer. Until tomorrow, farewell, little sister.

Janie: Farewell, St. Philomena. Thank you for everything.

Spiritual Blessings for Your Spiritual Director

February 5, 1997

St. Philomena: *Greetings from Heaven, little sister.*

Janie: Ave, St. Philomena.

St. Philomena: *My little sister, your spiritual director receives special blessings every day for he is one of Our Master's representatives. Our Master loves him very much.*

Janie: St. Philomena, I know that my spiritual director is blessed, but I thought, maybe today, he would receive more blessings.

188

St. Philomena: *He will, little sister, he will, for God knows how much you care about your spiritual director. Today, show Our Master your gratitude for blessing you with such a caring and prayerful spiritual director. Until tomorrow, farewell, little sister.*

Janie: Farewell, St. Philomena. Thanks for everything.

The Suffering of the Two Hearts

February 6, 1997

St. Philomena: *Greetings from Heaven, little sister.*

Janie: Ave, St. Philomena.

St. Philomena: *Today, spend time praying for the intentions of the Sacred Heart of Our Master and the Immaculate Heart of Our Lady.*
Our Master and His Mother suffer for all the sinfulness in the hearts of humanity. Console Our Master and His Mother, Our Beloved Queen, through your prayers. Know, little sister, that if you could experience, truly, the suffering of the Two Hearts of Jesus and Mary, you would not be able to live through this day. This is why God allows you to experience only what your heart can endure. Love Our Master and His Most Suffering Mother. Console them through your prayers. Until tomorrow, farewell, little sister.

Janie: Farewell, St. Philomena. I will do as you ask of me for the Two Hearts of Jesus and Mary.

One Day at A Time

February 7, 1997

St. Philomena: Greetings from Heaven, little sister.

Janie: Ave, St. Philomena. My little heavenly helper, please pray

189

for me that I may accomplish all things in preparation for Our Lady's anniversary. I have people coming and I know that this week, we will be busy.

St. Philomena: *Do not worry, little sister, but take one day at a time as Scripture guides you. Surrender everything to God, for He is in charge of all things. Our Lady will so arrange everything in such a way if you allow her to do so.*

Janie: Dear St. Philomena, how much wisdom you have. Thank you for reminding me to live one day at a time. I will do so.

St. Philomena: *Until tomorrow, farewell, little sister.*

Janie: I love you, St. Philomena.

Your Attitude Towards Holy Mass

February 8, 1997

St. Philomena: *Greetings from Heaven, little sister.*

Janie: Ave, St. Philomena. How are you doing this morning?

St. Philomena: *I am doing quite well, and yourself?*

Janie: I am also doing quite well and I am happy because, after my visit, I am going to Mass. I cannot wait to receive Our Master.

St. Philomena: *My little sister, you glorify God by your attitude towards Holy Mass. Many are the blessings that you will receive today. I will not keep you, but ask you to offer your prayers for all the unbelieving families in this world. Their souls are in dire need of prayer. Until tomorrow, farewell, little sister.*

Janie: St. Philomena, I love you. Farewell.

This Hurts God So Much

February 9, 1997

St. Philomena: *Greetings from Heaven, little sister.*

Janie: Ave, St. Philomena! Today, I am excited, for in five more days Our Lady will come to see me. I am so blessed by God. Please pray for me that I always remember how much God loves me. I desire to love Him, also, all the time.

St. Philomena: *My little sister, indeed, God loves you with such immense love! He has chosen you to help His lost families through your prayers and sacrifices. So many families in the world have forgotten God. Because they have forgotten God, they do not believe in the existence of God. This hurts God so much. Your prayers and sacrifices bring God comfort.*

Janie: St. Philomena, what you say is true. Many claim that there is no God, and that man is in control of everything. It is so sad to have this mentality, but I know that God understands the human heart.

St. Philomena: *Yes, my little sister! Only God understands and knows the human heart. Man has created a world without God. That is why there is no love and peace in so many souls. For those souls who believe in God, their fruit is love and peace. For those souls that do not believe in God, there is darkness and despair. Pray every day for all the unbelievers. Until tomorrow, farewell, little sister.*

Janie: Farewell, St. Philomena.

A Private Message

February 10, 1997

The message for today was personal.

191

Conversations With St. Philomena

Three Days of Suffering

February 11, 1997

St. Philomena: *Greetings from Heaven, little sister.*

Janie: Ave, St. Philomena. Today is the day before Ash Wednesday. I am excited about this time. I know that I will suffer, but it is suffering that purifies my sinful soul.

St. Philomena: *Little sister, during this time of Lent you will suffer and your suffering will be intense. There will be three days in which you will suffer the most. On Mondays: these days are for the purification of the Bride of Our Master; on Wednesdays: this was the day when Judas, one of the twelve, betrayed Our Master; on Fridays: you will unite with and suffer the Passion of Our Master.*

Janie: St. Philomena, please pray for me, that I may endure my suffering with love in my heart.

St. Philomena: *Do not worry, little sister, I shall be doing all I can to help you during this time of Lent. Until tomorrow, farewell, little sister.*

Janie: Farewell, St. Philomena.

They Do It To Me

February 12, 1997

St. Philomena: *Greetings from Heaven, little sister.*

Janie: Ave, St. Philomena. Please pray for me, for my soul is in such distress.

St. Philomena: *Do not worry, little sister, be at peace. Our Master will come to visit you in a short while. Unite your suffering with His. I shall be with Him during this time. Until then, farewell, little sister.*

192

Later that morning, St. Philomena and Our Lord came to me. These were His words: "Console Me, console Me. See how My beloved brothers treat Me."

I saw a bishop scourging Our Lord. The lashing was so severe that Our Lord was bathed in blood. Then, it wasn't Our Lord, but a priest whom I knew. This priest was being scourged by the bishop. Our Lord said to me: "Know, My humble servant, that when My brothers mistreat and do evil to one another, they do it to Me. Pray for My Bride and all My innocent brothers who are being persecuted for My Name's sake."

Be At Peace

February 13, 1997

St. Philomena: *Greetings from Heaven, little sister.*

Janie: Ave, St. Philomena. Please pray for me, because I have a very busy schedule. Many people are coming to Austin to join us for Our Lady's anniversary.

St. Philomena: *My little sister, I will intercede for all your needs. Be at peace. Enjoy your visit with your spiritual director. You are most blessed to have him guiding you. Until tomorrow, farewell, little sister.*

Janie: Farewell, St. Philomena.

Our Master is Coming

February 14, 1997

St. Philomena: *Greetings from Heaven, my little sister.*

Janie: Ave, St. Philomena! Today my soul is suffering again. Only God understands. It's so hard because I have people around me. What shall I do?

Conversations With St. Philomena

St. Philomena: *Remain quiet and peaceful, my little sister. Our Master is coming in the third hour of this very afternoon. I shall also come with Him. Until then, peace, little sister, peace. The Divine Spirit will give you strength.*

Later that day, at 3:00 p.m., Our Lord came with St. Philomena. I immediately felt my entire body racked with pain. Then I saw Our Lord bound to a column and two men had whips in their hands. They began whipping Our Lord. They each took turns. The whips were made of leather and at the end of the strings of the whips, there were steel balls with spikes all over the steel balls. Our poor Lord was bathed in blood. My body also was in extreme pain. I felt the scourging of Our Lord. I was also on the ground being scourged with Our Lord. While Our Lord was lying on the ground, covered with blood, He lifted His head and looked at me, then said, *"Thank you for being here for Me."* I was so overwhelmed with sorrow. St. Philomena stood by in a prayerful attitude.

Great Joy

February 15, 1997

St. Philomena: *Greetings from Heaven, little sister.*

Janie: Ave, St. Philomena! I am so happy.

St. Philomena: *Yes, little sister. One can see the great joy in your happy face. Today indeed, is a joyful day for you and all who have come to be with you. Many blessings and graces will be the result of the visit from Our Lady. Rejoice, little sister, and know that you are loved by Heaven. Until tomorrow, farewell, my little sister.*

Janie: Farewell, dear St. Philomena.

[Note: This day is the Anniversary of the Visit of Our Mother of Compassion and Love.]

A Blessed Day

February 16, 1997

St. Philomena: *Greetings from Heaven, little sister.*

Janie: Ave, St. Philomena. Today is a beautiful day I am so happy after being with Our Lady yesterday.

St. Philomena: *My little sister, you are a delight to Our Lady. Today she will visit with you as soon as you arrive at your property. Be prepared and give thanks to God for all the blessings which He is bestowing on you.*

Janie: St. Philomena, I am ever grateful to God for everything. Today, my husband and I are together; he is not working. Today we are going to have a great day.

St. Philomena: *Yes, my little sister, this will be a blessed day for you and your spouse. Until tomorrow, farewell, little sister. Recommend all the unbelievers to God in your prayers.*

Janie: Farewell, St. Philomena.

Our Lady Is Very Happy

February 17, 1997

St. Philomena: *Greetings from Heaven, little sister.*

Janie: Ave, St. Philomena! Please pray for me, St. Philomena, because I am very tired from working so hard for the anniversary of Our Lady.

St. Philomena: *My little sister, know that Our Lady is very happy with all the efforts that it took to bring about a glorious anniversary. She is very pleased with all her children.*

Conversations With St. Philomena

Janie: Oh, St. Philomena! I am so happy that She is pleased with our work. Everybody gave their best to make Our Lady happy.

St. Philomena: *My little sister, know for certain that Our Lady is happy. Rest now, my little sister. Until tomorrow, farewell, little sister.*

Janie: Farewell, St. Philomena.

Pray for All the Troubled Youth

February 18, 1997

St. Philomena: *Greetings from Heaven, little sister.*

Janie: Ave, St. Philomena.

St. Philomena: *My little sister, you are still tired from Our Lady's anniversary celebration. Rest, my little sister. I shall intercede for you. Our Master will renew you and relieve your tiredness.*
I ask you to pray for all the youth during your night prayers. So many young people live in darkness because their parents have abandoned them. These poor young souls have no one to turn to and God does not exist for them. Oh! pray for all the troubled youth! Until tomorrow, farewell, my little sister.

Janie: St. Philomena, thank you for caring and loving the youth so much.

Priests Who Have Turned Against Our Master

February 19, 1997

St. Philomena: *Greetings from Heaven, little sister.*

Janie: Ave, St. Philomena.

St. Philomena: *My little sister, today offer all your prayers and sacrifices for all the priests who have turned against Our Master. This hurts Him so much. Console Our Master through your prayers. Farewell, little sister.*

For Priests Who Have Abandoned Their Vows
February 20, 1997

St. Philomena: *Greetings from Heaven, little sister.*

Janie: Ave, St. Philomena.

St. Philomena: *My little sister, continue to pray for all the priests who have abandoned their priestly vows. Our Master is so much offended, so much offended. Until tomorrow, farewell, little sister.*

I Unite in Your Suffering
February 21, 1997

St. Philomena: *Greetings from Heaven, little sister.*

Janie: Ave, St. Philomena.

St. Philomena: *Little sister, know that I unite in your suffering. Do not despair. Until tomorrow, farewell, little sister.*

Helping Young Mothers
February 22, 1997

St. Philomena: Greetings from Heaven, little sister.

Janie: Ave, St. Philomena.

St. Philomena: *My little sister, know that your suffering is helping*

Conversations With St. Philomena

young mothers who need much love. They are young and so alone. Your suffering is love for these young mothers who are trying to find love in unhealthy relationships. Never forget all these poor mothers. Until tomorrow, farewell, little sister.

Janie: Farewell, St. Philomena.

I Will Intercede

February 23, 1997

St. Philomena: *Greetings from Heaven, little sister.*

Janie: Ave, St. Philomena. St. Philomena, please intercede for me that I may suffer with joy in my heart.

St. Philomena: *I, St. Philomena will intercede for your special intentions. Until tomorrow, farewell, little sister.*

Offer Your Daily Masses and Rosaries

February 24, 1997

St. Philomena: *Greetings from Heaven, little sister.*

Janie: Ave, St. Philomena. St. Philomena, pray for my special intentions for my sons. I will truly appreciate it.

St. Philomena: *Little sister, continue offering your daily Masses, Rosary and special prayers for your family. I will intercede for your sons. Until tomorrow, farewell, little sister.*

Have Courage in Your Suffering

February 25, 1997

St. Philomena: *Greetings from Heaven, little sister.*

Janie: Ave, St. Philomena.

St. Philomena: *Little sister, my visit will not be long, for I know that your suffering continues. I am asking Our Master to give you all the strength that your need. Have courage in your suffering; you are helping many souls. Until tomorrow, farewell, little sister.*

Janie: Thank you, St. Philomena, for all your prayers.

Remain Strong in Faith

February 26, 1997

St. Philomena: *Greetings from Heaven, little sister.*

Janie: Peace, St. Philomena.   St. Philomena, I ask again for your prayers, for during this season of Lent my suffering is heavy.   I don't mind and I am not complaining, I just need your prayers.

St. Philomena: *Little sister, I know that you are not complaining about your cross. You are very wise to ask for prayers, for prayers bring you many graces and blessings from heaven. Remain strong in faith during your suffering and know that all the assistance from Heaven is at your side. Until tomorrow, farewell, little sister.*

Janie: Thank you, St. Philomena. I know that God is my strength. I abandon myself completely to His care.

I Am Happy to Help

February 27, 1997

St. Philomena: *Greetings from Heaven, little sister.*

Janie: Peace, St. Philomena. St. Philomena, today I ask you please to pray for all those souls who embrace you as their patron saint. So many people are anxious to know more about you.   I redirect

Conversations With St. Philomena

everyone who asks about you to your intercession, and I give them a brief summary about your life.

There are so many young people who like you as soon as I tell them a little about you. Pray for all these young people. They have good intentions to lead holy lives, but they fear the temptations in the world. I encourage them to pray and not to worry but to trust in your intercession.

St. Philomena: *Little sister, I will intercede for all who ask for my intercession. I am happy to help all souls who ask for my assistance and I quickly respond. I especially assist the young people who trust in my intercession to maintain the spirit of purity and holiness. Encourage everyone to trust in my intercession. I welcome all devotees with love and place them in the hands of Our Holy Mother and Our Master. Until tomorrow, farewell, little sister.*

Janie: Thank you, St. Philomena.

At Your Disposal

February 28, 1997

St. Philomena: *Greetings from Heaven*

Janie: Peace to you, St. Philomena.

St. Philomena: *Little sister, I am deeply grateful for all that you do to spread devotion to me. You are very dear to my heart and I am always interceding for all your good works of charity. You give of yourself no matter how much you may be suffering. Continue, little sister, to love all souls and to pray for them. Remember, little sister, a generous and loving soul is pleasing to Our Master. Your have these qualities.*

Janie: St. Philomena, you are so kind to say all this to me. I am delighted to make you more well known. In this way, you can help

200

other souls as you have helped me and my family. I will spend my days on earth spreading devotion to you. I love you very much.

St. Philomena: *Little sister, I too, love you dearly. Know that my intercession is always at your disposal. Until tomorrow, farewell, little sister.*

Janie: Thank you, St. Philomena.

Simply By Praying Your Rosary

March 1, 1997

St. Philomena: *Greetings from Heaven, my little sister.*

Janie: Ave, St. Philomena.

St. Philomena: *Little sister, God knows that you are suffering for your own continuous conversion and that of your family. The evil one has been very strong in his attacks on your family. You, little sister, weaken his attacks as you implore the intercession of Our Lady and all of Heaven, simply by praying your Rosary with your husband.*

You glorify God, little sister, when you turn towards prayer as you seek God's intervention in your family crises. You see how quickly God comes to the rescue of those who turn to Him. He is the Source of all wisdom, all knowledge, the Source of all healing, the Source of all things. Remember this which I, St. Philomena, share with you, and let it penetrate your heart. Prayer is the answer to all things, for God is prayer. To pray means to be in union with God. Until tomorrow, farewell, little sister.

Janie: Farewell, St. Philomena.

201

Conversations With St. Philomena

To Pray and to Trust God

March 2, 1997
Mt. Pleasant, Texas

St. Philomena: *Greetings from Heaven, my little sister.*

Janie: Ave, St. Philomena.

St. Philomena: *Know that I am interceding for you. Have no worry; God will help you to prepare for tonight. Your only responsibility is to pray and to trust God. Until tomorrow, farewell, little sister.*

    These are words from St. Philomena as I am preparing for my talk tonight in Mt. Pleasant, Texas. I was invited here to give mission talks for four nights.

Give Him Everything of Yourself

March 3, 1997
Mt. Pleasant, Texas

St. Philomena: *Greetings from Heaven, my little sister.*

Janie: Ave, St. Philomena.

St. Philomena: *My little sister, God is pleased that you are preparing through your prayers to speak to His people tonight. Trust in Him completely and surrender everything to Him. He will fill you with His love, wisdom and knowledge, so that all who hear you tonight will know in their hearts that God sent you. Give Him everything of yourself, everything. I, St. Philomena will be interceding for you as you speak to God's people. Until tomorrow, little sister, farewell.*

Janie: Farewell, St. Philomena.

Prayer Frees You of Worry

March 4, 1997
Mt. Pleasant, Texas

St. Philomena: *Greetings from Heaven, my little sister.*

Janie: Ave, St. Philomena.

St. Philomena: *My little sister, observe the freshness of this morning and the beauty of today. Know that when you are united with Our Master, not even the freshness of the morning or the beauty of this day can compare to the freshness that comes from Our Master's Sacred Heart and to the beauty of His love for you.*

Little sister, do not be concerned about your little grandson or your son. Your family is in God's care. Spend today in prayer, surrendering all to God. Offer all your prayers to the Holy Spirit, that He may enlighten every fiber of your being.

Remember, little sister, prayer frees you of all the worries in your soul; prayer unites you to God. Until tomorrow, farewell, little sister.

Janie: Farewell, St. Philomena.

God Reminded Me of His Great Love

March 5, 1997

St. Philomena: *Greetings from Heaven, my little sister.*

Janie: Ave, St. Philomena.

St. Philomena: *My little sister, you are suffering for the conversion of poor sinners.*

Janie: St. Philomena, I was so scared after being attacked by the evil one.

St. Philomena: *My little sister, know that I was also scared when I*

203

was suffering from torture. My body was racked with pain; I was weak. Several times I felt as though I was at the point of death, but God gave me His strength through the visits of Our Lady and the angels. Like you, little sister, I, too, was scared at times of my torturers, but God reminded me, as He reminded you, of His great love. I knew that He was with me, so I endured everything for His glory.

Janie: Oh, St. Philomena, what you shared with me is so beautiful. Will I remember all this after our visit? (I said this because I had had no sleep, as I was attacked by the evil one. I was tired and exhausted.)

St. Philomena: *My little sister, you will remember everything. Write it down right after our visit. Remember, Heaven is at your disposal; surrender all to God and trust Him in everything. Until tomorrow, farewell, little sister.*

Janie: Farewell, St. Philomena.

The Archangels Will Share With You

March 6, 1997

St. Philomena: *Greetings from Heaven, little sister.*

Janie: Peace to you, St. Philomena.

St. Philomena: *Little sister, prepare for your visit with the three Archangels. Today, God will bless your special intentions for those suffering souls who have entrusted themselves to your prayers. The Archangels will share important things with you and ask a special request of you. Prepare, little sister, prepare. Until tomorrow, farewell, little sister.*

Janie: I will prepare! Thank you, St. Philomena.

Have No Worry

March 7, 1997

St. Philomena: *Greetings from Heaven, little sister.*

Janie: Peace, St. Philomena. Please pray for me that I can fast today. I am not feeling well and I am suffering. Please pray for me.

St. Philomena: *Little sister, I will intercede for you. Have no worry. Be at peace. Until tomorrow, farewell, little sister.*

Janie: Farewell, St. Philomena.

Trust in Your Prayers

March 8, 1997

St. Philomena: *Greetings from Heaven, little sister.*

Janie: Peace, St. Philomena. St. Philomena, I need your prayers for special intentions. There is a symposium of the Two Hearts in Rome and I've been invited. I have mixed feelings about going. Please present this special intention to Our Lord.

St. Philomena: *Little sister, do not worry. You will have a better understanding about this trip in a matter of days. Trust in your prayers. Until tomorrow, farewell, little sister.*

Janie: Thank you, St. Philomena.

For Children With No Families

March 9, 1997

St. Philomena: *Greetings from Heaven, little sister.*

Janie: Peace, St. Philomena.

Conversations With St. Philomena

St. Philomena: *Little sister, offer your Mass for all the children in the world who have no families. This is a special request which I ask of you. Until tomorrow, farewell, little sister.*

I saw a vision of many children, young and old, who were suffering because they had no parents.

Abandoned By Their Parents

March 10, 1997

St. Philomena: *Greetings from Heaven, little sister.*

Janie: Peace to you, St. Philomena. St. Philomena, yesterday you asked me to offer my Mass for all children who have no parents. I had a vision and saw many children, young and old, suffering. Were these children orphans?

St. Philomena: *Little sister, the reason I requested this of you is because there are so many children suffering from lack of parental love. Many parents abandon their children, for they have no love in their hearts. The children you saw in your vision are not orphans. They are all the children who have been abandoned by their parents. These children live in the streets; they are victims of drug abuse, prostitution and homosexuality. Many have had abortions at a very young age; many are victims of sexual abuse and emotional abuse.*
    Little sister, the injustice that the parents have put their children through is horrible. Please, I beg you, pray for these poor little ones. Please, little sister.

St. Philomena was very sad today. I was also sad.

His Love Is What Is Lacking

March 11, 1997

St. Philomena: *Greetings from Heaven, little sister.*

Janie: Peace, St. Philomena. St. Philomena, I am sorry that you were so sad yesterday. I understand your love for little children and young people. I prayed and prayed for your special request. I promise to keep praying for this special intention.

St. Philomena: *I am so grateful, little sister. I have much love for all of God's children but I especially am sad when little children and young people suffer because their parents do not love them.*

Little sister, love is important to the human heart, but many souls in the world have no love in their hearts, because they do not believe in God. God is love. There is no other true love, except for God's love. His love is what is lacking in millions of souls. Pray that people will return to God's love and children can be happy again. Until tomorrow, farewell, little sister.

Janie: St. Philomena, I will pray with you for our world to turn back to God's love.

Trust Him

March 12, 1997

St. Philomena: *Greetings from Heaven, little sister.*

Janie: Peace to you, St. Philomena.

St. Philomena: *Little sister, I know that you are concerned about whether you should go on the trip to Rome in a few weeks. Our Master will let you know soon. Trust Him. Until tomorrow, farewell, little sister.*

Janie: Thank you, St. Philomena.

Continue to Pray and Trust

March 13, 1997

St. Philomena: *Greetings from Heaven, little sister.*

Conversations With St. Philomena

Janie: Peace, St. Philomena. St. Philomena, I believe that I am going to Rome, Italy. Our Lord is preparing everything for me. I have never gone to Rome by myself. I am a bit nervous.

St. Philomena: *Little sister, you will receive many graces and blessings on this trip. Continue to pray and trust Our Master. He will give you more direction. I am happy for you. Until tomorrow, farewell, little sister.*

Janie: Thank you, St. Philomena.

In Reparation for the Whole World

March 14, 1997

St. Philomena: *Greetings from Heaven, little sister.*

Janie: *Peace to you, St. Philomena.*

St. Philomena: *Little sister, you are suffering much today, and your suffering will increase. These next days are marked with intense suffering for you. You are being prepared to unite with Our Master in His Passion. You will suffer in reparation for the whole world, for the evil in the world has spread like a plague. You also are being prepared for your journey to Rome.*

Yes, my little sister, you are going to Rome. Our Master has answered your prayers. While you are in Rome, you will visit my shrine, and you will receive an abundance of graces and blessings. I will be with you in a very special way.

Little sister, you will suffer greatly before your trip. Do not become discouraged, but remain strong in your faith. The devil will try to put every obstacle in your path to keep you from going on the trip to Rome, Italy. Little sister, I will be praying for you every day.

You will not be able to write anything which I share with you because of the pain in your hands. Do not write anything until the first of next month. By this time you will be in Rome, Italy. I shall come every day, and you and I will pray for special intentions. Through my prayers, you will bear your suffering with more peace.

208

I will be with you, little sister, and I will also console you in your suffering. Remember, you are suffering for the sake of Our Master's great love. Special favors will be granted to you while you visit my shrine.

Until tomorrow, little sister, farewell. Remember, you do not need to write down anything until the first of next month. I am reminding you, for I know that you are very tired. Peace, little sister, peace.

Janie: Thank you, St. Philomena. I am happy about Rome and about visiting your shrine, but I am tired and am having a hard time writing.

No Messages

March 15 -30, 1997

[St. Philomena visited daily, and they prayed together while Janie suffered during Lent. There were no messages.]

The Trip to Rome

March 31, 1997

9:45 a.m.

Today, everything that could go wrong is going wrong. Already, I have missed my flight to Dallas, Texas. I was under the impression that I would leave Austin at 12:55 p.m., but I was wrong. This is the information that I had received when I talked to the travel agent. Besides this, I have been under satanic attack since Good Friday. It was my own fault for not looking at the tickets. I kept hearing a voice within my heart that said, "Check your ticket, check your ticket." So finally I listened, and was I angry at myself for not listening to my guardian angel earlier!

Conversations With St. Philomena

11:00 a.m.

I missed my second flight, but through no fault of my own. I got to the airport at 10:15 a.m. There was but one attendant, and when the second attendant came, she said that I was fine, and that I could make the second flight. When I got to the gate, I was informed that the flight had just taken off. The attendant there sent me to US Air to see if they could help me.

11:45 a.m.

I am still here. American Airlines and US Air have been talking concerning whose fault it is that I didn't make my second flight. Nobody wants to compromise. I am praying hard, asking St. Philomena to fix things up, so that I'll make my third flight.

Finally, US Air is charitable. They are paying for me to fly on American Airlines from Austin to Dallas, then to Philadelphia.

12:20 p.m.

I boarded my third flight to Dallas. Thank you, St. Philomena.

1:50 p.m.

I boarded the flight to Philadelphia. Again, thank you, St. Philomena.

6:10 p.m.

We are still aboard the American Airlines plane. We cannot land. There is a severe snow storm and we are not cleared for landing. I am praying my Rosary and, again, begging the intercession of St. Philomena.

7:00 p.m.

We just landed. The snow storm is very bad. We had a difficult flight. I have 20 minutes to check in and go to my gate. Again, I beg St. Philomena to help me to walk fast.

7:15 p.m.

Finally I checked in and went to my gate. The plane to Rome, Italy is delayed, and we won't board until 8:00 p.m.. Our flight will depart at 8:20 p.m.. Thank you, St. Philomena. There have been obstacles on top of obstacles.

8:30 p.m.

I am on board the flight to Rome, Italy. Fr. X is nowhere to be seen. He and Father Y and his group missed their flight to Philadelphia due to the snow storm. Now what? I have no one; I am all alone and I am seated at the very end of the plane.

10:00 p.m.

We are still on board. We cannot leave because of the snow storm. It seems that all the east coast is having severe weather. I am wondering how I will get to the shrine of St. Philomena. I have no information about where I am staying. Fr. Y has all the information. I am feeling so alone with nobody to talk to on this long flight. I continue to pray my Rosary, fasting for Fr. X and Fr. Y. I haven't eaten all day.

10:30 p.m.

We are on our way to Rome, Italy. There is a priest right across from me with two ladies. I believe they are also going to Rome, Italy. I'll talk to them later. I am so tired and I am missing everyone. I have suffered extremely throughout this day.

Conversations With St. Philomena

You Have Endured Many Crosses

April 1, 1997
Domus Mariae Convent, Rome, Italy

St. Philomena: *Greetings from Heaven, little sister. Welcome to this holy city.*

Janie: Ave, St. Philomena. Thank you for everything you have done for me.

St. Philomena: *Little sister, you have endured many crosses during your journey to this holy city. Do not be concerned about your spiritual director. He will join you soon. I, St. Philomena, am with you and with him in a most special way. You and he will visit my shrine in Mugnano as I promised you.*

Peace, little sister. Rest now and know that Our Master and His Most Holy Mother will be with you later today. I, St. Philomena, shall come also.

Janie: St. Philomena, I love you.

I spent the rest of that day in prayer. I am so grateful to God for His love and mercy.

This has been truly a day filled with God's Spirit.

Fr. X's plane did not make it in time due to severe weather conditions. I had to fly to Rome alone and without anyone I knew. This was a quite a journey for me. The flight attendants were ever so nice, checking to see if I needed anything. I prayed and prayed that Fr. X's plane would hurry, so that I could be with someone I knew.

This is the first time I have written what St. Philomena shared with me since March 14. From March 14 to March 31, St. Philomena visited me every day, but we prayed together while I was suffering during Lent.

Love the Two Hearts Together With St. Joseph
April 1, 1997
Domus Mariae Convent

Our Lord: *Our humble servant, we have brought you here to unite you with this holy gathering and all those souls who have devotion to the Two Hearts.*

It will be here in this holy city where my Vicar resides that you will understand in a deeper way the great importance of the Two Hearts. Understand, beloved of Our Two Hearts, that St. Joseph was chosen by My Mother to be My foster father and to embrace Me as his own. His intercession has great power before the throne of My Father. Love the Two United Hearts together with St. Joseph, and we will protect you from harm.

St. Philomena will help you, Our humble servant, to embrace everything which We wish to teach you concerning the Two Hearts united with the heart of St. Joseph.

Our Lady: *Our angel, look to Us for everything. Rest now, our little one. You have suffered so much to make this journey to this holy city where great saints have lived and visited. Tomorrow, you will have an audience with My Son's Vicar. You wondered in prayer if tomorrow you could have a general audience with him. We arranged it for everyone here who has great love for the Two Hearts. Good night, Our angel; sleep now. My angel will keep watch over you.*

St. Philomena: *My little sister, I shall intercede for you and keep vigil as you rest. Until tomorrow, farewell, little sister.*

An Audience With the Holy Father
April 2, 1997
Domus Mariae Convent, Rome

Today, I was up early praying. St. Philomena has been with me in a most powerful way.

We had an audience with the Holy Father. What a great gift!

213

Conversations With St. Philomena

Already St. Philomena has been with me in prayer for three hours, including Adoration. St. Philomena, together with my guardian angel, woke me up at 4:20 am Rome time. Praise God, forever and ever. Amen.

I will have my visit with St. Philomena this evening when my spiritual director arrives. We are on our way to the Basilica to attend the general audience with the Holy Father.

Later that evening, 6:40 p.m.

I am back from being with Our Holy Father for two and one-half glorious hours. It has been such a holy day for me, filled with prayer. The Holy Father talked with us about Our Most Holy Mother. He loves her so much, as she loves him.

I have offered Our Lord and Our Lady 16 Rosaries, praying for everybody's intention, and especially those whom God chose, through the intercession of St. Philomena, to make this trip possible for me.

I was just informed that my spiritual director arrived this morning. Praise be God and all the intercession of heaven.

How You Earn Your Sanctification

April 2, 1997

St. Philomena: *Greetings from Heaven, little sister.*

Janie: Ave, St. Philomena.

St. Philomena: *My little sister, you have continued to endure many crosses to have your visit with me.* (She said this because my spiritual director and I couldn't find a quiet place for my private visit with St. Philomena.)

Janie: Yes, St. Philomena! This is true and I am also extremely tired. (She smiled.)

214

St. Philomena: *Little sister, this is how you earn your sanctification, through all your suffering.*
Know, little sister, that tomorrow you and your spiritual director will journey to my shrine in Mugnano. I am preparing everything for you. I shall be with you in a most special way, paving your journey through my intercession. Until tomorrow, farewell, little sister.

Janie: Farewell, St. Philomena.

Today I visited the Sistine Chapel and went to Confession in the Vatican. The Holy Father blessed all the petitions and religious articles that people sent to take to the Shrine of St. Philomena. I will have my visit with St. Philomena and the Archangels in Mugnano at the Shrine of St. Philomena. Praise be God, forever and ever.

At the Shrine of St. Philomena

April 3, 1997

My spiritual director and I left Domus Mariae Convent at 8:40 am. We took a taxi to the train station. Not knowing the train schedule, we arrived at the train station at 9:10 am. We bought our ticket to Naples. The train was to leave in 5 minutes. We made the train. St. Philomena's first miracle!
The second miracle: Fr. X and I, not knowing the difference between first class and second class, sat in first class. When the conductor came for the tickets, we were almost arriving at our destination. He looked at our tickets and said, "You are sitting in the wrong class." He could tell that we did not know the difference. We apologized and asked how much we owed him. He looked at us, smiled and said, "Nothing! Stay where you are, don't worry."
The third miracle of St. Philomena: We arrived at Napoli. We went to the information counter, again not knowing the train schedule. We were guided to the train station to buy our ticket. We had to find out where to go next. There was a man at the information

215

area who was trying to give us the wrong information because he wanted to take us and cheat us out of money. I recognized Satan in him and rebuked him away from us. Quickly we were redirected to the train which was scheduled to leave in 10 minutes to Baiano, Italy. We did not have to wait at all. Thank you, Jesus, Mary and St. Joseph through the prayerful intercession of St. Philomena.

Fourth miracle of St. Philomena: We arrived at Baiano, Italy and went to get information. We did not know whether to take a taxi or bus to Mugnano del Cardinale to St. Philomena's Shrine. The man there was not too helpful. I don't think that he really knew where to send us. Fr. X asked him if we should go to a tobacco office. (This is where tickets are obtained.) The man quickly said yes, as if trying to get rid of us.

We got off the steps where the train had left us. Feeling a bit confused, we really did not know where to go. Right in front of the steps was an old school bus, parked with lots of teenagers. Outside a sign read, "Mugnano." Fr. X asked him if he was going to Mugnano. He answered, "You want to go to St. Philomena? Come, come, I take you." He asked two girls to give us the two first seats. He took us all the way, right in front of the Shrine of St. Philomena. We arrived at 2:00 p.m.. The bus driver did not charge us anything. He refused to take any money. Fr. X and I were overwhelmed with the powerful help of St. Philomena. Only she could do all this! I love you, St. Philomena.

We walked inside the shrine. I immediately went to her statue. I knelt down almost in tears. My heart was pounding at a hundred miles a minute. St. Philomena spoke to me.

St. Philomena: *I, St. Philomena, welcome you and your spiritual director to my shrine. You see, little sister, how I arranged everything for you to get here? Know that during your stay here, I shall visit with you. Pray now and show your gratitude to God Who loves you and your spiritual director so much, so much.*

We immediately met Sister X who came to greet us. We introduced ourselves and told her where we were from. We asked if there was room available for us. She said yes.

She asked how our devotion to St. Philomena had started. Fr. X very gently told her that his devotion to her had begun through me. Sr. X looked at me and asked me to share with her. I was shocked as Fr. X began to tell her about my visitations with St. Philomena. He told her that he had been my spiritual director for five years. I kept praying quietly, "Please, St. Philomena, I did not come for this. Please do not let him say anymore." Fr. X continued sharing with the sister, who listened patiently while looking at me. I wanted to run and hide. I begged St. Philomena to bring this conversation to an end, but nothing happened.

Sr. X immediately said to us that I must document all this. She told us that she was going to call her secretary, because she (sister) could not understand English very well. I asked Fr. X, "Why did you share with her?" He responded, "I was moved to." Then I shared with him how I felt and my prayer to St. Philomena, asking her to keep him from sharing about me with the sister. Fr. X said, "Be at peace. This is all God's doing." With that I relaxed and submitted to his request of me.

The secretary came. Sr. X, Fr. X and I sat down to share with Y, the secretary, about my visitations with St. Philomena. Y told Sr. X all we said. Sr. X told the secretary to tell us that all of this must be documented and given to the Rector, that he may examine all these accounts with St. Philomena. After examining these messages that St. Philomena gave to me, the Rector would go to the bishop in Napoli. Sr. X believed that these accounts must also go to the Holy See. (At this point, I am scared stiff.) Sr. X believed that all these accounts should come out of Mugnano del Cardinale, so that people could begin to have more devotion to St. Philomena.

Fr. X said to her that we would send the Rector everything, but we didn't have anything to do with the bishop in Napoli , Italy.

I told the secretary to please tell Sr. X that it was not my intention in coming to St. Philomena's Shrine to share all this. Fr. X told the secretary that he felt moved to speak of these accounts with St. Philomena. The secretary told this to Sr. X who said that St. Philomena brought me to her shrine, no doubt to share all this, because this was very important to the devotion of St. Philomena. Fr. X invited Sr. X to be present during my visit with St. Philomena.

217

Conversations With St. Philomena

Sr. X agreed. We prepared in front of where St. Philomena's remains are. These are the words of St. Philomena.

St. Philomena: *Greetings from Heaven, little sister.*

Janie: Ave, St. Philomena.

St. Philomena: *My little sister, I, St. Philomena, brought you and your spiritual director here as I promised.*
I, St. Philomena, wish to assure Sr. X and the Rector not to be concerned with anything.
I, St. Philomena, am constantly making intercession for all their hard work and efforts.
I, St. Philomena, know how much they suffer to make me more known. I wish to convey to them that all their hard efforts will be rewarded.
I, St. Philomena, will help them to accomplish everything according to the Holy Will of God.
I, St. Philomena, am always interceding for the city of Mugnano and all of Italy.
I, St. Philomena, wish to express my deep gratitude to the Rector and Sr. X for all their work and for taking such good care of my little shrine. I am forever grateful to the both of them.
Little sister, I need your help. Please be a benefactor by spreading devotion to me, St. Philomena. There is so much evil in the world. I want to help all those who turn to me, St. Philomena, for help. I will help them to combat the evil which surrounds them. Will you please be a benefactor to help spread devotion to me, St. Philomena?

Janie: My dear little St. Philomena, tell me what you need and I will be at your disposal with all my heart and soul.

St. Philomena: *Thank you, little sister, thank you. I knew that I could count on your help. This is why God chose you. During your stay here, I shall visit with you. Until tomorrow, farewell, little sister.*

Janie: Good night, sweet St. Philomena.

These Accounts Are Very Important

April 4, 1997
Mugnano, Italy

I was awakened by my guardian angel through St. Philomena to record everything which I was receiving during my stay here. I began to write and immediately lights began to appear in my room. These lights were all over. They were the angels that came with St. Philomena. Then, on the wall there was a great light which covered a great portion of the wall.

St. Philomena: *I am here, little sister helping you to accomplish writing everything. These accounts are very important. You do not understand this now, but one day you will. For now, be obedient to the Holy Spirit and write everything I, St. Philomena, share with you.*

The lights were gone; my little sister would return later. I felt her presence so strongly with me. I had been recording ever since 4:00 am. Later, I went and spent time with her, praying before her altar for all her special intentions.

I Will Remain With You

April 5, 1997
Mugnano, Italy

I was praying before her altar for the many special requests I had been given when she came.

St. Philomena: *Greetings from Heaven, little sister.*

Janie: Peace to you, St. Philomena. St. Philomena, please help me. I brought so many requests from different people; you know who

219

Conversations With St. Philomena

they are. I have one request, in particular, from a dear friend. I love him very much. He suffers from migraine headaches and has had this suffering for a long time, many years, in fact. I told him that I would pray for him during my stay here. He also has devotion to you. Will you ask Our Master to find favor in his request through your intercession?

St. Philomena: *Little sister, do not give this request a second thought. Your friend's request will be answered. I, St. Philomena, will help him. Be at peace.*

I will pray with you to Our Master for all your special intentions. You will be leaving soon, little sister, but I will remain with you. Hold dear to you all that I shared during your stay here. Until tomorrow, farewell, little sister.

Janie: Farewell, St. Philomena and thank you for answering my dear friend's request.

With the Vicar of Our Master

April 6, 1997
Rome, Italy

St. Philomena: *Greetings from Heaven, little sister.*

Janie: Peace to you, St. Philomena.

St. Philomena: *Little sister, today you have a busy day. I will be with you in prayer. Until tomorrow, farewell, little sister.*

Janie: St. Philomena, today is Mercy Sunday and we are supposed to go to St. Peter's Square for Our Holy Father to bless us. Please pray for us, so that this may be accomplished.

St. Philomena: *Do not worry, little sister. God has already provided you and your friends a way to be with the Vicar of Our Master.*

Anchor of Hope from Heaven

On this Mercy Sunday we received the Holy Family's blessings. What a great day! Now, I must pack for tomorrow. I return to the states. Thank you, Jesus, for everything.

A Safe Journey Home

April 7, 1997
Rome, Italy

St. Philomena: *Greetings from Heaven, little sister.*

Janie: Peace, St. Philomena. St. Philomena, I have to go to the airport in a little bit. Keep us in your prayers.

St. Philomena: *Little sister, I wish to express my deep gratitude to you for visiting my little shrine and meeting the Rector and Sr. X. I love them both dearly. Always keep them in your prayers; they work hard to make me more known. Until tomorrow, farewell, little sister. You will have a safe journey home.*

Janie: Thank you, St. Philomena.

Blessed With So Many Graces

April 8, 1997

St. Philomena: *Greetings from Heaven, little sister.*

Janie: Ave, St. Philomena. Please pray for me; I am so tired. I think that I am experiencing jet lag.

St. Philomena: *My little sister, you have been blessed with so many graces. Know that these graces will help you while you are recovering from your trip to Rome, Italy. Remain steadfast and know that I am interceding for you. Rest, little sister, rest. God has accomplished much because of your "yes" to Him while you were at my shrine. Rejoice! Until tomorrow, farewell, little sister.*

221

Conversations With St. Philomena

Janie: Farewell and thank you, St. Philomena, thank you for everything.

I Embrace All Who Turn To Me

April 9, 1997

St. Philomena: *Greetings from Heaven, little sister.*

Janie: Greetings, St. Philomena and peace to you.

St. Philomena: *My little sister, I wish to express my gratitude to you for all that you are doing for me. Your heart burns with much love for Our Master for you know that He is the One Who is helping you to have a stronger devotion to me.*

Janie: St. Philomena, I am very grateful to you as well because you are helping me to draw closer to Our Master through your intercession. Tonight, I will talk to my family more about you so that they may embrace you more. I want everyone in the world to know you and to have more devotion to you.

St. Philomena: *Little sister, I will embrace all who turn to me and ask me to intercede for them. I invite parents and children to seek my intercession. I will help them to love God more and more every day. Until tomorrow, farewell, little sister.*

Janie: Farewell, St. Philomena.

I Will Help Them

April 10, 1997

St. Philomena: *Greetings from Heaven, little sister.*

Janie: Peace to you, St. Philomena.

St. Philomena: *Little sister, again, I wish to thank you for introducing me to all the people here.* (We were giving a talk on my trip to St. Philomena's shrine.)
I want to be friends with all who embrace devotion to me, St. Philomena. I will help them in times of distress. I will help them to pray with faith in their hearts. I will help them grow more towards holiness and purity of heart. I invite everyone here to be one of my little friends in Our Master and in Our Lady. Until tomorrow, farewell, little sister.

Janie: Thank you, St. Philomena.

For the Purification of Your Family and Poor Sinners
April 11, 1997

St. Philomena: *Greetings from Heaven, little sister.*

Janie: Peace, St. Philomena.

St. Philomena: *My little sister, you have been suffering because your little grandson is ill. You love him so much and you give of yourself to him. Do not be concerned, he will recover quickly. Endure your suffering for the purification of your family and poor sinners throughout the world.*

Janie: St. Philomena, please intercede for X.

St. Philomena: *My little sister, I will intercede for all your special intentions Until tomorrow, farewell. Rest, little sister, for you are tired from your suffering. I will be at your side interceding for you.*

Janie: Thank you, St. Philomena.

Conversations With St. Philomena

Private Messages for the Group

From April 12 through April 14 I was invited to Newark, New Jersey to give talks on the family. During this time St. Philomena came, but the messages were for that group.

In Reparation for the Bride of Our Master

April 15, 1997

St. Philomena: *Greetings from Heaven, little sister.*

Janie: Peace, St. Philomena. Today, again, I ask for your intercession. I am very tired from my trip.

St. Philomena: *Little sister, you have a busy day ahead of you. Offer your suffering in reparation for the Bride of Our Master. In doing this you will console His Sorrowful Heart. Until tomorrow, farewell, little sister.*

Janie: Thank you, St. Philomena.

Trust God in Your Suffering

April 16, 1997

St. Philomena: *Greetings from Heaven, little sister.*

Janie: Peace to you, St. Philomena.

St. Philomena: *My little sister, you have been suffering much for your family. Do not become discouraged in your suffering. Your suffering is bringing about good fruit.*

Janie: St. Philomena, I try not to become discouraged, but I am so tired. I do a great deal of traveling to help families draw closer to

224

God. God knows that I do not like to travel, but I do it out of love and obedience to God. He has been so good to me and my family. Pray for me; these are difficult times for me.

St. Philomena: *Little sister, continue to trust God in your suffering. He will provide you with all that you need. Until tomorrow, farewell, little sister.*

Janie: Farewell, St. Philomena.

For All the People You Will Meet

April 17, 1997

St. Philomena: *Greetings, from Heaven, little sister.*

Janie: Peace to you, St. Philomena.

St. Philomena: *Little sister, offer your suffering for all the people you will meet during these next few days. God is going to help many families through your suffering. Your talk will draw many families back to God. Be at peace, little sister. Until tomorrow, farewell, little sister.*

Janie: Thank you, St. Philomena.

All Fifteen Decades of the Rosary

April 18, 1997

St. Philomena: *Greetings from Heaven, little sister.*

Janie: Peace, St. Philomena. Please pray for my talk tomorrow.

St. Philomena: *Little sister, tomorrow, pray all fifteen decades of your Rosary, offering it to Our Lady. This will help you. Do not worry about your talk. Until tomorrow, farewell, sleep now. You*

225

Miraculous Statue of St. Philomena - exuded "Manna,"
a Miraculous Oil, on August 10, 1823

Janie in front of the Miraculous statue of St Philomena which exuded
"Manna," a Miraculous Oil, on August 10, 1823

Conversations With St. Philomena

have a busy day tomorrow.

Words to Touch The Hearts of God's Children
April 19, 1997
Detroit, Michigan

St. Philomena: *Greetings from Heaven, little sister.*

Janie: Peace, St. Philomena.

St. Philomena: *Little sister, abandon yourself completely to God. He will send you His Holy Spirit to help you. The Holy Spirit will give you His words to touch the hearts of God's children. Remember, little sister, pray your Rosary before you talk.*

Janie: St. Philomena, I will do as you say.
I did all that St. Philomena asked of me. I was filled with power from Heaven as I spoke. I received many compliments on my talk. Praise God!

See Their Woundedness
April 20, 1997
Detroit, Michigan

St. Philomena: *Greetings from Heaven, little sister.*

Janie: Peace to you, St. Philomena.

St. Philomena: *Dear Janie, my sweet little sister, offer your prayers for all the youth in the world who are walking in darkness. See their woundedness.*

In a vision I saw many young people suffering from a lack of love from their parents. Many of these young people were victims of child abuse and sexual abuse. They were suffering so much.

St. Philomena: *Little sister, pray for the parents of these young people. They have abandoned their responsibilities as parents. Many of their offspring are on their way to perdition. Pray with me for this special intention. Until tomorrow, farewell, little sister.*

Janie: Farewell, St. Philomena. I'll pray with you.

Anchor of Hope From Heaven

April 21, 1997

St. Philomena: *Greetings from Heaven, little sister.*

Janie: Peace to you, St. Philomena. St. Philomena, please pray for me, because I am not feeling too well. I don't know what is wrong, maybe a virus.

St. Philomena: *Little sister, I will pray for you. I ask you again to please keep in mind all the young people who are suffering. They need much love and prayers.*

Janie: St. Philomena, are you a patron of the youth and children?

St. Philomena: *Little sister, I embrace all souls who turn to me for assistance and invoke my intercession. I help many souls to convert. I love babies, children, the youth and all people. I love all of God's children and my love is demonstrated in all the assistance which I render to souls when they turn to me. Love, little sister, cannot be isolated to just one cause. **I am St. Philomena, "Anchor of Hope from Heaven," helping all souls in these troubled times. I am the solace of the suffering and sick. I help draw poor sinners to the love of Our Master and His Most Holy Mother.** Encourage souls to trust in my intercession. Until tomorrow, farewell, little sister.*

Janie: Farewell, St. Philomena.

The Shrine Church of St. Philomena located in Mugnano, Italy
in the diocese of Nola, near Naples.

The Original tiles found marking St. Philomena's tomb.

Janie, standing in front of Relics of various saints
in the Shrine of St. Philomena

Conversations With St. Philomena

Offer Your Prayers

April 22, 1997

St. Philomena: *Greetings from Heaven, little sister.*

Janie: Peace to you, St. Philomena. St. Philomena, I am not feeling well today. I believe I do have a virus.

St. Philomena: *Little sister, try to stay in bed and rest. Offer your prayers for the conversion of poor sinners. Until tomorrow, farewell, little sister.*

Janie: I will rest, St. Philomena.

Call Upon St. Michael the Archangel

April 23, 1997

St. Philomena: *Greetings from Heaven, little sister.*

Janie: Peace, St. Philomena. St. Philomena, please pray for me. The devil is telling me that it is not important to write down anything that you tell me. He says no one will believe that you come to visit me. His words are convincing and he constantly bothers me with these thoughts.

St. Philomena: *Little sister, do not listen to his lies. Call upon St. Michael, the Archangel, for support and prayer. Remember, little sister, that Satan hates anyone who prays. He knows that you pray all the time and your prayers help poor sinners to convert. You send your prayers to every soul in the world. You forget no one because you know in your heart that when a soul turns to God in prayer, that soul has God's total attention. The devil is a liar. Until tomorrow, farewell, little sister.*

Janie: Thank you, St. Philomena.

I Will Pray for You

April 24, 1997

St. Philomena: *Greetings from Heaven, little sister.*

Janie: Peace, St. Philomena. St. Philomena, I am very sick today. Please pray for me.

St. Philomena: *Little sister, I will pray for you. Stay in bed and rest. Until tomorrow, farewell, little sister.*

Janie: Thank you, St. Philomena.

No Messages

April 25-30, 1997

From April 25 to April 30 St. Philomena came to me and prayed for me. I have been ill with fever and suffered much. During this time I couldn't write anything.

Embrace Everything St. Joseph Shares With You

May 1, 1997

St. Philomena: *Greetings from Heaven, little sister.*

Janie: Peace to you, St. Philomena. St. Philomena, today I am happy, for St. Joseph will visit with me.

St. Philomena: *Little sister, today you will receive much joy. Embrace everything that St. Joseph shares with you. Until tomorrow, farewell, little sister. Pray for poor, poor sinners.*

Janie: Thank you, St. Philomena.

The Cure of Ars and St. Philomena's Shrine,
Mugnano, Italy

Janie praying over a soul who is a victim of cancer - standing in front of the Chapel of St. Philomena within the Shrine Church at Mugnano, Italy

Janie's husband was moved to take a second picture. The Pillar of Cloud Appeared - The presence of God. Exdous 13:21-22

Conversations With St. Philomena

The Sacred Heart Living in Your Midst

May 2, 1997

St. Philomena: *Greetings from Heaven, little sister.*

Janie: Peace to you, St. Philomena. Today is First Friday and I am offering my prayers for Our Lord's Most Sacred Heart. I am going to make my Holy Hour after our visit.

St. Philomena: *Little sister, this will make Our Master so happy for He loves all souls who embrace Him in Perpetual Adoration. He is able to help all those souls you recommend to His Most Sacred Heart. Little sister, always visit Our Master in the Most Blessed Sacrament, for the Most Blessed Sacrament is the Sacred Heart of the Master living in your midst. Love Him always, by visiting Him daily in the Most Blessed Sacrament. Until tomorrow, farewell, little sister.*

Janie: Thank you, St. Philomena.

The Sacrament of Reconciliation

May 3, 1997

St. Philomena: *Greetings from Heaven, little sister.*

Janie: Peace to you, St. Philomena. St. Philomena, please pray for me. I am preparing to go to Confession and then to Holy Mass in honor of Our Lady's request for First Saturday. I hold this devotion dear to my heart.

St. Philomena: *Little sister, preparing to go to Confession is pleasing to God. He desires that all souls prepare by making a good examination of conscience before receiving the sacrament of Reconciliation. Many special graces are given to souls who prepare well before going to be reconciled to God through the sacrament of Reconciliation. Many healings take place as well in the soul and in the*

230

mind and body. God is pleased with you, little sister. Live to please God. Until tomorrow, farewell, little sister.

Janie: Farewell, St. Philomena.

In God's Hands
May 4, 1997

St. Philomena: *Greetings from Heaven, little sister.*

Janie: Peace to you, St. Philomena. St. Philomena, please keep me and my family in your prayers. We are preparing to make a pilgrimage to the shrines in Rome, Italy, then to Medjugorje. We are all very happy about this trip, but I don't want to leave our little grandson behind. He will stay with his natural mother, and though she does love him very much, we have never left him for two weeks.

St. Philomena: *Little sister, I will intercede for the safety and wellbeing of your little grandson. Remember, he is, also and first of all, in God's hands. He will do well. Be at peace. Until tomorrow, farewell, little sister.*

Janie: Thank you, St. Philomena.

For All the Young People Who Live By Faith
May 5, 1997

St. Philomena: *Greetings from Heaven, little sister.*

Janie: Peace to you, St. Philomena.

St. Philomena: *Little sister, unite your prayers with mine and let us pray for all the young people who live by faith and have embraced the virtues of purity and holiness. These precious souls suffer much*

231

The Garza's,
Fr. Giovanni and
Marco from Rome,
Italy.(close and dear
friend to Marcelino
and Janie)

Marcelino, Janie Garza, Fr. Henry (Janie's spiritual director)
Fr. Giovanni Braschi, Rector of St. Philomena Shrine and Sister Bartellina

The Garza's, Fr. Giovanni, Fr. Henry and friends in front of
the Chapel of St. Philomena within the Shrine Church.

Fr. Giovanni, Sister Bartellina and Janie in front of
the chapel of St. Philomena.

Conversations With St. Philomena

persecution from other young people. It is very difficult for these young people, since they are constantly being tempted. Our prayers will help these souls in a special way. Until tomorrow, little sister. Remain in prayer with me.

Janie: St. Philomena, I will pray for these special intentions.

Christian Education

May 6, 1997

St. Philomena: *Greetings from Heaven, little sister.*

Janie: Peace to you, St. Philomena.

St. Philomena: *Little sister, let us continue to pray for all parents in the world that through our prayers, parents may give their children the Christian education which is so vitally needed for their spiritual well-being.*

Janie: St. Philomena, I know how powerful your intercession is before God. Please, I beg you, to always intercede for the world and all our sinfulness. You, who suffered so much for the sake of purity, pray, so that we may obtain purity of mind, body and spirit. I love you so much, and I truly trust in your intercession. Keep us all in your prayers.

St. Philomena: *Little sister, you have a loving heart. God has blessed you with a loving heart because of all your prayers and sacrifices. You busy yourself by constantly praying for yourself, your family, Our Master's Bride and all the world. Little sister, you do so much for the reign of Our Master through your prayers. Prayer, little sister, is the great force in the world that is helping to convert many hearts. Pray always. Until tomorrow, little sister, farewell. I will intercede for your intentions.*

Janie: Farewell, St. Philomena.

232

Helping Many Priests and Religious

May 7, 1997

St. Philomena: *Greetings from Heaven, little sister.*

Janie: Peace to you, St. Philomena.

St. Philomena: *Little sister, you are suffering much today. I will intercede for you. Know that you are helping many priests and religious to draw closer to the love of Our Master. I will intercede for you. Until tomorrow, farewell, little sister.*

Janie: Thank you for your prayers and support.

An Abundance of Graces

May 8, 1997
Solemnity of the Ascension

St. Philomena: Greetings from Heaven, little sister.

Janie: Peace to you, St. Philomena. Today, I am so happy for in a little while, I will be with Our Lord when He comes to visit with me.

St. Philomena: *Little sister, you will receive an abundance of graces through Our Master's heavenly visit. I will intercede for you. Until tomorrow, farewell, little sister.*

Janie: Farewell, St. Philomena.

Trust in the Love of Our Master During Suffering

May 9, 1997

St. Philomena: *Greetings from Heaven, little sister.*

Conversations With St. Philomena

Janie: Peace to you, St. Philomena.

St. Philomena: *Little sister, I won't stay long for I know that your suffering is intense. I encourage you to trust in the love of our Master during your suffering. Until tomorrow, farewell, little sister.*

Janie: Thank you, St. Philomena.

Have No Worry as You Suffer

May 10, 1997

St. Philomena: *Greetings from Heaven, little sister.*

Janie: Peace to you, St. Philomena. St. Philomena, I am still suffering. Keep me in your prayers.

St. Philomena: *Little sister, I will pray for you during your suffering. Have no worry as you suffer. God is with you. Until tomorrow, farewell, little sister.*

Janie: Thank you, St. Philomena. I will trust my God and my All.

He Loves All Mothers Unconditionally

May 11, 1997
Mother's Day

St. Philomena: *Greetings from Heaven, little sister.*

Janie: Peace to you, St. Philomena.

St. Philomena: *Little sister, a most happy Mother's Day to you. Today, I salute all mothers in the world. Being a loving mother is very special. Mothers are special to God for He knows just how*

234

very much mothers suffer with love for their children and their husbands.

Today, little sister, I will be interceding for all mothers in the world, so that children and spouses everywhere will see their mothers and their wives as God sees them. God is pouring His blessings upon all mothers, for He loves all mothers unconditionally.

Little sister, I know that you are sad and that you miss your mother. Please do not be sad. Your mother is home in Heaven. Rejoice so that your children will see you happy. I'll intercede for you. Until tomorrow, farewell, little sister.

Janie: Thank you, St. Philomena. I will enjoy Mother's Day with my family.

Blessings, Simply By Listening

May 12, 1997

St. Philomena: *Greetings from Heaven, little sister.*

Janie: Peace to you, St. Philomena. Please pray for me as I prepare to give my talk on the family. I am feeling better, but it seems that I always suffer just before I travel to different places to give talks on the messages of the Holy Family.

St. Philomena: *Little sister, do not be concerned. All will go well and many people will receive special blessings, simply by listening to what you share with them. Until tomorrow, farewell, little sister.*

Janie: Thank you, St. Philomena.

Personal Messages

May 13 - May 18, 1997

Because of my traveling, St. Philomena came to pray with me early every morning. Her messages were personal.

235

Conversations With St. Philomena

Your Prayers Will Help Thousands of Souls

May 19, 1997

St. Philomena: *Greetings from Heaven, little sister.*

Janie: Ave, St. Philomena.

St. Philomena: *My little sister, I wish to thank you for offering up your sleep in reparation for Our Master's Bride and for poor sinners.*

Janie: St. Philomena, I was very tired and wanted to go back to sleep, but instead I decided to stay awake and pray. My days are so busy, but God occupies my mind throughout my day.

St. Philomena: *Little sister, you have reached a spiritual level at which you are united with heavenly impulses and inspirations. You have been able to obtain this spiritual growth through your constant prayers.*
   Oh, that souls would understand the importance of prayer! Through prayer, souls are in union with their Creator. Prayer brings about spiritual maturity; prayer leads souls to holiness and purity of heart.
   Little sister, offer your prayers, today, so that more souls will be moved to pray more, especially those souls who do not believe in prayer.
   So many people throughout the world have life without God. This is so sad, for these are the people who are on their way to perdition unless they repent. These souls are the slaves of Satan, and he has all these poor souls under his power. Please, little sister, always embrace these poor sinners in all your daily sacrifices and prayers.

Janie: St. Philomena, if these people do not believe in God, how will my prayers help them?

St. Philomena: *Oh, my sweet little sister! God's love and mercy is without limit. God will take your prayers and sacrifices and help*

236

these poor souls. God accepts your prayers and sacrifices as an act of love, and God is love. Please do not ever let the evil one deceive you by telling you that you cannot save others through your prayers.

Remember, your prayers will help thousands of souls, and Satan knows this. This is why he will attempt to discourage you from praying for poor sinners. Until tomorrow, little sister, farewell.

Janie: Farewell, St. Philomena. I love you.

For Unwed Expectant Mothers

May 20, 1997

St. Philomena: *Greetings from Heaven, little sister.*

Janie: Peace to you, St. Philomena.

St. Philomena: *My dear little sister Janie, offer your prayers for all young, unwed, expectant mothers who are contemplating the evil of aborting their unborn babies. Oh, if you only knew how many unborn babies are killed every second that goes by, you would be shocked! The world has abandoned the spirit of purity. The young people lose their virginity at such a young age.*

Janie: St. Philomena, why is this happening?

St. Philomena: *My dear little sister, this happens because many parents encourage their young sons and daughters to have safe sexual relationships by educating their young children about birth control. This encourages the youth to enter into relationships which include sexual relationships. It is for this very reason that many young people end up having children out of wedlock.*

These methods which the world teaches to prevent getting pregnant is the very reason why young girls become pregnant. There is no protection that is guaranteed to be absolutely effective, except God's protection.

Janie: St. Philomena, I understand what you are telling me. I, my-

self, used to believe in birth control when I was under the influence
of Satan's power. I am forever grateful for God's love and mercy
in saving me from going to hell. I will offer up all my prayers and
sacrifices each day for these intentions.

*St. Philomena: My little sister, I am most grateful to you for your
honesty and for recognizing that all people that believe in using
birth control, as you call it, are under the influence of Satan. Life is
a gift from God. The desire to destroy life comes from Satan. Until
tomorrow, little sister, farewell.*

Janie: Farewell, St. Philomena.

Offer Your Rosary for the Salvation of Families
May 21, 1997

St. Philomena: *Greetings from Heaven, little sister.*

Janie: Ave, St. Philomena.

St. Philomena: *My little sister, know that God is pleased with the
responsibility which you take so seriously towards the care of your
little grandson. God knows how exhausting it can be to care for
children, especially very young children. You have embraced the
responsibility for your grandson with love and patience. Your
grandson will remember the love that you embrace him with.
Know, my little sister, that God chose you and your family to
propagate the importance of family prayer, family love and forgiveness.*

*My little sister, God knows how difficult it is for you to have
time for yourself. The time that you have alone, you spend with Our
Master. Rejoice and remain steadfast during trials and tribulations,
trusting God with all your needs. He will take care of you. Offer
your Rosary for the salvation of families everywhere.*

Until tomorrow, farewell, little sister. Remain peaceful.

Janie: Farewell, St. Philomena.

Never Lose Focus

May 22, 1997

St. Philomena: *Greetings from Heaven, little sister.*

Janie: Peace to you, St. Philomena. I am so glad that you are here with me, St. Philomena. Please pray for me.

St. Philomena: *My little sister, you are suffering for the love that you have in your heart for your grandson. Recall Our Master's words to you while you were in Adoration during Holy Hour: "My humble servant, your grandson is always under my protection and the protection of the Holy Family because of your constant prayers. Your little grandson is our property, for you gave him to us. No harm will come to him."*
 Little sister, in times of suffering, never lose focus on the trust that you have in God. It is during these difficult times that you must remain steadfast. God will pour the love of the Holy Spirit upon your entire being and fill you with His peace. Always keep in mind how much God loves you and your family. Until tomorrow, farewell, little sister.

Janie: Peace, St. Philomena and farewell.

People See Themselves As Gods

May 23, 1997

St. Philomena: *Greetings from Heaven, little sister*

Janie: Ave, St. Philomena. My little friend, I am so concerned about the world that I live in. I had never realized before just how much people do not believe in God. It is scary!

St. Philomena: *My little sister, this is the very reason why so many souls are on their way to perdition. Many people have forgotten about God and see themselves as gods. These souls are living their*

Conversations With St. Philomena

lives without God, and their souls are in great danger.
God has blessed all of humanity with different gifts so that they may help one another. Many people abuse their gifts, especially the intellectual souls. These souls use the gifts that God blesses them with to do evil to others.
Many are the evils today because of the mentality of humanity. Among many of these great evils is technology, a technology that is used to do great evil to others. The evil of the technology of humanity is what is destroying the world, for it is used to control mankind, to exploit, to enslave and do great injustice.
Little sister, please pray for all the people who use their intellectual gifts to do evil to other innocent souls. These souls are Satan's disciples.
I am sad to say that many of these evil souls are those who pledge to be God's representatives. These souls are working for the beast and are found in many areas throughout the world. Until tomorrow, farewell, little sister. Pray for these intentions.

The Holy Obedience of Our Master's Vicar

May 24, 1997

St. Philomena: *Greetings from Heaven, little sister.*

Janie: Peace to you, St. Philomena.

St. Philomena: *My little sister, continue to pray for Our Master's Vicar. He suffers much and the attacks and persecutions against him are enormous.*

Janie: St. Philomena, where do these attacks come from?

St. Philomena: *The attacks come from many of Our Master's beloved brothers and religious.*

Janie: Why do his own attack him?

St. Philomena: *These attacks come because your Pope is doing*

240

the Holy Will of the Father. He walks in the footsteps of St. Peter, whom Our Master chose as His first Vicar on earth.

Janie: St. Philomena, I will intercede for him, as I always do.

St. Philomena: *Little sister, increase your prayers and sacrifices for Him. This Pope has been chosen in a special way for these sinful times. God is saving many priests and religious through the holy obedience of Our Master's Vicar. Oh, blessed is he who walks in the path that leads towards holiness! Pray for him. Until tomorrow, farewell, little sister.*

Janie: Farewell, St. Philomena.

Encouraging the Importance of Family Prayer
May 25, 1997

St. Philomena: *Greetings from Heaven, little sister.*

Janie: Peace to you, St. Philomena.

St. Philomena: *Little sister, you and your family are being blessed for all the prayers that you offer as a family. Family prayer brings conversion to the family members who are distant from God, and it brings God's peace to the household.*
Encourage the importance of family prayer wherever you travel; this is so important. Remember, as I said in the past, that prayer is the greatest force in the world to purify and convert hearts. The Rosary is a very powerful prayer to pray as a family. If only souls would know the power of prayer, they would spend more time in prayer and less time worrying. God is pleased with the way that you pray together as a family. Until tomorrow, farewell, little sister.

Janie: Farewell, St. Philomena. Thank you for all that you share with me. It's so helpful.

Conversations With St. Philomena

God Will Provide Everything

May 26, 1997

St. Philomena: *Greetings from Heaven, little sister.*

Janie: Peace to you, St. Philomena. St. Philomena, please pray for my husband. He is having a hard time finishing our home. He never gets time to rest. Pray for him.

St. Philomena: *Little sister, your husband is suffering for all the souls that will be blessed in visiting your new home. Tell him not to become discouraged, that God is with him and will provide him with everything that he needs. Until tomorrow, farewell, little sister.*

Janie: Thank you, St. Philomena. I'll keep my husband in my prayers.

Embrace the Young People through Prayer

May 27, 1997

St. Philomena: *Greetings from Heaven, little sister.*

Janie: Peace to you, St. Philomena. St. Philomena, today I am praying for all the people who are going to Medjugorje and to Rome, Italy. Please keep this pilgrimage in your prayers.

St. Philomena: *Little sister, I am interceding for this special intention. There will be young people on this pilgrimage. Embrace these young people through your prayers for the devil will be very active, putting temptations in their paths. You will suffer much on this pilgrimage. Be prepared and remain steadfast. Until tomorrow, farewell, little sister.*

Janie: Thank you, St. Philomena. I will prepare with prayer.

Pray for Masonic Cardinals, Bishops, and Priests
May 28, 1997

St. Philomena: *Greetings from Heaven, little sister.*

Janie: Peace to you, St. Philomena.

St. Philomena: *Little sister, today let us both pray for all the Masonic cardinals, bishops and priests who have allowed themselves to be enslaved by the devil. Through these poor sinful souls, the devil has entered into the hearts of many of God's representatives within the Bride of Our Master. Please, little sister, pray for this special intention. Our Master is so offended by the actions of these disobedient souls who are against His Vicar on earth. Until tomorrow, farewell, little sister.*

St. Philomena was very sad today.

For the Bride of Our Master
May 29, 1997

St. Philomena: *Greetings from Heaven, little sister.*

Janie: Peace to you, St. Philomena.

St. Philomena: *Little sister, today again, I am asking you to pray for the Bride of Our Master. Until tomorrow, farewell, little sister.*

St. Philomena and I prayed together for a short while for the intentions above. St. Philomena has great love for our Holy Father and all the Church.

The Spirit of Apostasy
May 30, 1997

St. Philomena: *Greetings from Heaven, little sister.*

Conversations With St. Philomena

Janie: Peace to you, St. Philomena. St. Philomena, I have been offering my prayers for your special intentions for Our Lord's Bride. I don't like to see you so sad.

St. Philomena: *Little sister, the love that Our Master has for His Bride is immense. He loves and loves, no matter how much He is rejected by His representatives in the Church. He is so merciful, so loving. See how His love and mercy are rejected. Our prayers can be very helpful; please continue to pray for these intentions. The schism and the spirit of apostasy is alive in the Church. Only consistent prayer and fasting can remedy this horrible situation. Until tomorrow, farewell, little sister.*

Janie: I will pray and fast for this situation. I promise!

My Dear Pauline Jaricot

May 31, 1997

St. Philomena: *Greetings from Heaven, little sister.*

Janie: Peace to you, St. Philomena.

St. Philomena: *My dear Janie, do not despair in your suffering. It is for your own purification, as well as for poor sinners. Offer your intense suffering for this friend for whom you and I are interceding, together with my dear Pauline Jaricot, who is interceding for your intentions as well.*

    The evil one is strongly trying to distract you to keep you from praying. Please pray more intensely. Call upon the Archangel St. Michael to protect you. I shall continue to intercede for your special intentions concerning your dear friend who is ill. Until tomorrow, farewell, little sister.

Janie: Farewell, St. Philomena.

The Power of Heaven At Your Disposal
June 1, 1997

St. Philomena: *Greetings from Heaven, my little sister.*

Janie: Peace to you, St. Philomena. St. Philomena, please pray for me. Ask God to give me the strength and courage to endure my suffering with peace in my heart.

St. Philomena: *Little sister, I am with you interceding for you as you go through your suffering. I know that sometimes it is unbearable. It was that way for me as I suffered in the hands of the evil one. Look to Our Master and spend time with Him, for this is when Satan will try to confuse you.*

Janie: St. Philomena, I will trust in Our Master, for He is my everything. Intercede for me, that I may remain strong as you when you were suffering.

St. Philomena: *Little sister, keep your eyes on Our Master and seek the intercession of Our Most Holy Mother, together with St. Joseph. You have the power of heaven at your disposal. Satan has no victory over you. Abandon yourself to the love of Our Master. He will see you through everything. Until tomorrow, farewell. Pray for those poor sinners who continue to reject Our Master.*

Janie: Farewell to you, St. Philomena. I will continue to pray.

Suffer With Joy in Your Heart
June 2, 1997

St. Philomena: *Greetings from Heaven, my little sister.*

Janie: Peace to you, St. Philomena.

St. Philomena: *Little sister, you are suffering in reparation for*

245

Conversations With St. Philomena

poor sinners, especially for the Bride of Our Master. Suffer with joy in your heart. Your prayers and fasting are helping many. Until tomorrow, farewell, little sister.

Janie: Thank you, St. Philomena.

Feast on the Bread of Angels

June 3, 1997

St. Philomena: *Greetings from Heaven, my little sister.*

Janie: Ave, St. Philomena, my heavenly sister. I am so happy and grateful to God. Yesterday, I went to Confession, then attended Holy Mass. I so needed to go to Confession. I go to Confession once a week. This helps me to keep my soul spiritually polished.
St. Philomena: *My little sister, God is pleased that you are so concerned about your spiritual well-being. You see how your daily prayers and sacrifices help you to mature more towards Our Master. You attend daily Mass and pray many rosaries throughout the day. You adore Our Master in the Blessed Sacrament and say your devotional prayers which you offer God in reparation for your own sins and those of poor sinners.*

Oh, little sister! Blessed are you who feast on the Bread of the Angels every day. Blessed are you, for you keep Our poor Master company in the Most Blessed Sacrament. Blessed are you for all your daily prayers and sacrifices. Blessed are you, for you make room for your Creator. Blessed are you, little sister, who cares so much for the salvation of poor sinners. Blessed are you, who demonstrates your love to the Almighty Heavenly Father through your prayers and perseverance.

I love you, little sister. Until tomorrow, farewell, little sister.

Janie: Thank you, St. Philomena. I love you, my heavenly little sister. I love you.

246

No Messages

June 4, 1997

On this day St. Philomena interceded for me. This was a busy day for me.

No Messages

June 5, 1997

Again, due to my busy schedule, St. Philomena interceded for me today.

Blessed Are Those Who Love and Honor the Two Hearts
June 6, 1997
Feast of the Sacred Heart

St. Philomena: *Greetings from Heaven, my little sister.*

Janie: Peace to you, St. Philomena.

St. Philomena: *Little sister, today is a special day for you. Today, Our Master will come to visit with you. Spend quiet time in Adoration, adoring Our Beloved Master.*
Meditate on the love of His Sacred Heart and how much He loves all of humanity. Little sister, always remember the tremendous love that He has for you. His love is your strength to endure any suffering, any persecution, any obstacle in your path.
Love the Sacred Heart of Our Master and honor First Fridays and First Saturdays as requested by Our Master and His Most Holy Mother. Honor these two days as a family devotion, keeping in mind the great love and honor you are giving to the Two Hearts. The graces and blessings which come from honoring this heavenly request are without limit.

247

Conversations With St. Philomena

Teach others to love and honor the Sacred Heart of Jesus, Our Master, and the Immaculate Heart of His Most Holy Mother. Oh, blessed are those souls who love and honor the Two Hearts; blessed are they, their rewards are great in Heaven. Until tomorrow, farewell, little sister.

Janie: St. Philomena, I will invite my family tonight to renew our consecration to the Two Hearts. We have devotion as a family to First Fridays and First Saturdays. We have completed this obligation as a family. We will always love the Two Hearts, and we will continue to invite others to the love and devotion of the Two Hearts.

St. Philomena: *Little sister, God is pleased with your family efforts. Until tomorrow, farewell, little sister.*

I Am With Them Through Love

June 7, 1997

St. Philomena: *Greetings from Heaven, my little sister.*

Janie: Peace to you, St. Philomena. My heavenly sister, I am so happy that you come every day. You have helped me so much, and others as well. So many of my friends have embraced you as their friend. This makes me most happy. I know that a lot of people know you and have devotion to you. I want every soul in the world to know you and to embrace you, that you may help them as you have helped my family and friends.

St. Philomena: *Little sister, you are so kind and your heart is full of charity and love. I am most happy to come to you every day. I look forward to our visits. I enjoy sharing heavenly signs and wonders. As for all your friends whom you love so much, know that I am close to them as well. I am with them through the love and devotion that they have for me.*
Little sister, you have so much to do today. I shall help you and your family to prepare for your spiritual journey together

248

through my intercession. Until tomorrow, farewell, little sister.

Janie: Farewell, St. Philomena.

Holy Time

June 8, 1997

St. Philomena: *Greetings from Heaven, my little sister.*

Janie: Peace to you, St. Philomena.

St. Philomena: *Little sister, God is most pleased with you and your family. He knows that you, as a family, work very hard to keep your relationship with Him pure. You pray as a family and love and support one another during hard times. This pleases God very much. Remember, little sister, that Our Lady said to you in 1989 that one day, you as a family, would visit Medjugorje and many more holy places. This prophecy is coming true today.*

You, as a family, will visit holy places where you will be blessed, and the graces poured upon you will be without limit. What a holy time this will be for you and your family. Rejoice and be grateful to God for everything. Until tomorrow, farewell, little sister.

Janie: Farewell, St. Philomena.

The Crosses Will Be Many

June 9, 1997
(Pilgrimage to Italy, Paris and Medjugorje)

6:30 a.m.

St. Philomena: *Greetings from Heaven, my little sister.*

Janie: Peace to you, St. Philomena.

249

Conversations With St. Philomena

St. Philomena: *My little sister, prepare for this pilgrimage on which you will embark. The crosses will be many and the crosses will be severe. Embrace this suffering with joy and trust in Our Master in the midst of your suffering. Remain faithful to Our Master and abandon yourself into His care. Until tomorrow, farewell, little sister.*

Janie: Farewell, St. Philomena.

Later that day, we experienced four trials en route to Italy. Our first trial began when my son's ticket was canceled from Newark to Paris. The airline couldn't give any explanation. My son had to be on stand-by. I gathered people to pray the Rosary with me, asking St. Philomena to help us. She did! Our son got on the plane without any problems.

Our second trial: When we arrived in Newark, New Jersey, my son's luggage was lost and we couldn't find it.

Third trial: We all boarded the plane to Paris at 4:20 p.m.. We remained on the plane until 7:30 p.m.. Then we had to get off due to problems with the plane. Again, I gathered everyone in our group to pray the Rosary. We did, and everybody was at peace. I had a feeling that we would fly to Paris that same night.

We boarded the plane again and left for Paris at 11:00 p.m.. We arrived in Paris at 11:30 am, Paris time. Three hours later at 3:30 p.m., we boarded the plane to Rome. We arrived in Rome at 5:00 p.m..

Fourth trial: When we arrived in Rome and went to the baggage claim, half of the people were missing their luggage, including my son and I. We were told that our luggage would come to our hotel that night.

Hearts Very Wounded

June 10, 1997
Rome, Italy

St. Philomena: *Greetings from Heaven, my little sister.*

250

Janie: Ave, St. Philomena.

St. Philomena: *My little sister, I know that your crosses have been difficult ones, but you have done well. You turned to prayer, and God gave you His peace and strength.*

I ask that you offer up your sufferings for there are some on this pilgrimage whose hearts are very wounded. These souls need the love of Our Master in their hearts. Be charitable, loving and a prayerful example for these souls, that they may desire the love of God in their lives.

Janie: St. Philomena, will more crosses continue? (St. Philomena smiled.)

St. Philomena: *Oh, yes, little sister, more crosses will continue! Do not fear, for these crosses will help you to draw closer to Our Master. Until tomorrow, farewell, little sister.*

St. Philomena gave words for my spiritual director and another priest in our journey.

A Personal Message
June 11, 1997
Rome, Italy

St. Philomena: *Greetings from Heaven, my little sister.*

Janie: Peace to you, St. Philomena. (The message is personal.)

Later that night, the lost luggage arrived at our hotel, but my son's and my luggage remained missing. We have no clothing to wear, and we will be traveling until June 24. In God we trust.

251

Conversations With St. Philomena

Reflect Our Love, Be Our Love, Live Our Love

June 12, 1997
Rome, Italy

I saw Our Lord, Our Lady and St. Philomena come to me with a multitude of angels.

Our Lord: *Our humble servant, good morning. You have suffered attack upon attack from Satan, but he has not broken your spirit. He will not harm you. You belong to Me.*

Janie: O dear and good Master! I want to go to Heaven. I will endure all the suffering with joy in my heart. I am so very happy that You and Our Lady came to me when I needed You most.

Our Lord: *My humble servant, the devil is trying desperately to destroy you and your family. He will not succeed, for you and your family are protected by Our love.*

At this time, St. Joseph came.

Our Lady: *Our dear sweet angel, you are so loved by Us (the Holy Family). We delight in your obedience to endure the most difficult suffering and to be joyful at a time in which you would rather be angry. Be a joy to others that they may see the glory of God in your attitude when difficulties come your way.*

Janie: Blessed Mother, I love you so much, please help me to truly be an instrument of your Son's peace, beginning with my husband and family. Blessed are they who turn to God in everything. My sweet Mother, I will do anything that is asked of me by Heaven.

Our Lady smiled.

St. Philomena: *Greetings from Heaven, little sister. I am here to help you to endure your suffering as well as I did. You are not alone; we are with you.*

252

Janie: St. Philomena, I love you, dear little sister. I love you.

St. Joseph: *My little one, I, St. Joseph, am here to tell you to pray and offer your suffering for all families in the world. You have been chosen by God to be a suffering victim of love for the family. Especially, embrace the families that are traveling with you. Let them see how much you love God through your attitude. Recall what I, St. Joseph, said to you, "The Holy Family will be with you, especially in times of great suffering."*

Janie: Beloved St. Joseph! Yes, I do remember. I love you and thank you for coming. I entrust to you my husband and all husbands in the world and all the families. I ask that you intercede for all the young people traveling with us, please!

St. Joseph: *My little one, I, St. Joseph, will gladly respond to your request. Now, listen to my foster Son, Jesus.*

Our Lady: *Listen to my Son.*

St. Philomena: *Listen to Our Master.*

Janie: Our Lord looked at me with His most compassionate eyes. His look pierced my heart. His look is so full of love and peace.

Our Lord: *My humble servant, know that I am always with you. I have poured My love into your heart. I have plunged you in My burning love for humanity, that you may embrace all souls you meet with My love.*
    As you embrace the freshness of the morning and its fresh fragrance, know that its beauty cannot compare to the freshness and fragrance of the love that you will find in the Two Hearts, together with the love of St. Joseph.
    My humble servant, nothing in the world can give you the love which We offer you. Reflect Our love, be Our love, live Our love. There is no greater love than the love that comes through the love of My Father. Peace, peace, peace.

253

Conversations With St. Philomena

Janie: Please, my Beloved Savior, help me, so that no material things or physical things interfere with my love for You. All I desire is Your love. This is my food, the air that I breathe, the water which I drink. Your love clothes my entire being. There is nothing else for me except Your love.

They blessed me as they left.

You Are My Spiritual Child

June 12, 1997 (6:00 a.m.)
St. Giovanni Rotondo

St. Philomena: *Greetings from Heaven, my little sister.*

Janie: Peace to you, St. Philomena.

St. Philomena: *Little sister, continue praying constantly. Your prayers are deflecting many attacks which the devil inflicts on this holy faith journey.*
See how your prayers have helped that young girl for whom you have been offering much prayer? Your prayers are melting her heart.
Pray especially and be thankful to Our Master for His two beloved brothers who are traveling with you. These two beloved priests are Our Lady's beloved sons. You and all souls on this pilgrimage are being blessed through these special priests.
Continue to open your heart to God, for the graces and blessings are being poured forth like rain drops from heaven on all on this pilgrimage. Until tomorrow, farewell, little sister.

As we were arriving at St. Giovanni, I saw Padre Pio in the sky. He was smiling. He was very translucent and I could see right through him. Later, as we were making our tour through his living quarters, he spoke to me.

Padre Pio: *My little spiritual child, I welcome you to St. Giovanni. I asked permission from God to let you come back to St. Giovanni to finish your tour which you did not complete the first time you visited St. Giovanni. When you left St. Giovanni at that time, you left with a sad and heavy heart.*

I wanted to bring you back to St. Giovanni to let you know that you are my spiritual child and I respond to every prayer in which you ask for my help. Your guardian angel quickly brings me your prayer for help, and I quickly respond.

Later that day, St. Philomena came a second time.

St. Philomena: *Greetings from Heaven, my little sister.*

Janie: Peace to you, St. Philomena.

St. Philomena: *Little sister, spend much time praying for all the young people traveling with you, for Satan will flood their paths with evil temptations. Satan is not happy that these young souls are on this journey of prayer. The temptations of Satan will be strong against these young souls. I am sad to tell you, little sister, that some will give into Satan's temptations. You will suffer, little sister. Oh, how you will suffer! These temptations will continue against all the young people who are traveling with you.*

Little sister, I come this second time so that you may pray more, even though you are very tired. Know that some of these young souls have much pride in their hearts, and stubbornness has taken root in their hearts. They will not listen and will reject any advice. Pray for them wholeheartedly, little sister.

I knew that these prayers were much needed for the young people. St. Philomena helped me to understand that the temptations would be strong, especially in Medjugorje and that our young people would fall prey to Satan's temptations. I prayed so much and so hard for their souls and protection over them.

255

Conversations With St. Philomena

Continue to Pray for the Youth

June 13-14, 1997

During these two days I was suffering in my hands and I didn't write. St. Philomena asked me to continue to pray for the youth. She and I prayed together for these special intentions.

Endure Your Suffering

June 15, 1997
On the Ferry to Split, Yugoslavia

St. Philomena: *Greetings from Heaven, my little sister.*

Janie: Peace to you, St. Philomena.

St. Philomena: *Little sister, continue to endure your suffering with joy in your heart. Many blessings and graces are being poured into all who are traveling with you. I am interceding for all your personal intentions. Until tomorrow, farewell, little sister.*

A Deeper Conversion

June 16, 1997
Medjugorje, Yugoslavia

St. Philomena: *Greetings from Heaven, my little sister.*

Janie: Peace to you, St. Philomena.

St. Philomena: *Little sister, God has brought you again to this place in which His Most Holy Mother is appearing every day. Open your heart and embrace the spirit of prayer. Enter deep into the narrow road that leads to holiness and to eternal life.*
Do not allow the evil one to distract you with all the materialism which surrounds you. Spend quiet time with Our Master adoring Him. Allow Him Who loves you so much to purify you. Do not resist what is holy and good, but abandon yourself to His eternal love.

While you are living in this holy place, rejoice and show God your gratitude for bringing you here safely. You have been living without your clothing during this time. You have been living like the birds in the air, depending totally on God. This is so good for you, my little sister, for God wants you to depend on Him for everything.

Give thanks to God for removing the material things from your path and calling you to a deeper faith, a deeper prayer life, a deeper conversion, to a deeper trust in God.

Pray, little sister, for all the people who make the journey to come to this place, that they may open their hearts to the messages which Our Most Holy Mother is giving to the world.

Many souls come without an understanding of why they came, why God brought them here. Many have moved to this holy place with only one intention: to make a profit from the poor souls who are so distracted with all the materialism which surrounds them.

Janie: St. Philomena, people come from so far. Is it wrong for them to want to buy something for their loved ones back home?

St. Philomena: *Little sister, please try to understand. It is not wrong for them to buy gifts for their loved ones, but so many spend their entire stay here consumed with buying and eating. They leave very little time for prayer and meditation. They do not give God the time to help them. When they do this, they allow Satan to deprive them of the graces and blessing which God wishes to give them.*

Little sister, I will remain with you in a special way. Spend time in prayer for the special intentions of Our Lady. Until tomorrow, farewell, little sister.

Janie: Farewell, St. Philomena.

Embrace This Bittersweet Love of the Heavy Cross
June 17, 1997
Medjugorje

St. Philomena: *Greetings from Heaven, my little sister.*

257

Conversations With St. Philomena

Janie: Peace to you, St. Philomena.

St. Philomena: *Little sister, much is the suffering which you are enduring during your journey as a pilgrim. Know that God has chosen you to be a victim soul to suffer for poor sinners. You are suffering for all those souls who are with you on this pilgrimage.*

Little sister, God is pouring His graces and blessings on each soul in a special way. This is why Our Most Holy Mother and her beloved Son are asking you to endure your suffering. Special blessings will be bestowed on all, especially the young people. God is drawing these precious young souls to His love and to the love of His Mother Mary.

Your suffering will not cease but only increase for the conversion of others, at the same time purifying your own soul. Rejoice and embrace this bittersweet love of the heavy cross which you are carrying. All of Heaven is rejoicing as your journey continues. Until tomorrow, farewell, little sister.

Satan Will Flood Your Path

June 18, 1997
Medjugorje

St. Philomena: *Greetings from Heaven, my little sister.*

Janie: Peace to you, St. Philomena.

St. Philomena: *Little sister, continue offering much prayer and sacrifices for your own protection, for Satan will attempt to flood your path with many evil attacks and distractions. Your suffering will continue, for you are suffering in reparation for poor sinners who do not yet know the love of Our Master. Until tomorrow, farewell, little sister.*

Janie: Farewell, St. Philomena.

Medjugorje As a Special Place of Prayer

June 19, 1997
Medjugorje

St. Philomena: *Greetings from Heaven, little sister.*

Janie: Peace to you, St. Philomena.

St. Philomena: *Little sister, be grateful to God for His Most Holy Mother for, through her, very special graces are being poured into each heart that is open. Our Most Holy Mother has such great love for her children and she is always at the Throne of Mercy interceding for all her children.*

God has chosen Medjugorje as a special place of prayer, a place of peace for all who make the great sacrifice to journey to this special place.

You, little sister, have visited Medjugorje several times and each time has been different for you. Each time, you have entered into a deeper level of conversion. You come with an open and trusting heart. This is why you gain such great wealth in graces and blessings.

Pray , little sister, for those souls who live in Medjugorje and show no respect for Our Lady, Queen of Peace. Pray also for the conversion of all who come to Medjugorje and do not believe.

Prayer is the answer to all the problems in the world. Prayer is the remedy that will heal the world. This is why Our Most Holy Mother bids all children to pray, pray, pray. This is what I, St. Philomena, invite you, little sister, to pray for Our Lady's special intentions for all her children. Until tomorrow, farewell, little sister.

Janie: Farewell, St. Philomena.

Satan Knows How Powerful Your Prayers Are

June 20, 1997
Medjugorje

St. Philomena: *Greetings from Heaven, little sister.*

259

Conversations With St. Philomena

Janie: Peace to you, St. Philomena.

St. Philomena: *Little sister, continue to trust in the love of Our Master and His Most Pure Mother. Rely on their love as you continue to suffer. Satan is trying so hard to distract you from praying for your own conversion and for peace in the world.*

Little sister, Satan knows how powerful your prayers are, for you pray with much love and faith in your heart. You believe in the power of prayer. This is why Satan's attacks are strong against you. He uses your family and others to distract you. Do not let him, but pray more and you will drive him away with your prayers. God loves you very much. Always remember this, especially in your suffering. Until tomorrow, farewell, little sister.

Janie: Farewell, St. Philomena.

Look To the Passion of My Son

June 21, 1997
Medjugorje, Mt. Krizevac

Our Lady and St. Philomena came to visit me when I climbed "Cross Mountain". Our Lady spoke first. I was suffering for Our Lord 's and Our Lady's personal intentions.

Our Lady: *My angel, I, your Heavenly Mother, have come to comfort you.* (At this time I talked to her about many personal things. She continued.) *Know, my angel, that God is pleased with your sufferings. Look to the Passion of my Son and unite your suffering with His. Many souls are coming close to my Son because of your suffering. We are with you. Be at peace.*

St. Philomena: *Greetings from Heaven, little sister. Know that I am interceding for you in your suffering and that your rewards await you in Heaven for all the suffering that you offer up for poor sinners. Rejoice and trust God in all your suffering. Until tomorrow, farewell, little sister.*

260

Janie: Farewell, St. Philomena.

I spent the rest of that day in prayer. This was our last day in Medjugorje. I was kind of sad, but joyful as well. Medjugorje is a beautiful oasis of peace, but this oasis of peace can exist in each soul if we follow and live Our Lady's messages of prayer, fasting, conversion, Holy Mass, praying the Rosary, Adoration, reading Holy Scripture and Confession. This is not, probably, in the order she would give, but this is her request. This is why I wasn't too sad to leave Medjugorje, because God lives in my heart, and where God is, there is His peace.

Rest

June 22, 1997

Janie: (3:15 a.m.) We got up to leave Medjugorje. We had breakfast and boarded the bus and left. Everyone was so sleepy, but I offered my sleep and prayed for 3 hours (my Rosary, chaplets, etc.). I was thankful for everything!

11:30 a.m.

We arrived in Paris, France and had a tour of Paris. We visited the Miraculous Medal at Rue du Bac, visited the incorrupt body of St. Catherine Laboure, and the incorrupt body of St. Vincent de Paul. We saw all the most important sites in Paris. Praise be Jesus.

I had a brief visit with St. Philomena. She does not visit while I am in the airplane. I had a short visit in the hotel.

St. Philomena: *Little sister, I am interceding for you. Rest. I know you are very tired. Peace, little sister, peace.*

Always Pray to God for Purity

June 23, 1997
Paris, France

St. Philomena: *Greetings from Heaven, little sister.*

261

Conversations With St. Philomena

Janie: Peace to you, St. Philomena.

St. Philomena: *My little sister, God has blessed you and your family with such rich blessings and graces. Continue to love God as a family and pray together every day. God will bless your family and His blessings will be without limit.*

Invite your sons to always pray to God for purity so that they will not fall into the temptations of the devil. Share with them the importance of continuously praying the Rosary, offering it up for purity of heart, body and spirit; of receiving the sacrament of reconciliation often; and of trusting also in my intercession.

Little sister, God is pleased with all your hard efforts. Continue to love purity and to pray for purity in all hearts. God loves purity. Remember this especially when Satan is putting temptations in your path. Until tomorrow, little sister, farewell.

Janie: Farewell, St. Philomena.

No Visit

June 24, 1997
Paris, France

St. Philomena only interceded for me and all who traveled with me. I received no visit because I was traveling home to America on the plane.

Illness

June 25, 1997

No visit today from St. Philomena, due to my being ill. She interceded for me.

This Great Tribunal of His Love and Mercy

June 26, 1997
Austin, Texas

St. Philomena: *Greetings from Heaven, little sister.*

Janie: Peace to you, St. Philomena.

St. Philomena: *Little sister, rejoice, for you can begin to see the fruit of your suffering. Many blessings came to all those traveling with you because of your suffering and prayers.*

Janie: St. Philomena, this pilgrimage was hard for me. I feel that perhaps I offended God.

St. Philomena: *Little sister, God understands well your heart. He knows that you have good and pure intentions. This is why the devil works tireless hours to attack you.*
Trust always in the love and mercy of God and bring all souls to this great tribunal of His love and mercy. God has given you custody of praying and suffering for the conversion of the family. Trust in His great love and mercy. He loves you very much. Until tomorrow, farewell, little sister.

Janie: Farewell, St. Philomena.

You Are Experiencing the Desert

June 27, 1997

St. Philomena: *Greetings from Heaven, little sister.*

Janie: Peace to you, St. Philomena.

St. Philomena: *Little sister, you continue to suffer and your suffering has increased. You are experiencing the desert where you are in desolation. You seek the love and the comfort of Our Master, but you feel nothing, only dryness in your soul. Little sister, as you suffer this dryness, you are maturing in your spiritual journey.*

Janie: St. Philomena, what you say is true; I feel so empty inside, and my soul is so dry. I know that Our Master is with me, even though I feel nothing. I am trying very hard not to allow the emptiness inside my soul to be a distraction for me. I must say, this is

263

very difficult. It's difficult for me to pray, so I just constantly think about God and all of the saints and holy angels in Heaven. This is my prayer during this difficult time. I do not resist this period of dryness, but trust God and abandon myself totally to Him, Who is everything to me.

St. Philomena: *Little sister, keep this attitude alive in your heart, and you will survive any suffering with joy in your heart.*

Janie: St. Philomena, please pray for me, for my personal intentions.

St. Philomena: *Little sister, I, St. Philomena, will be praying for you. Until tomorrow, farewell, little sister.*

Janie: Farewell, St. Philomena.

Trusting God

June 28, 1997

St. Philomena: *Greetings from Heaven, little sister.*

Janie: Peace to you, St. Philomena. St. Philomena, please pray for me and my family. We are trying to return to our normal time here in the United States. I think that jet lag has set in. I am very tired and sleepy today.

St. Philomena: *Little sister, do not be concerned. God is taking care of all your family's needs. Trust Him. Until tomorrow, farewell, little sister. Rest!*

Janie: Thank you, St. Philomena.

Pray for All Babies, All Children and Youth

June 29, 1997

St. Philomena: *Greetings from Heaven, little sister.*

Janie: Peace to you, St. Philomena.

St. Philomena: *Little sister, you are doing better today.*

Janie: Yes, St. Philomena! Your prayers helped. My family is doing better, also. We are grateful to God and to you for your intercession. Is there anything which I can do for you?

St. Philomena: *Little sister, how kind of you to ask. I would be grateful if you would continue to pray for all babies, all children and the youth. Through our prayers, we will protect them from the hands of the devil and all his evil forces. Let us, together, unite in prayers for these precious souls. Until tomorrow, farewell, little sister.*

Janie: St. Philomena, I will pray with you for all these intentions.

Satan Lies To the Young People

June 30, 1997

St. Philomena: *Greetings from Heaven, little sister.*

Janie: Peace to you, St. Philomena. St. Philomena, please intercede for my family. It's been almost a week since we returned from our pilgrimage, and we need your prayers to help us. We have had many attacks since we came back. We know that Satan is trying to distract us from prayer. Help us to continue to do the Holy Will of the Father as a family.

St. Philomena: *Little sister, Satan's goal is to destroy families who are living according to the Holy Will of the Father. Prayer is the weapon to counter all his evil attacks. The families who allow his attacks to weaken their family prayer will be destroyed.*
    Satan knows that it takes great effort and commitment to pray together as a family. He also knows the weakness in each one of the family members. It is this weakness that he uses to attack the family

265

and discourage them from praying. He especially concentrates on the young people in the family. He seduces them with many temptations. He tells the young people terrible lies about their parents and teaches the young to hate their parents. This is one of the many ways he destroys the family.

Satan lies to the young people that it is not important to pray. He tells them that prayer is a waste of time. Once he stops young people from wanting to pray, he takes away their purity through drugs, fornication, profanity, stealing, violence, hate towards themselves, their parents and others. His attacks on humanity are so evil; he destroys millions upon millions of precious young people, all because they lose their desire to pray.

Please, little sister, do not let him do this to your family. Pray together every day, love one another and talk about God every day. Spend time as a family thanking God for all His blessings and everything which He gives. Please, do not allow Satan to rob you and your family of God's love, peace and joy. Pray always and never allow your feelings, your tiredness or anything to keep you from praying as a family.

I love you, my little sister, and I am interceding for all your intentions. Until tomorrow, farewell, little sister.

Janie: Farewell, St. Philomena. Thank you for everything. I shall do my best not to disappoint God.

Helping the Reign of Our Master By Suffering
July 1, 1997

St. Philomena: *Greetings from Heaven, little sister.*

Janie: Peace to you, St. Philomena. St. Philomena, please pray for us and for the completion of our new home. Today, my suffering for the Bride of Our Lord is intense. Pray for me.

St. Philomena: *Little sister, you are always in my prayers for I know that you suffer much. Remember how much you are helping the reign of Our Master by suffering in reparation for poor sinners.*

266

Until tomorrow, farewell, little sister.

Janie: Thank you, St. Philomena. I will embrace my suffering without complaining.

Souls Devoted to My Intercession

July 2, 1997

St. Philomena: *Greetings from Heaven, little sister.*

Janie: Peace to you, St. Philomena. St. Philomena, there are so many people who are interested in knowing more about your life. I don't have much to share with them since my spiritual director has not read or approved any of the things which you have shared with me. I share everything with him, but I have not shown him the journals in which I write our conversations.

St. Philomena: *Little sister, you are wise in always embracing the virtue of obedience by being obedient to your spiritual director. This is pleasing to God.*
Redirect my devotees to trust in my intercession and to read what has already been written about me. What I have shared with you will be published when I am finished revealing all that God has permitted me to share with you. Until then, let us continue to pray together for all those souls devoted to my intercession. Until tomorrow, farewell, little sister.

Janie: Thank you, St. Philomena, what you say helps me.

Never Give Up on Prayer

July 3, 1997

St. Philomena: *Greetings from Heaven, little sister.*

Janie: Peace to you, St. Philomena.

267

Conversations With St. Philomena

St. Philomena: *Little sister, you have just been visited by the three Archangels. They have given you much to think about concerning your country. They have also shown you how powerful prayer is and how God responds immediately to those who have faith in their prayers.*

Little sister, always encourage people to have faith in their prayers. Tell them how much God loves them. So many souls are starving for love, but they do not recognize or understand that true love only comes from God. They will find God in their prayers.

Oh, little sister, there is so much healing that comes through prayer! Those souls who pray with faith in their hearts find out that they are able to love others with unconditional love; they are able to forgive. Through prayer these souls find freedom. God helps these souls to abandon everything to Him. He delivers them from their many burdens and worries.

Little sister, never give up on prayer, never give up on God, for He will never give up on you. Remember, pray always. Until tomorrow, farewell, little sister.

Janie: Farewell, St. Philomena. Thank you for everything.

Do Not Be Too Hard on Yourself

July 4, 1997

St. Philomena: *Greetings from Heaven, little sister.*

Janie: Peace to you, St. Philomena.

St. Philomena: *Little sister, do not be sad about X. Pray for the pain of his family. He is not suffering anymore. Accept God's Holy Will and be at peace. Do not question God's Holy Will and do not try to understand God. He is beyond human comprehension. Trust Him in all things. Any peace will be the fruit of your trust for Him. Continue to pray for X. Your prayers and sacrifices will help him. Little sister, God knows of your suffering but keep in mind that He will never test you beyond your strength.*

Janie: St. Philomena, it seems to me that I am not praying as much as I did before. I have not been attending Holy Mass daily. I am deeply concerned about my spiritual life.

St. Philomena: *Little sister, do not be too hard on yourself. You have been ill for almost two weeks. Your spiritual life is pleasing to God. He knows that you are weak from your illness. God does not expect you to do anything beyond your capabilities. Offer this suffering for the intentions of the Sacred Heart of Our Master. He is your strength, your everything. Until tomorrow, farewell, little sister.*

Janie: Thank you, St. Philomena, farewell to you, my heavenly little sister. St. Philomena, I thank God for you. You have helped me, my family and all whom I recommend to your intercession. Today, I am so moved with love for God for allowing you to come to me. I will write in blood the prayer that Our Master taught the world, the Lord's Prayer. This is in honor of the Eternal Father. From now on I shall pray this prayer with much love and reverence to God Who loves me.

[Note: In Janie's journal the Lord's Prayer followed, written in her blood.]

I Was Surrounded With the Love of God

July 5, 1997

St. Philomena: *Greetings from Heaven, little sister.*

Janie: Peace to you, St. Philomena. St. Philomena, help me to suffer with joy in my heart. I feel like I do not suffer with joy in my heart. How were you so brave in your suffering?

St. Philomena: *Little sister, I was surrounded with the love of God during my suffering because of my faith and my trust in God. Our Most Holy Mother had assured me that the Archangel Gabriel and my guardian angel would help me. God took care of me because I trusted in Him. My faith and love for Him helped me and gave me His strength. The emperor subjected me to various torments, but nothing broke my spirit or my trust for God.*

Little sister, you have nothing to be concerned about. You suffered well for Our Master, and He is always with you because of your faith and trust. Be at peace; you are a humble suffering servant of God. Until tomorrow, farewell, little sister.

Janie: You have helped, St. Philomena. Thank you.

So Many Families Have Abandoned the Spirit of Prayer
July 6, 1997

St. Philomena: *Greetings from Heaven, little sister.*

Janie: Peace to you, St. Philomena. St. Philomena, today after Mass, my family and I are going to work on our home out in the country. Keep us in your prayers. Any special prayers or intentions for today?

St. Philomena: *Little sister, you are sweet to ask. In your family prayers, keep all the families in mind. There is so much evil in the world. So many families have abandoned the spirit of prayer, because they have no faith. Pray for this intention. Until tomorrow, farewell, little sister.*

Janie: I will pray with my family for this intention.

For All Who Are Dying of Serious Illnesses
July 7, 1997

St. Philomena: *Greetings from Heaven, little sister.*

Janie: Peace to you, St. Philomena.

St. Philomena: *Little sister, I know that you are ill. I am interceding for you. Offer your suffering for all who are dying of serious illnesses. Until tomorrow, farewell, little sister.*

Janie: Thank you, St. Philomena. I will pray for the sick and for those who are dying from terminal illnesses.

This Title Is Appealing to Me

July 8, 1997

St. Philomena: *Greetings from Heaven, little sister.*

Janie: Peace to you, St. Philomena. St. Philomena, when will your conversations with me be published? I have a title for your little book. I'll tell you, but first, please answer my question if it's in God's Holy Will.

St. Philomena: *Little sister, I will let you know soon, but not today.*

Janie: Very well, St. Philomena, I accept your answer with peace in my heart. Now for the title of your book. How does this title appeal to you, "Conversations with St. Philomena?" It's simple and not too long. Do you like it?

St. Philomena: *Little sister, I like it very much. This title is indeed appealing to me.*

Janie: St. Philomena, I hope the public likes it.

St. Philomena: *Little sister, do not worry about that. It's a lovely title. Rejoice! Until tomorrow, farewell, little sister.*

Janie: Farewell, St. Philomena.

Conversations With St. Philomena

All Will Go Well

July 9, 1997

St. Philomena: *Greetings from Heaven, little sister.*

Janie: Peace to you, St. Philomena. St. Philomena, pray for me. I have to prepare for my son is coming to visit with us. I haven't seen him in a long time. I am excited. This is special to me.

St. Philomena: *Little sister, I will intercede for you and for your time with your son. All will go well. Until tomorrow, farewell, little sister.*

Janie: Thank you, St. Philomena.

More Devotees

July 10, 1997

St. Philomena: *Greetings from Heaven, little sister.*

Janie: Peace to you, St. Philomena. St. Philomena, I am thinking of perhaps starting a confraternity in your honor, so that we may draw more devotees to you. Pray for this special intention.

St. Philomena: *Little sister, I will intercede for you. I am grateful for all that you do to bring more devotees to me. God will provide you with all that you need. Until tomorrow, farewell, little sister.*

Janie: Farewell, St. Philomena.

Division Within the Church

July 11, 1997

St. Philomena: *Greetings from Heaven, little sister.*

Janie: Peace to you, St. Philomena.

St. Philomena: *Little sister, today I ask you once more to pray for all the Masonic activity within the Bride of Our Master. This situation is causing much division within the Church. Encourage your family to pray for this intention. Until tomorrow, little sister, farewell.*

Janie: I will pray together with my family for this serious situation.

Suffering For the Vicar of Our Master
July 12, 1997

St. Philomena: *Greetings from Heaven, little sister.*

Janie: Peace to you, St. Philomena.

St. Philomena: *Little sister, I am here to tell you that in the next few days you will undergo intense suffering for the Vicar of Our Master. You will suffer for all the cardinals, bishops and priests whose hearts have grown cold towards the love of Our Master. Our Master, out of the great love that He has for His Bride and for your willingness to suffer, will subject you to intense suffering. You will unite in Our Master's suffering, and the suffering will be difficult. Are you ready to accept and to be subjected to this intense suffering for the Bride of Our Master?*

Janie: Yes, St. Philomena, I accept whatever Our Lord asks of me, for I know that Our Lord will be with me.

St. Philomena: *Little sister, your "yes" has pleased Our Lord. For the next five days you will suffer. I will come and pray for you to give you courage. Your suffering will help Our Master's Bride. Our Most Holy Mother will come to visit you on the fourth day of your suffering. Until tomorrow, farewell, little sister.*

Conversations With St. Philomena

Janie: Farewell, St. Philomena.

I Am Here to Pray for You

July 13, 1997

St. Philomena: *Greetings from Heaven, little sister.*

Janie: Peace to you, St. Philomena.

St. Philomena: *I know, little sister, that your suffering is intense. I am here to pray for you.*

Janie: St. Philomena, my suffering is indescribable. I feel like I am taking my last breath, but I trust My Jesus, My Jesus, My Jesus.

St. Philomena: *I will pray for you, little sister.*

Accepting Your Suffering

July 14, 1997

St. Philomena: *Greetings from Heaven, little sister.*

Janie: Peace, St. Philomena.

St. Philomena: *Little sister, you are doing well in accepting your suffering. Our Master is pleased with your sacrifices.*

Janie: Thank you, St. Philomena, your words are consoling.

St. Philomena: *Until tomorrow, farewell, little sister.*

Janie: Farewell, St. Philomena.

Protection and Support of the Three Archangels

July 15, 1997

St. Philomena: *Greetings from Heaven, little sister.*

Janie: Peace to you, St. Philomena.

St. Philomena: *Little sister, know that you have the protection and support of the three Archangels. Trust in their support. You are helping many of Our Master's representatives. Until tomorrow, farewell, little sister.*

Janie: Thank you, St. Philomena.

Strength to You in Suffering

July 16, 1997

St. Philomena: *Greetings from Heaven, little sister.*

Janie: Peace to you, St. Philomena.

St. Philomena: *Little sister, rejoice, for Our Most Holy Mother will come to visit with you later this morning. She will bring her Son, the Christ, as a Child. They both will bring much joy and strength to you in your suffering. Prepare for their visit. Until tomorrow, farewell, little sister.*

Janie: Thank you, St. Philomena, so very much.

The Last Day

July 17, 1997

St. Philomena: *Greetings from Heaven, little sister.*

Janie: Peace to you, St. Philomena.

St. Philomena: *Little sister, today is your last day of intense suffer-*

275

ing. You have been courageous in your suffering. You have done well. You will be able to sleep tonight and you will feel refreshed in the morning. Thank you, little sister, for the love that you demonstrated towards Our Master. You have brought much consolation to Our Master. Thank you. Until tomorrow, farewell, little sister.

Janie: Thank you, St. Philomena, for being my heavenly sister. I send Our Lord my love and my all. I'll do anything for Him Who died for me.

My Call Comes with Immense Grace

July 18, 1997

St. Philomena: *Greetings from Heaven, little sister.*

Janie: Peace, St. Philomena. St. Philomena, I am beginning to realize more and more how important my task is in making you more known. Please help me to do you justice and teach me all that I must know about you. As you know, the Rector has nominated me and authorized me to spread devotion to you in my state. I have begun to put together a confraternity in your honor. I will also build a small shrine in your honor, but I will need a statue of you. Please help me to accomplish all that I need, to bring more devotees to you.

St. Philomena: *Little sister, have no worry. I, St. Philomena, am at your side, interceding for you every day. Your task is important and my call comes with immense grace; therefore, know that everything which you need to make me more known, you will have.*
Little sister, you have had a most intense suffering in the past few days, as you suffered with your little grandson. God has filled your heart with His immense love. This is why you were able to overcome the attacks which you received from the devil while you were suffering.

Anchor of Hope from Heaven

Little sister, doing the will of God is important to you. This is why God will accomplish much work through you. He chose you, because He knows that you respect and honor the virtue of obedience.

Janie: St. Philomena, I will do whatever God asks of me.

St. Philomena: *Little sister, I am pleased to be your heavenly little sister. I will always be at your side, helping you to obtain holiness and purity of heart. Until tomorrow, little sister. I have so enjoyed our visit. Until tomorrow, farewell, little sister.*

Janie: Farewell to you, dear St. Philomena, I love you.

I Am at Your Side

July 19, 1997

St. Philomena: *Greetings from Heaven, little sister.*

Janie: Peace, St. Philomena.

St. Philomena: *Little sister, I will intercede for your intentions today. Continue to pray and remain steadfast.*

Janie: Thank you. St. Philomena. You are such a comfort to me. Thank you, my little sister.

St. Philomena: *I am at your side, little sister, I am at your side. Until tomorrow, farewell, little sister.*

Janie: Farewell, St. Philomena.

I was going through a suffering for a special soul.

Conversations With St. Philomena

Bringing Glory to His Name

July 20, 1997

St. Philomena: *Greetings from Heaven, little sister.*

Janie: Peace, St. Philomena. Thank you for helping me to go through my suffering, but I have a special request for X. Please intercede for this special intention.

St. Philomena: *Little sister, I will help you with your special intention. You have a kind and loving heart and this pleases God very much. God has blessed you with special gifts and you use these gifts only to glorify God. God always helps His children who bring glory to His Name. This is why your prayers are answered. God is pleased with your kindness towards others. Until tomorrow, farewell, little sister.*

Janie: Farewell, St. Philomena.

(I had made plans for myself, but a soul, who was in such pain, called me for assistance, and I canceled all my plans in order to help this soul. This is what St. Philomena was referring to).

I Will Pray for Your Son

July 21, 1997

St. Philomena: *Greetings from Heaven, little sister.*

Janie: Peace to you, St. Philomena. Please ask Our Master to bless my son today; it's his birthday. We will have a little party for him. I don't think he suspects anything. Pray for him, St. Philomena. He is special to my heart.

St. Philomena: *Little sister, I will pray for your son. I know you have a busy day. Until tomorrow, farewell, little sister.*

Janie: Farewell, St. Philomena.

Many New Devotees

July 22, 1997

St. Philomena: *Greetings from Heaven, little sister.*

Janie: Peace to you, St. Philomena. St. Philomena, thank you so much for helping X. with his illness. I am so grateful to you for responding to my prayer request.

St. Philomena: *Little sister, I am more than happy to assist anyone who turns to me for my intercession. You, little sister, have helped me to be more known. You have introduced me to many, many people. I have many new devotees, all because of your love for me. I am truly grateful to you for the tireless hours that you spend introducing me to hurting souls.*

Janie: St. Philomena, I love you so much and I am so aware of how powerful you are before God. I know that you are dear to Our Master and His Most Holy Mother. I know that you will help anyone who trusts in your intercession. I am so happy to introduce you to everyone that I meet. I want you to be known all over the world.

St. Philomena: *Little sister, you are so dear to me, St. Philomena. You have much work ahead of you in making me more known. I will always be at your side helping you to do the Holy Will of the Father. I will help you to truly abandon yourself to the Most Sacred Heart of Our Master and to the Immaculate Heart of His Mother. I, together with all the saints and angels in heaven, will intercede for all your petitions. Do not worry about X obtaining transportation. It is in the hands of Our Master. Until tomorrow, farewell, little sister.*

Janie: Farewell, St. Philomena.

My Little Shrine

July 23, 1997

St. Philomena: *Greetings from Heaven, little sister.*

Conversations With St. Philomena

Janie: Peace to you, St. Philomena.

St. Philomena: *My little sister, you have concerns over my little shrine; have no concerns. I, St. Philomena, will obtain a statue of myself. I will help you in all that you need to make me more known and to build my little shrine.*

For Unconverted Souls

July 24, 1997

St. Philomena: *Greetings from Heaven, little sister.*

Janie: Peace to you, St. Philomena.

St. Philomena: *Little sister, I am here to help you in your suffering. Remain steadfast and trust God. Your suffering is for the good of unconverted souls. Until tomorrow, remain peaceful, little sister.*

Janie: Thank you so much St. Philomena.

Prepare With Strong Prayer

July 25, 1997

St. Philomena: *Greetings from Heaven, little sister.*

Janie: Peace to you, St. Philomena. St. Philomena, I am so excited, for tomorrow is my birthday, and I will be visited by the Holy Family.

St. Philomena: *Little sister, tomorrow will be a day with many blessings upon your entire household. Everyone who is present will be blessed by the presence of the Holy Family. Prepare with strong prayer for this heavenly visit. Know that the joy that awaits you tomorrow is beyond your comprehension. Until tomorrow, farewell, little sister.*

280

Janie: Thank you, St. Philomena.

Pay No Attention to the Devil

July 26, 1997

St. Philomena: *Greetings from Heaven, little sister.*

Janie: Peace to you, St. Philomena.

St. Philomena: *Little sister, today is your birthday, and you are having a difficult time. Rejoice, little sister, and pay no attention to the devil. He knows that today you will be visited by many heavenly visitors, including the Holy Family. I, myself, will come to you again during your visit with the Holy Family. Peace, little sister, peace. I will be with you later.*

Janie: Thank you, St. Philomena.

Remain on God's Level Path

July 27, 1997

St. Philomena: *Greetings from Heaven, little sister.*

Janie: Peace to you, St. Philomena. St. Philomena, I thank you from the bottom of my heart for helping me today. You saved me from going in the opposite direction which would have caused me to deviate from doing the Holy Will of God. I was so distracted with my own emotions and this interfered with my trusting in God.

St. Philomena: *My little sister, God has allowed me, St. Philomena, to help you to remain on God's level path; this is my task. In your suffering, you asked me to please help you, and so I did.*

Janie: St. Philomena, you helped me in such a powerful way. You led me right to Holy Mass and then to Adoration. From there Our

281

Conversations With St. Philomena

Master took over for the next two and a half hours. I was so filled with His love and mercy. Again, thank you so much.

St. Philomena: *My little sister, it is for your own sake and all of humanity that Our Master died. He died to give you life. He remained in the most Holy Eucharist to feed and quench your hunger for His love. He chose to remain disguised in Eucharistic Adoration to fill you with His grace of salvation.*

Yes, little sister, you are so loved by Our Master. Always turn towards Him in your great distress. He will renew your spirit and fill you with His love. Trust Him always! Until tomorrow, little sister, farewell.

Janie: Thank you, my heavenly friend and farewell to you.

So Much Evil in Your Country

July 28, 1997

St. Philomena: *Greetings from Heaven, little sister.*

Janie: Peace to you, St. Philomena. Thank you so much for coming to me, and again thank you for yesterday.

St. Philomena: *My little sister, yesterday was a most difficult day for you. You suffered much for the salvation of your family.*

Janie: St. Philomena, why is Satan always attacking my family?

St. Philomena: *Little sister, Satan knows that you and your family love one another. You pray together; when you have difficulties, you forgive each other. As a family you are joyful, always doing things together.*

Your home has the spirit of joy and Satan hates this. He hates that you often attend Holy Mass and receive the sacrament of Reconciliation. You pray your family Rosary daily and always ask the Holy Spirit to guide you. As a family you bring others closer to God through your prayers. Know, little sister, all your good and holy deeds are most disturbing to Satan. This is the reason for his numerous attacks. He is trying very hard to distract your family prayers.

Little sister, God is pleased with you and your family. He has shown you as a family the importance of family prayer, and your family prayers help you to stay on God's level path. Little sister, please intercede with me for all the poor families who do not believe in God, for those families who never take the time to thank God for all their blessings.

Little sister, when you pray, ask Our Master to shower His mercy on your country. There is so much evil in your country. Much prayer and fasting is required to help unconverted souls. The spirit of paganism is annihilating many souls. Remember this special intention in your prayers. Until tomorrow, farewell, little sister.

Courageous in Your Suffering

July 29, 1997

St. Philomena: *Greetings from Heaven, little sister.*

Janie: Peace to you, St. Philomena. St. Philomena, please intercede for me, so that I may be ever so ready to embrace any suffering which Our Lord sends me. I want to imitate your courage and your faith. Please intercede for me. I need your prayers.

St. Philomena: *Little sister, know that Our Master is pleased in the way in which you accept your suffering. Our Master has given you the grace to be courageous in your suffering.*

Little sister, I am always interceding for all your special intentions. Trust in my intercession always.

Little sister, offer your prayers and suffering that souls may open their hearts to God's love and mercy. Many souls suffer so much because they do not know how to turn to God and trust Him with their prayers. Your prayers and suffering help souls to turn to God. Pray for this special intention, little sister. Until tomorrow, farewell, little sister.

283

Conversations With St. Philomena

Janie: I will pray, St. Philomena.

Mothers Contemplating Abortion

July 30, 1997

St. Philomena: *Greetings from Heaven, little sister.*

Janie: Peace to you, St. Philomena.

St. Philomena: *Little sister, please join me in your prayers and let us pray for all the mothers who are contemplating abortion. This is a horrible evil which is most offensive to God. So many babies are being killed in their mothers' wombs because these mothers are under the influence of the devil. Many parents are on their way to perdition, for many have killed their unborn babies and have not repented.*

Please, little sister, let us bring these poor unconverted souls to the mercy of Our Master through our prayers. Prayer is the answer to lessen all the evil in the world. Until tomorrow, farewell, little sister.

Janie: St. Philomena, I will pray with you for these special intentions.

Our Master's Vicar Is Suffering Much

July 31, 1997

St. Philomena: *Greetings from Heaven, little sister.*

Janie: Peace to you, St. Philomena.

St. Philomena: *My little sister, continue to pray for Our Master's Vicar on earth. He is suffering much and needs much prayer.*

Janie: St. Philomena, I will pray for our Pope in all my prayers. Please pray for me that I may be able to fast on bread and water only. I need this grace. I am very grateful tonight to Our Lord, Our

Lady and St. Joseph and all of Heaven. Our son was able to get a car today. Our Master had told me that our son would get a car and he did. I thank God and you, as well, for your intercession. Thank you.

St. Philomena: *Little sister, God loves you very much. You have been praying for a long time for your son. You did not give up. Now you are beginning to see the fruit of your prayers. Keep praying, little sister. Your prayers help many souls. Until tomorrow, farewell, little sister.*

Prepare to Have Them Published

August 1, 1997

St. Philomena: *Greetings from Heaven, little sister.*

Janie: Peace to you, St. Philomena. St. Philomena, do you have a request of me? My guardian angel woke me up at 4:00 a.m., letting me know that I must get up to have my visit with you.

St. Philomena: *Little sister, I know that you have been suffering from illness, but I did wish to speak to you*

Janie: Tell me, St. Philomena, what do you wish to speak to me about?

St. Philomena: *Little sister, you have begun your fourth journal of our visitations. It is time to begin to prepare the other three journals so that you may have them published.*

Janie: St. Philomena, if this is your wish, I will do as you request. Do you have any publisher in mind?

St. Philomena: *The Holy Spirit through my intercession will guide you, and you will know who the publisher will be.*

285

Conversations With St. Philomena

Janie: St. Philomena, I will carry out your request without delay. Please intercede for me for you know how busy I am with my little grandson and family tasks.

St. Philomena: *Have no worry, little sister, I will help you with everything through my intercession. I know that you will give it your all. Until tomorrow, farewell, little sister.*

Janie: Farewell, St. Philomena, my heavenly little sister.

Thank You for Your Obedience
August 2, 1997

St. Philomena: *Greetings from Heaven, little sister.*

Janie: Peace to you, St. Philomena.

St. Philomena: *Little sister, you made Our Lady very happy today by making every effort to attend First Saturday Mass. In your doing this, you demonstrated how much you honor her.*

Janie: St. Philomena, I thank you for telling me but I know that you helped me to do this. I remember asking you to please help me to find somebody to take me to Holy Mass. I felt the presence of Our Lady in a profound way.

St. Philomena, please help me to find guidance to buy a statue of you. Should I buy the statue which I was informed about?

St. Philomena: *Little sister, do what your guardian angel asked you to do. You shall receive your answer.*

Janie: Thank you, St. Philomena, I will do this.

St. Philomena: *Little sister, thank you for your obedience in wanting to do me justice. Your obedience will be rewarded. Until tomorrow, farewell, little sister.*

Janie: Farewell, St. Philomena.

Interceding For His Bride

August 3, 1997

St. Philomena: *Greetings from Heaven, little sister.*

Janie: Peace to you, St. Philomena.

St. Philomena: *Little sister, today let us devote our prayers for the Bride of Our Master, that through our prayers those souls who are weak may be strengthened in faith.* (St. Philomena refers here to the priests and religious whose faith is weak).

Little sister, our prayers will help the Bride of Our Master to love Our Master more and to trust Him. He loves His Bride with immense love. Let us console Our Master by interceding for His Bride. Until tomorrow, little sister, farewell.

Janie: Thank you, St. Philomena, I enjoy praying with you.

As St. John Vianney Did

August 4, 1997

St. Philomena: *Greetings from Heaven, little sister.*

Janie: Peace to you, St. Philomena. St. Philomena, today we celebrate the feast of Saint John Vianney. He was devoted to your intercession. I am devoted to him. Please salute him for me.

St. Philomena: *Little sister, St. John Vianney loved Our Master and His Most Holy Mother when he lived on earth. He was indeed a holy, humble servant of God. His suffering, prayers and sacrifices bore much fruit for those souls for whom he interceded. He gave all his time to God by helping poor sinners to convert. God rewarded all his hard efforts, and now he is with me in Heaven, living in his*

287

Conversations With St. Philomena

heavenly home.
Little sister, imitate the call to holiness just as St. John Vian-
ney did, and you too shall someday be in Heaven with us. Never
grow tired of living a life of purity and holiness but live Heaven on
earth. You shall not regret it. Until tomorrow, farewell, little sister.

Janie: Thank you, St. Philomena.

Remain Steadfast

St. Philomena: *Greetings from Heaven, little sister.*

Janie: Peace to you, St. Philomena. St. Philomena, please pray for
my very special intentions.

St. Philomena: *Little sister, I will intercede for you. I know that you*
are suffering. Remain steadfast. Remember, your suffering is help-
ing to bring peace to many souls. Until tomorrow, farewell, little
sister.

Janie: Thank you, St. Philomena.

He Will Fill Your Heart With Joy

August 6, 1997

St. Philomena: *Greetings from Heaven, little sister.*

Janie: Peace to you, St. Philomena.

St. Philomena: *Little sister, rejoice, for in a short while Our Mas-*
ter will come to visit you. He will fill your heart with joy. Until to-
morrow, farewell, little sister.

Janie: St. Philomena, I am very happy that Our Lord is coming.

288

Holy Mass Is the Ultimate Prayer

August 7, 1997

St. Philomena: *Greetings from Heaven, little sister.*

Janie: Peace to you, St. Philomena.

St. Philomena: *Little sister, let us pray today that more souls will believe in the Real Presence of Our Master in the Holy Eucharist. Let us offer our prayers that more souls will believe in the Sacrifice of the Holy Mass and its powerful healing.*

Oh, that souls would turn to Our Master in the Holy Sacrifice of the Holy Mass and realize that Mass is the ultimate prayer, the source of all healing and the source of everything in the world!

Let us pray that souls will understand that the Holy Eucharist is a constant reminder of Our Master's love for a world walking in darkness. Through the Holy Eucharist Our Master reminds the world, "My love shall never leave you." Let us pray hard, little sister, for this special intention.

Janie: St. Philomena, I will pray intensely for this intention.

A second message (below) was given this day.

Protection and Support of the Archangels

August 7, 1997

St. Philomena: *Greetings from Heaven, little sister.*

Janie: Peace to you, St. Philomena. St. Philomena, please pray for my very special intentions.

St. Philomena: *Little sister, embrace all that the Archangels share with you. I know that you are suffering for Our Master's special intention. The Archangels will give you guidance. Always trust in the powerful intercession of the Archangels and encourage everyone whom Our Master puts in your path to trust in the protection and support of the Archangels. God has invested the Archangels with great power to help all His children. Until tomorrow, farewell, little sister.*

Janie: Farewell, St. Philomena. I will follow your heavenly guidance.

The Guidance of the Holy Spirit

August 8, 1997

St. Philomena: *Greetings from Heaven, little sister.*

Janie: Peace to you, St. Philomena.

St. Philomena: *Little sister, today I wish to share with you that God is pleased with you for invoking the power of the Holy Spirit in all your prayers. You have great faith in the guidance of the Holy Spirit. Always keep in mind that the Holy Spirit is the Advocate which Our Master speaks of in Holy Scripture.*
The Holy Spirit is the Spirit of Truth, and He will guide you to all truth. He will enlighten you and declare to you the things that will happen. Always trust in the power of the Holy Spirit, always! Until tomorrow, farewell, little sister.

Janie: Thank you so much, St. Philomena. You help me so much.

Erase Hatred and Pride

August 9, 1997

St. Philomena: *Greetings from Heaven, little sister.*

Janie: Peace, St. Philomena.

St. Philomena: *Little sister, let us pray that hatred and pride will disappear from all hearts. Let us ask Our loving Master to take away all hatred and pride and replace them with His love and*

290

peace. Oh, if only hatred and pride would not exist in so many of God's children, there would be no need for wars and violence.

Please pray with me, little sister, that our prayers will erase hatred and pride from all who harbor this horrible spirit. Until tomorrow, farewell, little sister.

Janie: Farewell, St. Philomena.

For All Families Who Do Not Believe in God
August 10, 1997

St. Philomena: *Greetings from Heaven, little sister.*

Janie: Peace to you, St. Philomena.

St. Philomena: *Little sister, I know that you are preparing to go to Holy Mass with your family. Offer your prayer of Holy Mass for all the families in the world who do not believe in God. Until tomorrow, farewell, little sister.*

Janie: Farewell, St. Philomena. We will offer our Mass for all families beginning with our own family.

Celebrate This Feast Day
August 11, 1997

St. Philomena: *Greetings from Heaven, little sister.*

Janie: Peace to you, St. Philomena. St. Philomena, my heavenly sister, I salute you, for today is the liturgical feast day in your honor. I am happy for you. I wish I could be there in Italy, rejoicing in this celebration.

St. Philomena: *Little sister, I am grateful to you for remembering this day. Much celebration is taking place in my shrine in Italy.*

291

Conversations With St. Philomena

Little sister, do not be sad, for one day you will celebrate this feast day at my shrine in Italy. For now, celebrate with your family. I will intercede for you and your family. Until tomorrow, farewell, little sister.

Janie: I love you, St. Philomena.

A Day of Many Blessings and Graces
                                    August 12, 1997

St. Philomena: *Greetings from Heaven, little sister.*

Janie: Peace to you, St. Philomena. St. Philomena, please pray for me and my son who is helping me to go out to our land to prepare it for August 15th. Our land and new house will be enthroned to the Sacred Heart of Jesus and the Immaculate Heart of Mary and to the heart of St. Joseph.

St. Philomena: *Little sister, I will be with you in prayer. The 15th day of this month will be a day of many blessings and graces. Until tomorrow, farewell, little sister.*

Janie: Thank you, St. Philomena.

Your Devotion to Me
                                    August 13, 1997

St. Philomena: *Greetings from Heaven, little sister.*

Janie: Peace to you, St. Philomena. St. Philomena, today your shrine in Italy celebrates your name. I, too, thank God for knowing you in the way that I do. You are a blessing to all your devotees and to our world. Praise be God, forever and ever for you.

St. Philomena: *Little sister, I am grateful that you are my little sis-*

292

ter. We share so much together, and you share your devotion to me with all you meet. You have brought many new devotees to me. I am deeply, deeply grateful. God's blessings on you, my little sister, for all your holy work. Until tomorrow, farewell, little sister.

Janie: I love you, St. Philomena.

For Your Intention

August 14, 1997

St. Philomena: *Greetings from Heaven, little sister.*

Janie: Peace to you, St. Philomena. St. Philomena, please pray for my son. He is visiting with us and it's been a joy for me. He is very special and I love him so much. I entrust him and his family to your powerful intercession. Help him to draw closer to the Holy Family, please.

St. Philomena: *Little sister, I will intercede for your intention for your son and his family. Until tomorrow, farewell, little sister. I will come with Our Most Holy Mother tomorrow.*

Janie: Thank you, St. Philomena, for everything.

Assumption of Mary

August 15, 1997

St. Philomena came with Our Lady today; no particular conversation. She was very happy in the company of Our Lady.

Always Be Grateful to God

August 16, 1997

St. Philomena: *Greetings from Heaven, little sister.*

Conversations With St. Philomena

Janie: Peace to you, St. Philomena. St. Philomena, yesterday was beautiful on the Solemnity of the Assumption of Our Lady. I am so happy. The Holy Family came. God blessed everybody.

St. Philomena: *Little sister, God loves His children with immense love. He constantly yearns for the conversion of all His children. Always be grateful to God for all His blessings. Until tomorrow, farewell, little sister.*

Janie: Thank you, St. Philomena. I love you.

St. Philomena: *I love you, little sister.*

Chosen to Be a Victim of Love

August 17, 1997

St. Philomena: *Greetings from Heaven, little sister.*

Janie: Peace to you, St. Philomena.

St. Philomena: *Little sister, you are sad today and much suffering is in your heart. I am here to pray with you. I know, little sister, that you are suffering for the lack of prayer in many families. Know, my little sister, that when souls do not value the power of prayer, it is because these souls do not have a relationship with Our Master. This is why you suffer so much, to help bring souls back to the love of Our Master.*
Little sister, from the very first time that you began to have heavenly visitations, you were chosen to be a victim of love to suffer for the conversion of poor sinners. There are souls who, like yourself, suffer for the sake of Our Master's love. I know that the sorrow in your heart is deep, but your suffering is redemptive, that is, it helps souls to convert. Until tomorrow, farewell, little sister. I love you.

Janie: I love you, St. Philomena.

Conversion of the Family

August 18, 1997

St. Philomena: *Greetings from Heaven, little sister.*

Janie: Peace to you, St. Philomena.

St. Philomena: *Little sister, you are still suffering for the conversion of the family. I am here to pray with you for all the families in the world.*

Janie: St. Philomena, thank you. I really need your visit to console me. I want to pray for families everywhere, starting with my own family.

My Prayer for all Families

Eternal Father, Giver of our very lives, our One True Love, please, I beg You, give all families a total infusion of Your love. My Lord, in Your goodness you allow me to see the great suffering in families through the many visions which You have shown me.

My heavenly Father, it is obvious to me how far from Your love we are. I know that the reason we are so distant from Your love is because we do not value prayer as the greatest power from Heaven. Forgive us, Father, for truly we do not know what we are doing.

I know that prayer is life to the soul. Please give us, as a world, the gift of prayer of the heart so that we may all turn to You and pray, "Abba, Father." We need your help to abandon our sinful ways.

O Father! Hear my poor humble prayer; do not turn away from my wretchedness, but hear the cry of this miserable worthless sinner. Help us to convert. Send us Your Holy Spirit and baptize us with an infusion of Your love. I ask this in the name of Your beloved Son, Jesus Christ, and through the intercession of all of Heaven and my beloved friends, the holy souls. Amen.

Conversations With St. Philomena

St. Philomena: *Little sister, know that God has heard your prayer for the family. Rejoice, little sister. Until tomorrow, farewell, little sister.*

Janie: Thank you, St. Philomena.

Continue Praying for the Conversion of All Families
August 19, 1997

St. Philomena: *Greetings from Heaven, little sister.*

Janie: Peace to you, St. Philomena.

St. Philomena: *Little sister, let us continue praying for the conversion of all families. Until tomorrow, farewell, little sister.*

Janie: Thank you, St. Philomena.

(Our Lord has been allowing me to see the suffering in families, so I have been praying for all these intentions.)

A Suffering For Mother Teresa
August 20, 1997

St. Philomena: *Greetings from Heaven, little sister.*

Janie: Peace to you, St. Philomena.

St. Philomena: *Little sister, prepare well in reparation for all the souls who will be helped when you go to give witness of your life.* (A reference to the Marian Conference in Pittsburgh.)
You will also undergo a suffering for Mother Teresa who is ill. Pray for her; God is preparing her soul in a special way. He will soon call her home. Until tomorrow, farewell, little sister.

296

Janie: St. Philomena, I have been planning to go to meet Mother Teresa when she goes to Washington. I would like to ask if she'll be my spiritual mother. I will pray for Mother Teresa.

Pope Pius Will Intercede

August 21, 1997

St. Philomena: *Greetings from Heaven, little sister.*

Janie: Peace to you, St. Philomena. St. Philomena, today is Pope Pius X's special day. He was one of your devotees. He was the one who elevated your pious archconfraternity into a universal pious archconfraternity. I have been praying about starting a confraternity in your honor. I am asking Pope Pius X for his intercession to accomplish this special task.

St. Philomena: *Little sister, Pope Pius will intercede for your special intention, trust in his assistance and in mine. Until tomorrow, farewell, little sister.*

Janie: Thank you, St. Philomena.

Live Our Lady's Messages

August 22, 1997

St. Philomena came with Our Lady today. No message today. St. Philomena only encouraged me to love Our Lady and to live and spread her messages.

For Mother Teresa and for Peace

August 23, 1997

St. Philomena: *Greetings from Heaven, little sister.*

Conversations With St. Philomena

Janie: Peace to you, St. Philomena.

St. Philomena: *Little sister, offer your prayers for Mother Teresa and for peace in all hearts. Until tomorrow, farewell, little sister.*

Janie: Thank you, St. Philomena, for you guidance.

(From what St. Philomena shared, I knew in my heart that Mother Teresa's time was very short and that she would soon be in heaven. I hope I get to meet her if it be God's Holy Will.)

For Mother Teresa

August 24, 1997

St. Philomena came to ask for special prayers for Mother Teresa and for her community.

God Is Preparing Her

August 25, 1997

St. Philomena: *Greetings from Heaven, little sister.*

Janie: Peace to you, St. Philomena. St. Philomena, please pray for me to suffer well for the Bride of Our Beloved Savior.

St. Philomena: *Little sister, I will pray for you and with you. Remember, you are also suffering for Mother Teresa and her community. God is preparing her and her community.*

Again For Mother Teresa and Her Community

August 26, 1997

St. Philomena came to encourage me again to pray for Mother

298

Teresa and her community.

St. Monica Will Help You

August 27, 1997

St. Philomena: *Greetings from Heaven, little sister.*

Janie: Peace to you, St. Philomena. St. Philomena, today I am asking St. Monica to intercede for me so that I may persevere in praying for my family as she did when she prayed for years for her son, St. Augustine. Her prayers helped him to convert. I have devotion to her and love her. We named one of our granddaughters after St. Monica.

St. Philomena: *Little sister, having devotion to the saints is pleasing to God. Always trust in their intercession. St. Monica will help you in your perseverance to pray for the conversion of your own family. Until tomorrow, farewell, little sister.*

Janie: Thank you, St. Philomena.

The Intercession of Heaven

August 28, 1997

St. Philomena: *Greetings from heaven, little sister.*

Janie: Peace to you, St. Philomena. St. Philomena, yesterday I asked St. Monica for her prayers. Today I also asked her son, St. Augustine. He can intercede for all the men in our whole family. He understands men and their life styles.

I have devotion to both of them. I thank God for you and for all the saints and the intercession of heaven.

St. Philomena: *Little sister, your prayers are always heard when you ask for the intercession of heaven. Until tomorrow, farewell, little sister.*

Conversations With St. Philomena

Janie: Thank you, St. Philomena.

Many Will Be the Favors

August 29, 1997

St. Philomena: *Greetings from Heaven, little sister.*

Janie: Peace to you, St. Philomena. St. Philomena, I am so excited because I put together your first newsletter and assigned the first day to form your confraternity. To me this was a great accomplishment. I know that I couldn't have done this without your help. Thank you so much. I will mail the Rector a copy of this letter to keep him informed of everything that we are doing to foster devotion to you.

St. Philomena: *Little sister, I am grateful for your love and dedication to foster devotion to me. You demonstrate much wisdom and prudence in keeping the Rector informed of all that you are doing to promote devotion to me. Your obedience to work under the direction and guidance of the Rector will bring blessings to all that you do for love of me.*

I will intercede for all your work, and many will be the favors granted to you and my devotees. Until tomorrow, farewell, little sister.

No Message

August 30, 1997

Today, I was ill. St. Philomena came to pray for me.

No Message

August 31, 1997

Due to illness, St. Philomena came to pray for me.

Suffering for the Bride

September 1, 1997

St. Philomena: *Greetings from Heaven, little sister.*

Janie: Peace to you, St. Philomena.

St. Philomena: *Little sister, prepare with strong prayer for all poor sinners. Until tomorrow, farewell, little sister. I know that you are suffering for the Bride of Our Master.*

Janie: I will be in prayer all day.

Wake Up To Pray

September 2, 1997

St. Philomena: *Greetings from Heaven, little sister.*

Janie: Peace to you, St. Philomena.

St. Philomena: *Little sister, know that God is pleased that you offered up your sleep for His special intentions. God needs your prayers to help souls to draw closer to Him. Prayer is the medicine that helps to heal souls. Your prayers have helped to remove many obstacles from the paths of many souls.*

God has delighted in your attitude this morning, little sister, for He knows that you were very tired and sleepy. As your little angel informed you, God wanted you to wake up to pray for special intentions. Your response to God was, in your own words: "Lord, if you want me to stay awake and pray for your special intentions, I will do so."

Janie: St. Philomena, I want to do my best for God. I know that He will provide for my own needs. My sacrifice for His special intentions is to give up my rest.

Please, St. Philomena, pray for my special intentions for my

301

little grandchildren. Ask God to protect them through your intercession. Today is a busy day for me, so intercede for me. Keep my family in your prayers and all those souls whom I recommend to you.

St. Philomena: *Little sister, I will bring all your intentions to Our Heavenly Queen. She will present them to her Son. Until tomorrow, farewell, little sister.*

Janie: Farewell, St. Philomena.

Before the Blessed Sacrament

September 3, 1997

St. Philomena: *Greetings from Heaven, little sister.*

Janie: Peace to you, St. Philomena.

St. Philomena: *Little sister, know that I am interceding for you to help you to prepare for your visit to the Marian Conference. Spend quiet time before the Blessed Sacrament. There Our Master and His Holy Mother will guide you regarding your talk to their children.*

Janie: St. Philomena, I know that Our Master and Our Heavenly Mother are present have with me. I will do exactly as you say. I wish to thank you for helping my son obtain a good job. I knew you would help; you never have not helped anyone who turns to you for help. You are indeed powerful with God.

St. Philomena: *Little sister, know that God grants me many favors for my devotees. He is a good and loving God. His gifts and blessings to all who ask through the intercession of Heaven are without limits. Until tomorrow, farewell, little sister.*

Janie: Farewell, St. Philomena; pray for my special intention.

Suffering for the Conversion of All You Meet
September 4, 1997

St. Philomena: *Greetings from Heaven, little sister.*

Janie: Peace to you, St. Philomena.

St. Philomena: *Little sister, know that I am praying for you. You are suffering much, but remember, your suffering is in preparation for all the souls that you will meet during your stay in Pittsburgh. Offer all your suffering for the conversion of all whom you meet. Until tomorrow, farewell, little sister.*

Janie: Peace to you, St. Philomena.

Embrace the Spirit of Obedience
September 5, 1997
Pittsburgh, Pennsylvania

St. Philomena: *Greetings from Heaven, little sister.*

Janie: Peace to you, St. Philomena.

St. Philomena: *Little sister, I know that you are very tired. I will intercede for you to help you to sleep well. Continue to embrace the spirit of obedience and love this virtue. When you are obedient to God, Satan cannot harm you. Until tomorrow, farewell, little sister.*

Janie: Thank you, St. Philomena.

(Today I had struggled because many people at the Marian Conference wanted me to pray for them. I wanted to make sure that it was alright with the people who invited me as a speaker. I wanted to follow their agenda, and I did not want to be a distraction. This is why St. Philomena was speaking to me on the virtue of obedience).

Conversations With St. Philomena

Personal Message

September 6, 1997
Pittsburgh, Pennsylvania

St. Philomena's visit took place when others were present for the visit. It was personal.

No Visit

September 7, 1997

No visit today because I was traveling.

The Feast of Our Lady's Birthday

September 8, 1997

Today was the Feast of Our Lady's birthday. I had a visit from Our Lady, but afterwards I was suffering. St. Philomena was with me for a moment to let me know that she was interceding for me.

Satan is Furious

September 9, 1997

St. Philomena: *Greetings from Heaven, little sister.*

Janie: Peace to you, St. Philomena. St. Philomena, please intercede for us (my family), for evil forces are trying to take our peace. The attacks have been harder.

St. Philomena: *Little sister, know that Satan is furious with you for your presence at the conference. The story of your life touched many families. The message on the importance of family prayer helped many souls. Many made a decision to begin to pray as a family. This is why Satan has attacked your family, because you destroyed his plan to attack families during the conference.*
Do not fear, little sister, and embrace your family in their suf-

304

fering. Remind them of the love and mercy of God.

Janie: St. Philomena, I am quite aware of how much more I have to pray and fast to thwart Satan's attacks on the family. Please help me in this effort.

St. Philomena: *Have no worry, little sister. I will be praying with you for your family. Until tomorrow, farewell, little sister.*

Janie: Farewell, St. Philomena.

Embrace the Guidance of the Heavenly Queen
September 10, 1997

St. Philomena: Greetings from Heaven, little sister.

Janie: Peace to you, St. Philomena. St. Philomena, thank you for the prayers. I can see the difference in my son. I am so happy for myself as well. I am being more consistent in Adoration which is so important to me. I am trying very hard to live the messages of Our Lady. Continue to make intercession for my family so that each one of us in a personal way will embrace Our Heavenly Mother.

St. Philomena, tomorrow we will begin your confraternity gathering. I am most excited, for I know how happy this will make you -- all your devotees coming together to pray so that we can make you more known.

St. Philomena: *Little sister, God is pleased with your dedication. You embrace the guidance of the Heavenly Queen. Many graces are being bestowed on you and your family. Continue to persevere on the path towards holiness.*

Little sister, I am grateful to you for all your hard work. Tomorrow will be a day filled with blessings and special graces. Prepare with strong prayer for protection over you and your family. The evil one is most upset with you and he does not want this con-

305

Conversations With St. Philomena

*fraternity to take place. I will intercede for you and your family.
Until tomorrow, farewell, little sister.*

Janie: Farewell, St. Philomena.

Remain Calm and Peaceful

September 11, 1997

St. Philomena: *Greetings from Heaven, little sister.*

Janie: Peace to you, St. Philomena.

St. Philomena: *Little sister, continue to offer your prayers and sacrifices for your grandchildren. You are their comfort and these
poor little children look to you for safety. I know that you are suffering with mixed emotions for what your grandchildren are going
through. Remain calm and peaceful. Trust Our Divine Master. He
is your strength. He will help you and your grandchildren. Until
tomorrow, farewell, little sister.*

Janie: Thank you, St. Philomena.

Your Holy Hour

September 12, 1997

St. Philomena: *Greetings from Heaven, little sister.*

Janie: Peace to you, St. Philomena.

St. Philomena: *Little sister, I am here with you as you visit Our Divine Master during your Holy Hour. You have pleased Our Beloved
Master. Listen to all that He speaks to you in your soul. Until tomorrow, farewell, little sister.*

Janie: Thank you, St. Philomena.

Pray for Italy

September 13, 1997

St. Philomena: *Greetings from Heaven, little sister.*

Janie: Peace to you, St. Philomena. St. Philomena, I am excited about being with Our Lady the day after tomorrow, but in a way, part of me wants to skip this visit because I don't want to see her sad.

St. Philomena: *Little sister, you will comfort Our Lady. She loves you so very much. You will embrace her in her sorrow. Do not be nervous about this day but prepare with prayer, and you will do well. Until tomorrow, farewell, little sister. Pray for Italy -- that region will undergo a suffering.*

Janie: Farewell, St. Philomena. I will pray for Italy.

Rejoice!

September 14, 1997
Triumph of the Cross

St. Philomena: *Greetings from Heaven, little sister.*

Janie: Peace to you, St. Philomena. St. Philomena, today I will have a visit from Our Lord. I am so excited.

St. Philomena: *Little sister, I will pray much for you on this day. Rejoice! Until tomorrow, farewell, little sister. Continue praying for Italy.*

Janie: Thank you, St. Philomena. I will do as you say.

307

Conversations With St. Philomena

Visit the Most Holy Virgin

September 15, 1997
Our Lady of Sorrows

St. Philomena: *Greetings from Heaven, little sister.*

Janie: Peace to you, St. Philomena.

St. Philomena: *Little sister, prepare for the visit of the Most Holy Virgin. She will share much with you. Until tomorrow, farewell.*

Janie: Thank you, St. Philomena.

Embrace Every Holy Hour

September 16, 1997

St. Philomena: *Greetings from Heaven, little sister.*

Janie: Peace to you, St. Philomena.

St. Philomena: *Little sister, you have brought much consolation to Our Master through the Holy Hour which you offered Him. He is abandoned and forgotten by so many. He remains alone in the Blessed Sacrament for endless hours, but He loves humanity with immense love.*

Janie: St. Philomena, I feel so bad because when I visit Him in the Blessed Sacrament, He is alone. When my time comes to leave, I am sad because I do not wish to leave Him alone. I always leave with a sad heart.

St. Philomena: *Little sister, Jesus delights in the time which you spend with Him. While you are keeping Him company in Adoration, He is blessing you and those intentions you bring with an abundance of graces.*
Being with Our Master in Adoration brings you to a greater

308

union with Him and His Most Holy Mother. Rejoice and embrace every Holy Hour which you make, for Our Master is embracing you and helping you to obtain love and peace in your family. Until tomorrow, farewell, little sister.

Janie: Thank you, St. Philomena.

Hidden in the Humble Host

September 17, 1997

St. Philomena: *Greetings from Heaven, little sister.*

Janie: Peace to you, St. Philomena.

St. Philomena: *Little sister, I am here to help you in your suffering. Keep your eyes on Our Divine Master. He will give you strength to endure your pain.*

Janie: St. Philomena, this is a most difficult time for me. I feel that no one really understands my spiritual journey and the suffering that comes with embracing the Cross. Help me, St. Philomena, please; I only want to do the Holy Will of the Father.

St. Philomena: *Little sister, you are in the True Presence of Our Divine Master as you make your Holy Hour. You have poured out your concerns to Mary, Our Heavenly Queen, who helps you to draw closer to her son.*
Know that your time spent here in consoling Our Divine Master is precious to Him. He also consoles you. Trust in His Eucharistic love. That is why He chose to remain hidden in the humble host: to help you and all who come to visit Him in Eucharistic Adoration.
Remember, little sister, few are the ones who visit Him. He is forgotten and abandoned. People are too busy, and many do not believe in His True Presence in Eucharistic Adoration. For this reason, your daily visits are so precious to Jesus. His Eucharistic Heart is so infinitely appreciative of the love you show Him by com-

309

ing to the Blessed Sacrament.
Everything will work out, little sister. Heaven is at your side.
Until tomorrow, farewell, little sister.

Janie: Thank you, my dear heavenly friend.

The Schism Will Be Great

September 18, 1997

St. Philomena: *Greetings from Heaven, little sister.*

Janie: Peace to you, St. Philomena.

St. Philomena: *Little sister, prepare with strong prayer, for in a matter of days, you will undergo a physical suffering that will last through the eleventh month of this year. Recall that Our Blessed Queen informed you that your suffering would also include physical illness in reparation for the conversion of poor sinners. Your physical suffering will make you very weak, and you will require bed rest. This physical illness will bring much anguish to your soul as well. This suffering will be hard for you.*
Little sister, offer this suffering for the Bride of Our Master and for all families in the world; especially keep in mind the leader of your own country. Many of his decisions are leading a multitude of souls to perdition. Little sister, the evil in the world is strong. This is why your suffering is so intense.
Little sister, remember that prayer is the great force that can bring about an interior change in hearts that live in darkness. Faith is very weak in many hearts and there are many who have no faith at all.
The coming of the new year will bring about much turmoil among the faithful. The devil will cause much confusion and division among different ministries. As I said before, apparition sites will be condemned by many of the faithful and much suffering will take place. The Bride of Our Master will suffer much as well. Many cardinals, bishops and priests will be disobedient to the Vicar of Our Master. The Vicar of Our Master will suffer much as

well. The schism will be great among many within the Bride of Our Master.

Little sister, do not be sad or concerned about what I share with you. I tell you this so that you will pray and ask Our Master for mercy on all whom the devil is trying to destroy. Remember, God loves His Church and people very much. His love and mercy cannot be outdone if souls pray and repent. God wants His children to have eternal life. He does not want their condemnation. This is why prayer is so important and so needed. Let us pray for the conversion of all souls. Until tomorrow, farewell, little sister.

Janie: St. Philomena, thank you for sharing all this.

For the Least of My Little Ones
September 19, 1997

St. Philomena: *Greetings from Heaven, little sister.*

Janie: Peace to you, St. Philomena.

St. Philomena: *Little sister, God is pleased with all the time which you are dedicating to your grandchildren. Although you are tired and suffering, you give of yourself continuously to your family. You have love and compassion for the suffering and rejected and God blesses all your efforts. Remember Our Lord's words: "Whatsoever you do for the least of my little ones, you do it to me."*

Continue to embrace the suffering, the abandoned, the rejected, the unloved, the discouraged in all little children, for in doing this you are pleasing God. You have much to suffer, little sister, because you love so much.

Janie: St. Philomena, I am happy that you tell me all this. I don't feel like I have the love which it takes to serve God. I pray so much for Jesus to give me His loving heart. I want to be gentle of spirit and have God's peace in my heart. I am doing my best to do the Holy Will of God and to let Our Lady lead me closer to her Son.

311

Conversations With St. Philomena

Please pray for my son. Today is his birthday. He is so special and I know that God loves him a lot. I love him, too. All my children and grandchildren are gifts from Heaven for me. Ask God to bless my son with a good, simple and prayerful life for his birthday.

St. Philomena: *Little sister, I will present your prayer to God. Until tomorrow, farewell, little sister.*

Janie: Thank you, St. Philomena.

Four Corners of the Earth

September 20, 1997

St. Philomena: *Greetings from Heaven, little sister.*

Janie: Peace to you, St. Philomena.

St. Philomena: *Little sister, you are concerned about your little granddaughter. Do not worry. She is under God's protection and loving power.*
You suffer so much, little sister, for the love of your family. You are constantly doing spiritual warfare for their souls. This is why Satan is so furious with you. He knows that you have great love for God and for your family. He knows that your prayers are powerful, because you pray with faith and trust in your heart.
Abandon yourself to Our Divine Master and ask Him and His Holy Mother to take you to the four corners of the world to share the heavenly teachings on the family. Know that as you do God's holy work of helping to save souls, as your share these heavenly messages, there will be many fruits from your witness.
Trust, little sister, trust God; do not listen to the devil. He is the father of lies; you belong to the truth. He cannot hurt you spiritually. Heaven is at your side. Fear nothing but trust God in everything.

312

Janie: St. Philomena, I will do everything to please God. Please intercede for my family while I am gone to give this retreat. I go in obedience. God knows that I do not like to travel, especially to be away from my family. I don't like to be away from my grandchildren. They are my treasures; I love them so much. Please pray for their constant protection. Pray also for my cat. His little paw is hurting. I love you, St. Philomena. I love you so much.

St. Philomena: *Little sister, your friendship is a treasure to me. I love you also, little sister. You are dear to me. I will present all your petitions to God. Until tomorrow, farewell, little sister.*

Janie: Thank you, St. Philomena.

Abandon Yourself to Him that He May Use You
September 21, 1997
Little Rock, Arkansas

St. Philomena: *Greetings from Heaven, little sister.*

Janie: Peace to you, St. Philomena.

St. Philomena: *Little sister, know that God is going to bless many souls through your "yes." Abandon yourself to Him that He may use you according to His most Holy Will.*

Janie: St. Philomena, I will do as you say.

St. Philomena: *Little sister, you bring much consolation to Our Master because of your "yes." Until tomorrow, little sister, farewell.*

Janie: Farewell, St. Philomena.

There were two close friends and my spiritual director present when I had my visit with St. Philomena. The rest of our conversation was personal, for my friends and spiritual director.

313

Conversations With St. Philomena

Total Commitment to Help Families

September 22, 1997

St. Philomena: *Greetings from Heaven, little sister.*

Janie: Peace to you, St. Philomena.

St. Philomena: *Little sister, I wish to express gratitude on behalf of Our Master for your total commitment to help families through your testimony. God's blessings will be bestowed on all who come with an open heart and those others who come because they were invited. All will receive special graces and blessings.*

God is pleased with all His poor humble children who suffer so much. God will give them hope through you. You are His instrument and His little servant. You have worked so hard in preparing yourself through prayer. God will pour out His wisdom, knowledge and strength. Trust Him; He has much to give His people through you. Until tomorrow, farewell, little sister.

Janie: Thank you, St. Philomena.

Spend Time in Adoration

September 23, 1997
Glenwood, Arkansas

St. Philomena: *Greetings from Heaven, little sister.*

Janie: Peace to you, St. Philomena.

St. Philomena: *Little sister, Our Master will bless all His children tonight. This little community will grow and many conversions will take place. Many more will join this community, and your spiritual director will be very busy helping his humble little flock. Prepare and spend time in Adoration with Our Master, for tonight much joy will fill many hearts. Until tomorrow, farewell, little sister.*

Janie: I love you, St. Philomena.

314

Private Visit

September 24, 1997
Glenwood, Arkansas

(Today, St. Philomena came to pray with me before I left home to Austin, Texas).

Your Physical Suffering Has Begun

September 25, 1997

St. Philomena: *Greetings from Heaven, little sister.*

Janie: Peace to you, St. Philomena.

St. Philomena: *Little sister, your physical suffering has begun. Rest and pray in thanksgiving for all that Our Master did for His children* (in Glenwood, Arkansas). *Until tomorrow, farewell, little sister.*

Janie: Thank you, St. Philomena.

For the Love of Our Master

September 26, 1997

St. Philomena: *Greetings from Heaven, little sister.*

Janie: Peace to you, St. Philomena.

St. Philomena: *Little sister, I am here to pray with you for Our Master's Bride. You are suffering much, little sister, but it is all for the love of Our Master.*

St. Philomena and I prayed while I was in bed with my cold.

315

Conversations With St. Philomena

No Messages

September 27-30, 1997

St. Philomena came to pray with me during this time. I have been sick with fever and chills.

Perpetual Adoration

October 1, 1997

St. Philomena: *Greetings from Heaven, little sister.*

Janie: Peace to you, St. Philomena.

St. Philomena: *Little sister, Our Divine Master is pleased that you are here adoring in Perpetual Adoration. Your time spent here will enrich your life, and Our Heavenly Queen will pour the love of her Son in your heart and soul. Rejoice!*
Little sister, Our Master knows that you are ill, and your visit consoles His Eucharistic Heart. He will console your heart and soul and soothe your aching heart.

Janie: St. Philomena, it is a great honor to come and adore Our Master. I have to have this meeting with my dear Jesus. He is my life and my all. I am grateful to God for giving us His only-begotten Son. Please pray for me, St. Philomena, that I may always keep this daily and hourly meeting with Jesus.

St. Philomena: *Do not worry, little sister. I will intercede for you. Until tomorrow, farewell, little sister.*

More Than A Cold

October 2, 1997

St. Philomena: *Greetings from Heaven, little sister.*

316

Janie: Peace to you, St. Philomena. Little sister, please pray for me. This cold seems to be lingering. I feel very weak and I cannot control my coughing.

St. Philomena: *Little sister, this is more than a cold. This is the physical illness which I spoke about. Remain steadfast and pray; it is all for the Bride of Our Master. I will be asking Our Master to give you His strength. Until tomorrow, farewell, little sister.*

Janie: Farewell, St. Philomena.

In the Midst of Your Suffering

October 3, 1997

St. Philomena: *Greetings from Heaven, little sister.*

Janie: Peace to you, St. Philomena.

St. Philomena: *Little sister, you are getting ready for Holy Mass. This will give you new strength. Today you will be visited by the three Archangels and by many angels. Rejoice, it will be a great day for you even in the midst of your intense suffering. Until tomorrow, farewell, little sister.*

Janie: Thank you, St. Philomena.

Love the Cross With All Your Heart

October 4, 1997
(Visit by St. Francis)
Feast of St. Francis

St. Francis: *Little daughter, the peace of God be with you and keep you in His loving care.*

Conversations With St. Philomena

Janie: St. Francis, I am most honored that you came on your feast day. I don't quite know what to say. Please tell me why you came at this time. You mean so much to me.

St. Francis: *Little daughter, God has allowed me to come to you to comfort you in your suffering with your grandchildren. You sacrifice so much for these little precious jewels from Heaven. Your grandchildren's suffering has become your suffering; their sorrow, your sorrow. You spend endless hours in prayers, offering God everything for the spiritual and physical well-being of your grandchildren. You are carrying the cross of your grandchildren with great love in your heart.*

Janie: St. Francis, I love my grandchildren with all my heart.

St. Francis: *Little daughter, your love for your grandchildren reflects the love of your Heavenly Mother. She stood by and watched her Son suffer. All she could do was pray and forgive her Son's offenders. You have done the same with your grandchildren by embracing them in their pain and praying for the people who are mistreating them.*

I assure you, little daughter, that you are doing so much more for these offenders than a jail sentence could do. God is listening with tender loving care to your prayers during this difficult time in your life and that of your grandchildren. You have taught your grandchildren to pray and not to hate their offenders. God is pleased with you, little daughter. He is most pleased.

Little daughter, you are living the gospel message with your heart and soul. You have embraced God through His Son's Cross. Remember that all the sufferings which come your way are steps that help you draw closer to God. Suffer with joy in your heart and love everyone, especially those souls who cause you so much pain, those who reject you and persecute you. Love these poor wounded souls and pray for them. These are the souls who need God's love and mercy.

Little daughter, I am close to your heart and I intercede for you in all your suffering. Love the Cross with all your heart, and you will know the joy which exists only in heaven. Blessings, little daughter, God's blessings to you.

St. Philomena came with St. Francis; no words from her. Later that day during Mass, as I was going to receive Communion, I was looking down and I saw two feet with the wounds. They were the feet of St. Francis. I knew this because I saw him to my right and St. Philomena to my left. As soon as I received Our Lord, they both disappeared.

The Horrible Evil of Abortion

October 5, 1997

St. Philomena: *Greetings from Heaven, little sister.*

Janie: Peace to you, St. Philomena.

St. Philomena: *Little sister, prepare to suffer during these next few days as you pray and fast to end the horrible evil of abortion. You will suffer much as you embrace the unborn through your prayers and sacrifices. I will intercede for you and all your special intentions for the unborn. Until tomorrow, little sister, farewell.*

Janie: Thank you, St. Philomena.

The Mass Is the Ultimate

October 6, 1997

St. Philomena: *Greetings from Heaven, little sister.*

Janie: Peace to you, St. Philomena. St. Philomena, I am offering Holy Mass for the protection of the unborn and to put an end to this evil.

St. Philomena: *Little sister, God knows that you are not well, but*

319

Conversations With St. Philomena

He is pleased with your perseverance in praying for all who participate in this horrible evil. Holy Mass is the greatest prayer to God; Holy Mass is the ultimate form of prayer, little sister. Your offering will bring about much fruit. Until tomorrow, farewell, little sister.

Janie: Thank you, St. Philomena.

Visit of Our Blessed Queen

October 7, 1997

St. Philomena: *Greetings from heaven, little sister.*

Janie: Peace to you, St. Philomena.

St. Philomena: *Little sister, you are preparing for Holy Mass and then for the visit of Our Blessed Queen. I will pray for you. Until tomorrow, farewell, little sister.*

Janie: Pray for me, St. Philomena.

God Is Pleased

October 8, 1997

St. Philomena: *Greetings from Heaven, little sister.*

Janie: Peace to you, St. Philomena.

St. Philomena: *Little sister, God is pleased with you for the way in which you prepare for Holy Mass despite your physical illness.*

Janie: St. Philomena, I care very much about the protection of the unborn. I'll make every sacrifice that I can to bring an end to this killing of the unborn. Knowing that Holy Mass is the highest form of prayer, I offer the Sacrifice of the Holy Mass for the unborn.

St. Philomena: *Little sister, God is pleased! Until tomorrow, fare-*

well, little sister.

Janie: Farewell, St. Philomena.

See All the Souls Whom You Are Helping
October 9, 1997

St. Philomena: *Greetings from Heaven, little sister.*

Janie: Peace to you, St. Philomena.

St. Philomena: *Little sister, you continue to suffer from your physical illness. Your fever continues to weaken you. Remain in bed and rest. I will pray for you. See all the souls whom you are helping.*

I saw a vision. In this vision I saw many cardinals, bishops, priests and religious who have returned to the love of God. All of these souls had stopped believing in the True Presence of Jesus Our Lord in the Eucharist. This made me want to suffer more to help these precious souls whom Our Beloved Savior loves so much.

St. Philomena: *Little sister, now you see why your suffering is so intense. Until tomorrow, farewell, little sister.*

Janie: St. Philomena, I understand a little bit, but I am willing to suffer for Our Lord.

Be Patient With Yourself
October 10, 1997

St. Philomena: *Greetings from Heaven, little sister.*

Janie: Peace to you, St. Philomena.

St. Philomena: *Little sister, your fever continues to weaken you.*

321

Conversations With St. Philomena

Know that your lungs are infected. You will visit your physician, and you will begin taking medication to help clear the infection in your lungs. You will continue to require bed rest.

Know, little sister, that you are frustrated, for you do not like being in bed. This is part of your cross, a great suffering for you.

Janie: St. Philomena, what you say about my frustration is true; pray for me, please. I am willing to suffer for Our Lord.

St. Philomena: *Little sister, this physical illness will linger to the eleventh month. Be patient with yourself. Until tomorrow, farewell, little sister, sweet suffering soul.*

Janie: I love you, St. Philomena. You bring me courage to suffer.

Recall the Vision

October 11, 1997

St. Philomena: *Greetings from Heaven, little sister.*

Janie: Peace to you, St. Philomena. St. Philomena, you were right. I did have infected lungs. I have pneumonia which my doctor said might have been caused by an upper respiratory infection, probably from the cold I had last month. I have to really stay in bed now. I am too weak to fight or to be stubborn! Please pray for me.

St. Philomena: *Little sister, remember that this suffering is to help the Bride of Our Master. Recall the vision which you saw on the ninth day of this month. Keep this vision in your heart. It will give you courage to suffer. Until tomorrow, farewell, little sister.*

Janie: Farewell, St. Philomena.

You Are Helping Many Priests

October 12, 1997

St. Philomena: *Greetings from Heaven, little sister.*

322

Anchor of Hope from Heaven

Janie: Peace to you, St. Philomena. St. Philomena, I have to get up and go to Holy Mass because nobody can bring me Our Lord.

St. Philomena: *Little sister, when you return from Holy Mass, go straight to bed. You need much rest. I am praying for you. You are helping many priests, many priests to draw closer to Our Master. Until tomorrow, farewell, little sister.*

Janie: Thank you, St. Philomena. I feel weak, but I'll be strong when I receive Our precious Lord in the Holy Eucharist.

An Attack on God Himself

October 13, 1997

St. Philomena: *Greetings from Heaven, little sister.*

Janie: Peace to you, St. Philomena.

St. Philomena: *Little sister, you are very ill today. For this reason, I wish you to recall the vision God allowed you to see a few days ago (10-9-97) and to pray for the Bride of Our Master and help all His representatives.*

Today, little sister, pray especially for all people in the world. The world has continued to move farther and farther away from God. The world does not respect the gift of life. This is demonstrated through prevalence of the evil of abortion, the use of contraception, euthanasia, infanticide and suicide. This mentality that has spread throughout the world today is indeed an attack on God Himself.

Your prayers, little sister, are necessary, as are the prayers of all who remain true to the love of God. Pray that the Bride of Our Master will continue to believe firmly in the presence of Our Master in the Holy Sacrifice of the Mass. Pray for those who no longer believe in the True Presence of Our Master in the Holy Eucharist. The Holy Eucharist is the heart of Our Master burning with love for man, for all humanity. Until tomorrow, farewell, little sister.

323

Conversations With St. Philomena

Janie: St. Philomena, I will ponder all of this deep in my heart.

The Eucharist Is the Greatest Force to Combat Evil
October 14, 1997

St. Philomena: *Greetings from Heaven, little sister.*

Janie: Peace to you, St. Philomena.

St. Philomena: *Little sister, offer your suffering for more people to embrace Our Master in the Sacrifice of Holy Mass. So many souls go to Mass unprepared, therefore, they do not understand the graces which Our Master gives to all souls. The Eucharist is the greatest prayer that can be offered for the conversion of all souls. The Eucharist can be used as a weapon for spiritual warfare. The Eucharist is the greatest force to combat evil in the world.*

Little sister, you are ill and suffering, and you are bringing much fruit to many souls beginning with your very own soul. Know that Our Holy Queen, Mary, and St. Joseph are ever so close to you. Until tomorrow, farewell, little sister.

Janie: Thank you, St. Philomena. I love you.

A Great Purification
October 15, 1997

St. Philomena: *Greetings from Heaven, little sister.*

Janie: Peace to you, St. Philomena.

St. Philomena: *Little sister, continue to pray that more and more souls may draw closer to God. The new year will bring much suffering. The calamities will be intense, and many will be left homeless; many will die. There will be much devastation, and many will blame God.*

Little sister, souls do not understand the love and the mercy of God because they do not believe in prayer. The spiritual war of good and evil continues to be fought. The Church and the world continue to fall into a great apostasy. There is a great loss of the sense of the sacred and a crisis of faith. The sinfulness of the world continues to increase. The world has fallen into danger as never before.

Little sister, you are living in times of great sinfulness. Divine intervention will come upon the world. God in His goodness will release a great purification to help His sinful children. Pray, little sister, pray and trust God with your prayers. Until tomorrow, farewell, little sister.

Janie: Farewell, St. Philomena.

The World Cannot Find Peace Unless It Turns To Our Master
October 16, 1997

St. Philomena: *Greetings from Heaven, little sister.*

Janie: Peace to you, St. Philomena. St. Philomena, I have been pondering all that you share with me. I have been praying very intensely. I especially offer Holy Mass and the Rosary as my prayers for conversion to take place in hearts. Please tell me more of the things to come.

St. Philomena: *Little sister, always remember that God is ever so good and merciful. He wants the conversion of all His children, but He cannot help unless intercessory prayers are being offered for poor lost sinners. The only way that humanity will save itself is to return to God. The world cannot find peace unless it turns to Our Master Jesus Christ by the participation in the sacraments and prayer. Let us pray for these special intentions. Until tomorrow, farewell, little sister.*

Janie: Thank you, St. Philomena.

325

Conversations With St. Philomena

O Jesus, good and loving Savior, help us to save our souls by returning back to you.

Your Prayers and Suffering Are Enough

October 17, 1997

St. Philomena: *Greetings from Heaven, little sister.*

Janie: Peace to you, St. Philomena. St. Philomena, ask Our Lord to give me His strength. My illness is so intense. I am not eating much because I am trying to fast to end all the sinfulness in the world.

St. Philomena: *Little sister, your prayers and your suffering are enough. You need food to sustain you physically. Rest, little sister. Until tomorrow, farewell, little sister.*

Janie: Thank you, St. Philomena.

Pray Your Rosary For Your Family

October 18, 1997

St. Philomena: *Greetings from Heaven, little sister.*

Janie: Peace to you, St. Philomena. St. Philomena, please continue to pray for my sanctification and my family's. Satan is trying so hard to destroy the peace in our family. I will not let him do this. That is why I am awake so early, to offer the prayers of my Rosaries to thwart all his attacks. Together with your intercession, I will storm heaven and plead to God for the spiritual well-being of my family.

St. Philomena: *Little sister, you are courageous and you have a loving heart. Although you are suffering from pneumonia, you are battling spiritually for those you love. Your prayers are powerful because you offer everything with such love in your heart. Your*

326

love for your family, especially your love for your grandchildren, pleases God.
   I shall be praying with you as you pray your Rosary for your family and for families everywhere. Continue to offer your illness for Our Master's Bride, for the unborn and for poor sinners everywhere. Until tomorrow, farewell, little sister.

Janie: Farewell, St. Philomena.

Pray Your Rosary For the Protection of the Unborn
October 19, 1997

St. Philomena: *Greetings from Heaven, little sister.*

Janie: Peace to you, St. Philomena. Thank you for praying for my family. Your prayers helped us.

St. Philomena: *Little sister, you are most welcome. Today, I invite you to pray your Rosary for the protection of the unborn. This great evil of abortion is destroying many lives. This evil that continues to grow has become legal throughout the world. This horrible crime is regarded throughout the world as a form of family planning, when, indeed, it is a direct attack on God Himself.*
   Little sister, the Rosary is a powerful weapon to combat this horrible crime. Our Heavenly Queen warns all her children to put an end to this evil through prayer and fasting and returning to the sacraments. ConsoleOurHeavenlyQueen and pray for the protection of the unborn. Until tomorrow, farewell, little sister.

Janie: I will pray for Our Lady's intentions.

How Much He Loves You
October 20, 1997

St. Philomena: *Greetings from Heaven, little sister.*

327

Conversations With St. Philomena

Janie: Peace to you, St. Philomena. St. Philomena, please pray for me. I have much pain in my hands; they hurt very much. Pray for enlightenment for me. I had a dream about my dear friend, Dorothy, who is on a pilgrimage. This dream disturbed me.

St. Philomena: *Little sister, do not worry about the pain in your hands. Our Master is reminding you of how much He loves you. As for your dream about you dear friend, pray for her. Until tomorrow, farewell, little sister.*

Janie: Thank you, St. Philomena.

Many Will Leave the Church

October 21, 1997

St. Philomena: *Greetings from Heaven, little sister.*

Janie: Peace to you, St. Philomena.

St. Philomena: *Little sister, as you continue to suffer from your physical illness, offer your suffering for Our Master's Bride. The work of the devil continues to infiltrate into many hearts of the representatives of Our Master. Many of Our Master's represent-atives accept compromises, and the devil presses on their souls to leave the service of Our Master. Many will leave the Church and abandon their priestly vows. Pray and fast, offering the Eucharist and the Rosary for these souls to return to God. Until tomorrow, farewell, little sister.*

Janie: I will pray very hard.

Parents Do Not Realize

October 22, 1997

St. Philomena: *Greetings from Heaven, little sister.*

328

Janie: Peace to you, St. Philomena.

St. Philomena: *Little sister, pray for parents to teach their children and young people about the virtue of purity and the power of prayer. Many parents give their young people so much freedom to participate in activities that will endanger their souls. So many parents do not realize how much they endanger their children by not taking the time to teach them about God's love. Pray for all parents. Until tomorrow, farewell, little sister.*

Janie: I will pray for parents, St. Philomena.

The Devil Continues to Stalk

October 23, 1997

St. Philomena: *Greetings from Heaven, little sister.*

Janie: Peace to you, St. Philomena.

St. Philomena: *Little sister, continue to pray for the Bride of Our Master. The devil continues to stalk many of Our Master's representatives. I know that you are suffering much today. I am with you in prayer. Until tomorrow, farewell, little sister.*

Janie: I'll pray.

Continue to Pray

October 24, 1997

St. Philomena: *Greetings from Heaven, little sister.*

Janie: Peace, St. Philomena.

St. Philomena: *Little sister, you are a bit stronger today. Continue to pray. I will pray with you. Until tomorrow, farewell, little sister.*

Janie: Farewell, St. Philomena

Conversations With St. Philomena

Their Belief in the Eucharist

October 25, 1997

St. Philomena: *Greetings from Heaven, little sister.*

Janie: Peace to you, St. Philomena.

St. Philomena: *Little sister, your prayers and sacrifices have helped many of Our Master's representatives. Many have renewed their faith and believe, once more, in Our Master's True Presence in the Eucharist. The devil, however, is determined to destroy their belief in the Eucharist. Let us embrace these priests through our prayers. Until tomorrow, farewell, little sister.*

Janie: Thank you, St. Philomena. I am happy for these priests, and I know that God will protect them, because they have faith again in Our Lord.

Preparing for Holy Mass

October 26, 1997

St. Philomena: *Greetings from Heaven, little sister.*

Janie: Peace, St. Philomena.

St. Philomena: *Little sister, you are preparing for Holy Mass. Rejoice! You will receive many graces. Until tomorrow, farewell, little sister.*

Janie: Farewell, St. Philomena. I am praying for all that you have shared with me.

Grieve For Your Friend

October 27, 1997

St. Philomena: *Greetings from Heaven, little sister.*

330

Janie: Peace to you, St. Philomena. St. Philomena, I just learned that my dear friend, X, went to Heaven last week while she was in Lourdes, France. I am happy, but I am also sad. She willed all her belongings to me. I have to go to Dallas, Texas to get everything. Pray for me.

St. Philomena: *Little sister, you will grieve for your dear friend, but Our Master and His Mother will see you through this difficult time. Until tomorrow, farewell, little sister.*

Janie: Thank you, St. Philomena.

Trusting God Will Bring You Peace

October 28, 1997

St. Philomena: *Greetings from Heaven, little sister.*

Janie: Peace to you, St. Philomena.

St. Philomena: *Little sister, you are preparing to go to your dear friend's home. Be at peace, little sister. All will go well.*

Janie: St. Philomena, I am having a hard time, but I will trust God to be my strength.

St. Philomena: *Little sister, you have made a good decision. Trusting God will bring you peace. Until tomorrow, farewell, little sister.*

Brief Visit

October 29, 1997

St. Philomena came to pray with me, because I was having a difficult time. She came before I left Austin.

Conversations With St. Philomena

Remember the Good Times

October 30, 1997

St. Philomena: *Greetings from Heaven, little sister.*

Janie: Peace to you, St. Philomena. St. Philomena, it is so hard being here in X's house. Her spirit seems so alive here; it's as if she is here with me. I miss her already, but I am happy for her. I am glad that all my family is here. This way I won't be alone in her home.

St. Philomena: *Little sister, your dear friend loved you and respected you. She trusted you with all her suffering and personal problems. She will always be with you in your prayers. Remember all the good times which you spent with each other and your phone conversations, but especially the prayer time you shared. Rejoice with her. Until tomorrow, farewell, little sister.*

Janie: Thank you for your kind words, St. Philomena. I love you.

Give Yourself Time

October 31, 1997

St. Philomena: *Greetings from Heaven, little sister.*

Janie: Peace to you, St. Philomena.

St. Philomena: *Little sister, you and your family have worked very hard in getting everything ready to return to your home. I know that your heart is sad; give yourself time, little sister. Trust God with your loss. Until tomorrow, farewell, little sister.*

Janie: Thank you, St. Philomena. I know that for a while I will miss X. I loved her a lot. Pray for me, my dear heavenly sister.

St. Philomena: *Little sister, you are in my prayers. Until tomorrow, farewell, little sister.*

Janie: St. Philomena, I have no doubt that you will help me. I love you so much, and I do not want to abuse our friendship by asking you to obtain these things for me. (Some requested items regarding devotion to St. Philomena). I want to do this by trusting in my prayers and maybe surprising you, my little sister, by doing things for you.

St. Philomena: *Little sister, you have already done me much justice by spreading devotion to me. I am your heavenly little sister. God sent me to you to help you in everything. This is my task, so we will both obtain these things which you need. Until tomorrow, farewell, little sister.*

Janie: Farewell, St. Philomena.

Adoring the Lord and Praying for All the Souls
November 1, 1997   Solemnity of All Saints

St. Philomena: *Greetings from Heaven, little sister.*

Janie: Peace to you, St. Philomena. St. Philomena, I am so happy. Today is a very joyful day for me. It is First Saturday and All Saints Day. I will have heavenly visits, and you are my first heavenly visit.

Oh, St. Philomena, I so trust in the intercession of all the saints in heaven! Although I do not know all the saints, I trust in their intercession.

St. Philomena: *Little sister, God in His goodness provides His children with all that they need for their sanctification. He puts the assistance and guidance of Heaven at His children's disposal. The saints spend all their time adoring God and praying for all the souls who turn to them for assistance. The saints pray for all souls, but they cannot help those souls who do not pray or trust in their intercession. Devotion to the saints is most pleasing to God. En-*

*courage souls to trust in the intercession of the saints. Until tomor-
row, farewell, little sister.*

Janie: Farewell, St. Philomena. Thank you for all your help.

Poor Souls Rely Totally on Your Prayers

November 2, 1997
All Souls Day

St. Philomena: *Greetings from Heaven, little sister.*

Janie: Peace to you, St. Philomena. Today is another wonderful
day for me because it is All Souls Day. I love the holy souls, and I
have such devotion to them because they help me and everybody
through their prayers. I am always offering all my Masses and
prayers to help them to enter the Kingdom of God quickly, so that
they may continue to pray for us.

St. Philomena: *Little sister, your prayers for the poor souls in Purgatory are so important. These poor souls rely totally on the
prayers of the faithful to help them. In Purgatory there are multi-
tudes of souls of all ages and conditions. They all are experiencing
terrible torments. Your prayers help them and many are released
daily from Purgatory.*
*Little sister, all prayers help the poor souls, but the greatest
prayer is the Sacrifice of the Mass. These poor souls suffer intensely the most excruciating pain and their suffering continues until they are released from Purgatory.*
*Little sister, encourage priests to always offer Masses for the
poor souls in Purgatory, not only on All Souls Day, but with every
opportunity that they have.*
*Little sister, God has allowed you to see the suffering of the
poor souls. God granted you this favor because you did not believe
in Purgatory. Now you have much love for them. Encourage the
faithful to offer always as many Masses as possible for the poor
souls. All the poor souls that you help enter heaven through your*

prayers will remain your heavenly friends. They will intercede for you as they live with Our Master in paradise. Until tomorrow, farewell, little sister.

Janie: Thank you for this heavenly knowledge, St. Philomena.

[Note: *Janie did not believe in Purgatory before her visitations began on February 9, 1989.]

Priests and Religious Who Suffer Much From Persecution
November 3, 1997

St. Philomena: *Greetings from Heaven, little sister.*

Janie: Peace to you, St. Philomena.

St. Philomena: *Little sister, as you suffer for the Bride of Our Master, offer your prayers for all the priests and religious who suffer so much from persecution. Through their suffering for the sake of love, they are helping those who are persecuting them. Pray for those who choose to suffer rather than disobey Our Master. Until tomorrow, farewell, little sister.*

Janie: St. Philomena, I will pray. I promise.

For Poor Lost Sinners
November 4, 1997

St. Philomena: *Greetings from Heaven, little sister.*

Janie: Peace to you, St. Philomena. St. Philomena, please pray for me. My soul is suffering so much anguish. I cannot concentrate on my prayers. Please help so that I can continue to pray.

St. Philomena: *Little sister, your soul is united with the sorrows of*

Conversations With St. Philomena

Our Master and His Most Holy Mother for the souls who choose to live in darkness. Do not worry; you will be able to continue to pray. Offer your prayers for poor lost sinners. Until tomorrow, farewell, little sister.

Janie: Thank you, St. Philomena.

These Thoughts Will Soon Leave

November 5, 1997

St. Philomena: *Greetings from Heaven, little sister.*

Janie: Peace to you, St. Philomena. St. Philomena, please intercede for me, so that I may persevere in my prayer life. I want nothing to interfere with my relationship with Our Lord. I try to always be in prayer by occupying my mind with heavenly thoughts. I try to be grateful for all the blessings that God gives me, especially the gift of my family and my spiritual family. I have so much to be grateful for. I am most grateful for my salvation. I find that when distractions enter my mind and I allow myself to entertain these distractions, I lose my peace.

St. Philomena: *Little sister, do not allow these distractions to be a concern for you. Simply continue to pray and these thoughts will soon leave. God is pleased that you are grateful. Be at peace. Your prayers are helping many souls. Until tomorrow, farewell, little sister.*

Janie: Thank you, St. Philomena.

The Three Archangels

November 6, 1997

St. Philomena: *Greetings from Heaven, little sister.*

Janie: Peace to you, St. Philomena.

336

Anchor of Hope from Heaven

St. Philomena: *Little sister, today you will receive your heavenly visit from the three Archangels. Embrace everything they share with you and always encourage others to trust in their powerful intercession. Until tomorrow, farewell, little sister.*

Janie: Thank you, St. Philomena. I will continue to spread devotion to the Archangels and guardian angels.

Snatch Souls from the Hands of the Devil
November 7, 1997

St. Philomena: *Greetings from Heaven, little sister.*

Janie: Peace to you, St. Philomena.

St. Philomena: *Little sister, you are suffering for poor sinners, and your suffering is intense.*
Little sister, the evil in the world continues to increase. Our Master is consoled when victim souls, such as yourself and many others, are willing to suffer to save poor sinners who are on their way to perdition. Your prayers and suffering help to snatch souls from the hands of the devil. Suffer with joy in your heart. Our Master loves you with immense love. Until tomorrow, farewell, little sister.

Janie: St. Philomena, you are so kind and you help me to have a better understanding of my suffering.

Parents Who Have Had Abortions
November 8, 1997

St. Philomena: *Greetings from Heaven, little sister.*

Janie: Peace to you, St. Philomena.

St. Philomena: *Little sister, I know that you are concerned*

337

about your husband and the completion of your new home. I am here to tell you that God will provide you and your husband with everything that you need. Continue to abandon everything to Him.

Today, little sister, please join me in praying for all the parents who suffer so much because they have had abortions. Our prayers will help these parents to see the wrong that they have done, and they will repent. Until tomorrow, farewell, little sister.

(St. Philomena speaks of "parents" because both parents consented to have their babies aborted.)

Rescue His Children

November 9, 1997

St. Philomena: *Greetings from Heaven, little sister.*

Janie: Peace to you, St. Philomena.

St. Philomena: *Little sister, let us continue to pray for poor sinners for the devil is very active, trying to destroy all souls who do not pray. Always encourage the faithful to pray every day and to guard their souls by means of prayers. Prayer is the strongest force in the world, for when the faithful pray they call upon the power of God to come to their aid. God never refuses anyone, but gladly and with great joy sends the assistance of His angels to rescue His children from the hands of the devil.*

Let us pray for poor sinners and bring souls to the love and mercy of Our Master. Until tomorrow, farewell, little sister.

Janie: I will pray for poor sinners.

For Our Holy Father

November 10-11, 1997

During these two days I was very sick and did not receive any prayer requests from St. Philomena. She prayed for me and asked me to offer my suffering for our Holy Father.

338

Attend Holy Mass Daily

November 12, 1997

St. Philomena: *Greetings from Heaven, little sister.*

Janie: Peace to you, St. Philomena.

St. Philomena: *Little sister, today, as you continue to pray and suffer for poor sinners, keep in mind how much God wants the salvation of all His children. Ask Our Master to help you to endure the cross that you carry for poor sinners.*

Little sister, you work very hard, guarding your soul by always remaining in the state of grace. You attend Holy Mass every day. You allow yourself to be fed by the Bread of Angels. This is why you are able to wage spiritual warfare for your family and poor sinners.

Little sister, your heart is open to God, and you allow yourself to be guided by the light and movement of grace. Our Master's love is strong in you, simply because you trust Him and claim Him as your strength.

Little sister, encourage souls to attend Holy Mass daily and to live in the state of grace, and they will be able to resist the devil. Until tomorrow, farewell, little sister.

Janie: Thank you, St. Philomena.

Eager to Please Our Loving Master

November 13, 1997

St. Philomena: *Greetings from Heaven, little sister.*

Janie: Peace to you, St. Philomena. St. Philomena, I am so grateful to God for you. You have helped me so much, and I will remain forever grateful to you. My prayer life has been strengthened because you have encouraged me to pray, to embrace all crosses with joy in my heart. Thank you, St. Philomena. Thank you from the depths of my heart.

339

Conversations With St. Philomena

St. Philomena: *Little sister, it is a joy to share all that God has allowed me to tell you. You are a good listener, and you embrace everything with faith in your heart. Even though the devil torments you with doubts about my visits, you choose to remain obedient and believe in all that I am sharing with you.*

You have a beautiful humble heart and a very simple disposition. This is so pleasing to God. You are like a little child who eagerly wants to please their parents. This is how you are eager to please Our loving Master.

I love you dearly, little sister. Until tomorrow, farewell, little sister.

Janie: Thank you, St. Philomena. I love you very much.

Endure Your Suffering

November 14, 1997

St. Philomena: *Greetings from Heaven, little sister.*

Janie: Peace to you, St. Philomena.

St. Philomena: *Little sister, your suffering is very intense. I will pray for you as you endure your suffering for poor sinners.*

Janie: Thank you, St. Philomena.

Poor, Poor Families

November 15, 1997

St. Philomena: *Greetings from Heaven, little sister.*

Janie: Peace to you, St. Philomena.

St. Philomena: *Little sister, pray for the families who do not believe in God. These poor families are these whom the devil devours*

340

because they are not in the state of grace. Poor, poor families, if only they would understand the reason they are so miserable is they have no relationship with God. Pray for these families. Until tomorrow, farewell, little sister.

Janie: I'll pray, St. Philomena.

Souls in Purgatory

November 16, 1997

St. Philomena: *Greetings from Heaven, little sister.*

Janie: Peace to you, St. Philomena. St. Philomena, I have continued to offer my Mass for poor sinners and for the poor souls in Purgatory.

St. Philomena: *Little sister, know for certain, that God is listening to your humble prayers and all your petitions. Much good fruit is taking place in the hearts of poor sinners. The holy souls in Purgatory are forever grateful for your prayers offered for them. Your prayers, little sister, helped release many souls from Purgatory today. Rejoice and be grateful to Our Master for His love and mercy. Until tomorrow, farewell, little sister.*

Janie: Thank you so much, St. Philomena, for your kind words.

No Other Way to the Cross

November 17, 1997

St. Philomena: *Greetings from Heaven, little sister.*

Janie: Peace to you, St. Philomena.

St. Philomena: *Little sister, today you are suffering for the Bride of Our Master. Know, little sister, that as you suffer, your own soul is*

341

Conversations With St. Philomena

being purified. Suffering, little sister, is the way to embrace Our Master's Cross. There is no other way to the Cross except through suffering.

Little sister, encourage souls to embrace the suffering in their lives and to allow God to purify them through their suffering. Little sister, trust God in all your suffering. Until tomorrow, farewell, little sister.

Janie: Peace to you, little sister.

Will Not Test You Beyond Your Limit
November 18, 1997

St. Philomena: *Greetings from Heaven, little sister.*

Janie: Peace to you, St. Philomena. St. Philomena, please pray for me. I don't believe that I have recovered from my illness completely.

St. Philomena: *Little sister, your illness has lasted, but soon you will feel stronger and better. You will have much to suffer in your lifetime and physical illness will be a part of your suffering. You have been chosen to suffer for poor sinners. Your prayers and suffering are helping many souls to convert.*

Little sister, keep in mind that Our Master will not test you beyond your limit. When you are undergoing a suffering, remember what I am sharing with you now. This will give you peace during your suffering. Until tomorrow, farewell, little sister.

Janie: Thank you, St. Philomena for sharing this with me.

Devotion to the Immaculate Heart of Mary
November 19, 1997

St. Philomena: *Greetings from Heaven, little sister.*

Janie: Peace to you, St. Philomena.

St. Philomena: *Little sister, today offer your prayers and sacrifices so that souls who do not have devotion to the Immaculate Heart of Mary will open their hearts to her motherly love. Many are the graces that come to those who practice this devotion and who spread this devotion.*

Little sister, encourage all who have this devotion to pray in reparation for poor sinners everywhere. There is so much evil in the world, but through Our Heavenly Mother's intercession many poor sinners will be converted.

Until tomorrow, farewell, little sister. I know that your hands are hurting. Offer this pain for poor sinners.

Janie: I will pray, St. Philomena.

They Would Pray All the Time!

November 20, 1997

St. Philomena: *Greetings from Heaven, little sister.*

Janie: Peace to you, St. Philomena.

St. Philomena: *Little sister, continue to pray for poor sinners. There is so much misery in many souls because they do not pray. God wants to bless all His children, but He cannot if they do not pray. Oh, if only poor sinners would understand the importance of prayers, they would pray all the time!*

Little sister, in your prayers, especially keep in mind all parents that they may teach their children how to pray. God blesses the family that prays together, and His peace dwells in their hearts. Until tomorrow, farewell, little sister.

Janie: Farewell, St. Philomena. I love you.

343

Conversations With St. Philomena

Suffering Is Intense Because of Evil

November 21, 1997

St. Philomena: *Greetings from Heaven, littl e sister.*

Janie: Peace to you, St. Philomena.

St. Philomena: *Little sister, you are suffering much this morning. The pains in your hands keep you from doing many of your household tasks. Know that your suffering is intense because of the evil in the world. Your suffering is helping poor sinners. Remain strong in your prayers during your suffering. I love you, little sister. Until tomorrow, farewell, little sister.*

Janie: I will remain strong in my prayers.

Those Who Have Abandoned Family Prayer

November 22, 1997

St. Philomena: *Greetings from Heaven, little sister.*

Janie: Peace to you, St. Philomena.

St. Philomena: *Little sister, continue to offer your suffering and prayers for peace in all families. Your prayers are powerful during your suffering, for you have said "yes" to be a victim of love and suffering for poor sinners. Pray, that families will begin to pray together, those who have abandoned family prayer. Pray, that these families will make peace with God, with others and with themselves. Until tomorrow, farewell, little sister.*

Janie: Thank you, St. Philomena.

Hunger for Purity and Goodness

November 23, 1997

St. Philomena: *Greetings from Heaven, little sister.*

344

Janie: Peace to you, St. Philomena.

St. Philomena: *Little sister, offer your Mass for all children and young people that they will hunger for purity and goodness. Pray for the young people to remain chaste and not to fall into temptation but to offer their purity to God. Until tomorrow, farewell, little sister.*

Janie: Peace to you, St. Philomena.

The Eucharistic Love of Our Master

November 24, 1997

St. Philomena: *Greetings from Heaven, little sister.*

Janie: Peace to you, St. Philomena.

St. Philomena: *Little sister, today as you suffer for the Bride of Our Master, pray that all the representatives of Our Master believe in the True Presence of Our Master in the Most Blessed Sacrament. Many do not believe in the True Presence, and this causes Our Master much sadness. Our Master has a deep hunger to be united with all His representatives who believe in His True Presence in the Most Blessed Sacrament.*

Little sister, you have a deep love for Our Master, and you believe in His True Presence in the Most Blessed Sacrament. My heart aches for all those who refuse to believe that Our Master is truly present in the Blessed Sacrament. Pray, so that these representatives of Our Master will soon realize that it is the Eucharistic love of Our Master Who motivates and urges His Bride to live for Him in their daily lives.

Little sister, these times are very important. There is great evil in the hearts of many people. This is why it is important for the Bride of Our Master to find its strength in the Eucharistic love of Jesus. Until tomorrow, farewell, little sister.

345

Conversations With St. Philomena

No Greater Love

November 25, 1997

St. Philomena: *Greetings from Heaven, little sister.*

Janie: Peace to you, St. Philomena. St. Philomena, thank you so much for sharing with me the importance of believing in the True Presence of Our Lord in the Blessed Sacrament. I know how Our Lord fills my heart when I go to make my Holy Hour. I do not even want to leave His side. He helps me so much.

St. Philomena: *Little sister, there is no greater love than that of Our Master. There is no greater time than the time you spend attending Holy Mass, Perpetual Adoration and prayer, especially praying your Rosary. All this deepens your union, not only with Our Master, but also with His Most Holy Mother. Until tomorrow, farewell, little sister.*

Janie: Thank you, St. Philomena.

This Divine Love

November 26, 1997

St. Philomena: *Greetings from Heaven, little sister.*

Janie: Peace to you, St. Philomena. St. Philomena, please pray for me that I may be able to prepare all the food for Thanksgiving, which is tomorrow. We have provided food for poor families so that they, too, may have a reason to give thanks to Our Lord.

St. Philomena: *Little sister, charity is most pleasing to God. Charity is the fruit of the love which God has blessed you with. It is this divine love that moves you to love your neighbor. Always pray for the love of Our Master to be poured into your heart. In this way your own heart will be filled with charity. Until tomorrow, farewell, little sister.*

346

Janie: Thank you, St. Philomena.

No One to Help Them

November 27, 1997

St. Philomena: *Greetings from Heaven, little sister.*

Janie: Peace to you, St. Philomena.

St. Philomena: *Little sister, pray for all families who have no one to help them. These poor families are in need of much prayer.* (St. Philomena is referring to the families who have very little food or no food). *Until tomorrow, farewell, little sister.*

Janie: I'll pray for these families.

For All the Troubled Spouses

November 28, 1997

St. Philomena: *Greetings from Heaven, little sister.*

Janie: Peace to you, St. Philomena.

St. Philomena: *Little sister, offer all your prayers and sacrifices for all the troubled spouses in the world. Many spouses are dissolving their marriages, not knowing what great harm and pain it causes their children. Pray to Our Master so that through your prayers these troubled marriages will be healed. Many spouses seek divorce instead of the forgiveness that comes through prayer. My heart aches for all the children and young people who suffer because their parents refuse to save their marriages. Pray with me for these poor families. Until tomorrow, farewell, little sister.*

Janie: St. Philomena, I will ask Our Lord to help these families.

Conversations With St. Philomena

For the Homeless and Hungry

November 29, 1997

St. Philomena: *Greetings from Heaven, little sister.*

Janie: Peace to you, St. Philomena.

St. Philomena: *Little sister, offer your prayers and sacrifices for all who are homeless and hungry. Pray, asking the intercession of the Heavenly Queen to protect all these suffering souls who suffer so much. Until tomorrow, farewell, little sister.*

Janie: Farewell, St. Philomena.

Much to Give to All Who Prepare

November 30, 1997

St. Philomena: *Greetings from Heaven, little sister.*

Janie: Peace to you, St. Philomena.

St. Philomena: *Little sister, offer your Mass so that you and your family will prepare for the holy season of Advent. Our Master has much to give to all who prepare to allow Him to be born in their hearts. Until tomorrow, farewell, little sister.*

Janie: Thank you, St. Philomena.

The Flock of the Bride of Our Master

December 1, 1997

St. Philomena: *Greetings from Heaven, little sister.*

Janie: Peace to you, St. Philomena.

St. Philomena: *Little sister, you have entered into the holy season of Advent. Today, as you offer your suffering for the Bride of Our Master, pray for all who are lukewarm and care very little about being Christ-like. Our Master loves His Bride with immense love and wants to pour His love into every heart. So many reject His love and choose the emptiness that the world offers them.* (Here St. Philomena is referring to all the priests and religious who have embraced materialism and all the ways of the world.)

Little sister, the Bride of Our Master must be strengthened so that she may guide and feed all the flock entrusted into her care. (Here St. Philomena continues to refer to those priests and religious who allow themselves to be consumed by their weakness.)

Little sister, the flock of the Bride of Our Master must be spiritually fed and guided on a level path which leads towards holiness. The flock must be protected by the representatives of Our Master. (St. Philomena refers to the flock as the people under the guidance of the Church.) *Pray for the Bride of Our Master. Until tomorrow, farewell, little sister.*

The Rosary in Family Crises

December 2, 1997

St. Philomena: *Greetings from Heaven, little sister.*

Janie: Peace to you, St. Philomena.

St. Philomena: *Little sister, rejoice and share the joy in your heart! Imitate the spirit of St. John the Baptist and through your prayers prepare the way of the Lord. May He find every heart waiting for His birth to take place in their hearts. May He find every heart rejoicing with all of the heavenly hosts.*

(Later that day)

St. Philomena: *Greetings from Heaven, little sister.*

Conversations With St. Philomena

Janie: Peace to you, St. Philomena.

St. Philomena: *Little sister, as you continue to prepare your heart during this holy season, encourage your family to abandon themselves to the intercession of their Heavenly Mother. She will help them draw closer to her Son and to prepare for His holy birth to take place in their hearts.*
Little sister, God is pleased with your prayers as a family. As a family, you have embraced the Rosary as your weapon. You use the power of the Rosary to help you in family crises. You are able to overcome many obstacles because you pray together as a family. Through praying the Rosary together as a family, you are learning the value of family prayer. God delights in family prayer. Share this with your family. Until tomorrow, farewell, little sister.

Janie: Thank you, St. Philomena.

Imitate Their Spirit As A Family

December 3, 1997

St. Philomena: *Greetings from Heaven, little sister.*

Janie: Peace to you, St. Philomena.

St. Philomena: *Little sister, offer your family prayer so that other families will begin to pray together. During this holy season reflect on how St. Joseph and your Heavenly Mother struggled to find a place for Our Master to be born. Both St. Joseph and Mary suffered so much for they were rejected when they asked for help. The spirit of charity was lacking in those souls who refused to help St. Joseph and Mary.*
Little sister, as St. Joseph and Mary suffered, they allowed nothing to interfere with following the will of God. No obstacle broke their spirit, because their hearts were full of holy love. They remained obedient to God until they accomplished their task. Imitate their spirit as a family and allow nothing to keep you from growing closer to God as a family. Little sister, the family is pre-

350

cious to God. Until tomorrow, farewell, little sister.

Janie: Thank you, St. Philomena.

Heavenly Guidance and Intercession

December 4, 1997

St. Philomena: *Greetings from Heaven, little sister.*

Janie: Peace to you, St. Philomena.

St. Philomena: *Little sister, today you receive your heavenly visit from the Archangels. Open your heart to all that they share with you. Always trust in their heavenly guidance and intercession. God sent them to you to receive many important things which they will continue to share with you. Until tomorrow, little sister, farewell. Prepare for the visit of the Archangels.*

Janie: Thank you, St. Philomena.

Have Devotion to the Sacred Heart

December 5, 1997

St. Philomena: *Greetings from Heaven, little sister.*

Janie: Peace to you, St. Philomena.

St. Philomena: *Little sister, you are suffering for the conversion of poor sinners. Unite your suffering with the suffering of Our Master. Offer your holy hour so that more souls will come to believe in the True Presence of Our Master in the Eucharist. Embrace the Sacred Heart of Our Master and console Him by spending time with Him in Perpetual Adoration. He remains a prisoner of love for humanity in the Holy Eucharist. Encourage souls to spend time with Our Master.*

351

Conversations With St. Philomena

Little sister, always encourage souls to have devotion to the Sacred Heart of Jesus. God the Father grants an abundance of graces and blessings to those who have devotion to the Sacred Heart of Jesus. Until tomorrow, farewell, little sister.

Janie: Thank you, St. Philomena.

World Peace Through the Two United Hearts

December 6, 1997

St. Philomena: *Greetings from Heaven, little sister.*

Janie: Peace to you, St. Philomena. St. Philomena, my family and I are getting ready to go to Confession, pray our Rosary and attend Holy Mass in honor of First Saturday. Pray for us that the Holy Spirit will help us to make a good confession.

St. Philomena: *Little sister, God is pleased with your efforts as a family to honor the request of your Most Holy Mother. Little sister, as a family your dedication to the First Saturdays will help many families who are in need of conversion. Pray your Rosary for peace in all families. Spread the devotion of the Immaculate Heart of Mary. Remember, God wishes to establish in all families in the world the devotion to the Immaculate Heart. Little sister, God gives graces through the Immaculate Heart of Mary. Share with families about these graces that come through the Immaculate Heart of Mary and tell them to ask for graces from her. Tell families to venerate the Sacred Heart of Jesus with the Immaculate Heart of Mary. Ask souls to pray for world peace through the Two United Hearts. Honor your Most Holy Mother and ask her to pray for world peace. The Lord, Himself, has confided the peace of the world to His Most Holy Mother. Until tomorrow, farewell, little sister.*

Janie: Thank you, St. Philomena. We will do as you say. We love the Two Hearts.

Children Who Are Without Parents

December 7, 1997

St. Philomena: *Greetings from heaven, little sister.*

Janie: Peace to you, St. Philomena.

St. Philomena: *Little sister, offer your Mass in preparation for tomorrow when you will receive the visit of your Most Holy Mother. I will come with Our Heavenly Queen tomorrow.*

Offer your Mass for all the children and youth in the world who are without parents. Their suffering is so intense. They feel abandoned by those around them. Embrace them through your prayers. Until tomorrow, farewell, little sister.

Janie: Farewell, St. Philomena.

Solemnity of the Immaculate Conception

December 8, 1997

St. Philomena came with Our Lady.

Young People Without Someone to Love Them

December 9, 1997

St. Philomena: *Greetings from Heaven, little sister.*

Janie: Peace to you, St. Philomena.

St. Philomena: *Little sister, continue to offer your prayers and sacrifices for children and young people who will be without someone to love them during this holy season. So many of these precious ones need love in their lives. You can love them by praying for them. Until tomorrow, farewell, little sister.*

St. Philomena looked so sad as she entrusted the children and

353

the youth to my prayers. She loves them so much.

Prepare for the Birth of Our Master

December 10, 1997

St. Philomena: *Greetings from Heaven, little sister.*

Janie: Peace to you, St. Philomena.

St. Philomena: *Little sister, pray that souls will prepare for the birth of Our Master. This is a time when many people are distracted by material things. These souls forget what this holy season is all about. Invoke the intercession of the Heavenly Queen and St. Joseph, so that they will help the world to prepare for the birth of Our Master.*

Little sister, spend quiet time in prayer with your family, preparing your hearts for the Savior of the world. Prepare your hearts that He may purge you in His love and cleanse you of everything. He is the light of the world Who rescues souls from the darkness of sin. Prepare your hearts to experience the fullness of His joy and gladness. Until tomorrow, farewell, little sister.

Janie: Farewell, St. Philomena.

Today we began to prepare for the feast of Our Lady of Guadalupe.

A Joyful Day

December 11, 1997

St. Philomena: *Greetings from Heaven, little sister.*

Janie: Peace to you, St. Philomena. St. Philomena, I am so excited, for tomorrow is the feast of Our Lady of Guadalupe. This is a special day for the Hispanic people. Many others embrace her under this title, but Mexico knows truly how to celebrate this special day.

354

I love her under this title.

St. Philomena: *Little sister, tomorrow I will come with Our Heavenly Queen. Prepare; it will be a joyful day for you and your family. Until tomorrow, farewell, little sister.*

Janie: Thank you, St. Philomena.

Feast of Our Lady of Guadalupe

December 12, 1997

St. Philomena came with Our Lady. No special message by St. Philomena was given.

Trust the Intercession of St. Joseph

December 13, 1997

St. Philomena: *Greetings from Heaven, little sister.*

Janie: Peace to you, St. Philomena. St. Philomena, please pray for my husband. He is working so hard to complete the house. It's been cold, and my husband is very tired. He needs your prayers so that he won't become discouraged.

St. Philomena: *Little sister, do not be concerned about your husband. St. Joseph is guiding him in a gentle way. St. Joseph is teaching your husband perseverance and patience. Your husband is in the care of St. Joseph.*
The house that your husband is building will bring blessings to many people. This is why the crosses are most difficult.
Continue to trust in the intercession of St. Joseph. I will intercede for your husband. Until tomorrow, farewell, little sister.

Janie: Thank you, St. Philomena.

355

Conversations With St. Philomena

Set Free From the Snares of the Devil

December 14, 1997

St. Philomena: *Greetings from Heaven, little sister.*

Janie: Peace to you, St. Philomena.

St. Philomena: *Little sister, as you prepare for Holy Mass, offer your prayers so that many souls will be set free from the snares of the devil. Pray that souls will open their hearts to the Savior of the world. Oh, little sister, pray that Our Master's love will melt away the darkness in sinful hearts. Until tomorrow, farewell, little sister.*

Janie: Farewell, St. Philomena. I will pray.

Helping the Bride of Our Master

December 15, 1997

St. Philomena: *Greetings from Heaven, little sister.*

Janie: Peace to you, St. Philomena.

St. Philomena: *Little sister, you are suffering today for the Bride of Our Master. Embrace your suffering and offer it so that the Church will help all the faithful to draw closer to Our Master. I know that you are suffering much and you feel very weak. I will intercede for you.*
   Remember, your suffering is helping the Bride of Our Master. Until tomorrow, farewell, little sister.

Janie: Thank you, St. Philomena, for understanding my suffering. You are a good example for those who suffer.

Very Weak in Their Faith

December 16, 1997

St. Philomena: *Greetings from Heaven, little sister.*

356

Anchor of Hope from Heaven

Janie: Peace to you, St. Philomena. St. Philomena, I am so tired and weak from my suffering yesterday. Today I continue to suffer, but not as much as yesterday. Our Master keeps bringing souls to me to pray for and to suffer for. I do not know these souls personally, but I can see them clearly.

St. Philomena: *Little sister, there are souls who are suffering much and who are very weak in their faith. Your suffering and prayers will help to strengthen their faith. I will pray with you for these souls.*

Resemble Him in All Your Suffering

December 17, 1997

St. Philomena: *Greetings from heaven, little sister.*

Janie: Peace to you, St. Philomena. St. Philomena, please pray for me, for I am suffering much from the attacks of Satan. He places many temptations before me and it takes great courage for me to remain prayerful during these attacks. I share these sufferings with my spiritual director, and he prays for me, but these attacks continue.

St. Philomena, I know that you have suffered much, so you understand suffering. This is why I need your powerful intercession, as I also turn to my spiritual fathers, St. Francis and Padre Pio. These temptations pursue me no matter what I may be doing. Some of these temptations are against faith and some are of judgmental thoughts about others. I suffer such agony that at times I feel like I am losing my mind. Satan tells me that my spiritual director is not a good spiritual director and not to share these temptations with Him, because he cannot help me.

Please, St. Philomena, I know that my soul is in the state of grace, but these attacks are so violent that, at times, I feel my body paralyzed. This is a hard suffering. Please help me.

St. Philomena: *Little sister, you are undergoing such trials for*

357

poor sinners. Satan knows how much you pray and offer sacrifices for poor sinners. He is angry with your love and concern for poor sinners. Have no worry, little sister. Our Master is with you, and it is He Who is leading you towards Calvary. Our Master permits the devil to attack you, just as He suffered the attacks and torments of the devil while in the desert and the Garden and on the Cross.

Your love and compassion for poor sinners make you so dear to Him. He wants you to resemble Him in all your sufferings. Little sister, abandon yourself to the love of Our Master and pray, that you may endure all that heaven permits you to suffer.

Janie: St. Philomena, thank you so much.

St. Philomena: *Little sister, know that I am praying with you. Until tomorrow, farewell, little sister.*

Janie: Farewell, St. Philomena.

The Devil Will Flee From Your Side

December 18, 1997

St. Philomena: *Greetings from Heaven, little sister.*

Janie: Peace to you, St. Philomena. St. Philomena, today my sufferings continue. Please pray for me. St. Philomena, sometimes I feel like I am suffering from hysteria. The devil continues his attacks on me and whispers terrible things about my heavenly visitations. He tells me that God has nothing to do with all that is happening to me spiritually. He tells me that all of this originates in my own mind and that I need help.

When I am before the Blessed Sacrament, making my Holy Hour, Satan tells me to leave, that Our Lord is not truly present in Perpetual Adoration. He tells me that I am wasting precious time praying for poor sinners. Satan makes every effort to induce my mind with all sorts of images of judgmental thoughts and ideas of despair. Sometimes this causes such fear in me, and I suffer much.

Sometimes I feel like hiding and not talking to anyone, but my guardian angel helps me and reminds me of my responsibility to God.

The spiritual path to which I am called is constantly enveloped in such thick darkness. I know that it is by God's grace and the gift of faith that I am able to endure all this. No one on earth seems to understand these sufferings I go through -- no one.

St. Philomena: *Little sister, know that your sufferings are helping poor sinners to convert. The devil is angry with you, and he will do everything to discourage you from prayer and doing God's Holy Will. Have no fear, for God will never test you beyond your strength. Continue praying for poor sinners and resist the attacks of the devil by blessing yourself with holy water, praying your Rosary and invoking the intercession of Our Holy Mother, St. Joseph and St. Michael the Archangel. Do this and the devil will flee from your side. Until tomorrow, farewell, little sister.*

Janie: Thank you, St. Philomena.

Your Suffering Will Help to Melt Away Darkness
December 19, 1997

St. Philomena: *Greetings from Heaven, little sister.*

Janie: Peace to you, St. Philomena.

St. Philomena: *Little sister, I know that your suffering continues. Offer your suffering today, especially for all those poor sinners who do not believe in the birth of Our Master. Your suffering will help to melt away the darkness from many souls.*

Little sister, for the rest of these next few days, you will suffer much. These sufferings will be a physical suffering. Until tomorrow, farewell, little sister.

(I know that St. Philomena means that I will suffer Our Lord's passion).

Conversations With St. Philomena

For All the Youth in the World
December 20, 1997

St. Philomena: *Greetings from Heaven, little sister.*

Janie: Peace to you, St. Philomena.

St. Philomena: *Little sister, endure your suffering today, especially for all the youth in the world. Offer your suffering and prayers, so that their young hearts will be open to the birth of Our Master. Ask Our Most Holy Queen and St. Joseph to help you to embrace your suffering, so that you may help all the youth in the world return to the love of Our Master. Until tomorrow, farewell, little sister.*

St. Philomena is referring to all the youth who do not believe in God and whose faith is weak.

Family Prayer Has Helped to Prepare Your Hearts
December 21, 1997

St. Philomena: *Greetings from Heaven, little sister.*

Janie: Peace to you, St. Philomena.

St. Philomena: *Little sister, you and your family have done well in preparing for the birth of Our Master. Your family prayer (the Rosary) has helped to prepare your hearts. Rejoice! God is pleased with your family efforts to pray together every day. Until tomorrow, farewell, little sister.*

Janie: Farewell, St. Philomena.

St. Philomena is always happy when the family prayers together. She and her family always prayed together.

360

How Heaven Is Preparing For the Bride

December 22, 1997

St. Philomena: *Greetings from Heaven, little sister.*

Janie: Peace to you, St. Philomena.

St. Philomena: *Little sister, rejoice and see how Heaven is preparing for the birth of Our Master!*

I then saw a vision of Heaven and there was great joy. I heard the choir of angels singing praises to the Lord. These are the words I heard them singing; the angels cried out these words in adoration:

"Hosanna in the highest, Hosanna in the highest, Hosanna, Hosanna, Hosanna in the highest. Blessed is He Who comes in the name of the Lord. Oh, all ye nations, embrace your King, the joy of every human heart! Hosanna in the highest. To Him all glory be."

All of this brought much joy to my heart.

The Blessings of Christmas

December 23, 1997

St. Philomena: *Greetings from Heaven, little sister.*

Janie: Peace to you, St. Philomena.

St. Philomena: *Little sister, the time is near when people in many parts of the world will celebrate the birth of Our Master.*

Pray, little sister, pray, that the blessings of Christmas will fall upon the world. Pray that people of all nations will be open to the love and compassion of God, for He has sent His only-begotten Son to free mankind from the power of death. Pray to the Holy Spirit and to all of Heaven to intercede for the whole world during this holy season. Until tomorrow, farewell, little sister.

Janie: St. Philomena, I will pray hard for all the intentions which you gave me.

361

Conversations With St. Philomena

All Families to Receive God's Blessings

December 24, 1997

St. Philomena: *Greetings from Heaven, little sister.*

Janie: Peace to you, St. Philomena.

St. Philomena: *Little sister, today is the eve of the birth of Our Master. Again, I ask that you continue to pray for all families in the world to receive God's blessings that will come through the birth of Our Master. Pray that families will be united and experience the glory of God's love in their hearts. Until tomorrow, farewell, little sister.*

Janie: Thank you, St. Philomena.

Behold the Joy of the Angels!

December 25, 1997

St. Philomena: *Greetings from Heaven, little sister.*

Janie: Peace to you, St. Philomena.

St. Philomena: *Little sister, today Our Master will come to visit you. Rejoice and behold the joy of the angels!*

Then I saw Our Lord in great splendor, wrapped in swaddling clothes in a manger. He was so beautiful and so tiny. St. Joseph and Our Lady were at His side. There was a great multitude of angels, and I heard them singing in a different language. This is what I heard. (I will spell it to the best of my ability):

> "Adeste fideles, laeti triumphantes
> Venite, venite in Bethlehem.
> Natum videte Regem angelorum.
> Venite adoremus, venite adoremus,
> venite adoremus Dominum."

The angels sang these verses over and over. It was so beautiful to hear them sing.

God Blessed the World With Peace

December 26, 1997

St. Philomena: *Greetings from Heaven, little sister.*

Janie: Peace to you, St. Philomena.

St. Philomena: *Little sister, you and your family had a blessed Christmas, and God gave you new strength through the birth of His Son. God blessed the world with peace. Pray that the world will continue to live in His peace and His love. Until tomorrow, farewell, little sister.*

Janie: Thank you, St. Philomena.

Reflect the Spirit of the Holy Family

December 27, 1997

St. Philomena: *Greetings from Heaven, little sister.*

Janie: Peace to you, St. Philomena. St. Philomena, I am so excited about my visit with the Holy Family tomorrow. I can hardly wait!

St. Philomena: *Little sister, tomorrow is truly a special day for all who embrace the feast of the Holy Family. Little sister, God invites all His children to reflect the spirit of the Holy Family. God wants the families of the world to live as the Holy Family lived. God has demonstrated the order of the family according to Holy Scripture.*
Husbands, being the head of the household, are to love their wives as Our Master loves the Church. Husbands should love their wives as they love themselves. Wives are to submit to their hus-

363

bands.

Both the husband and wife should love and respect each other, being good and holy examples for their children. Parents must teach their children to obey them as their parents, for this is their duty as children. Parents should bring up their children with the training and holy instruction which are pleasing to God.

Little sister, pray for these intentions, so that through your prayers, families will be blessed. Remember, always call upon the intercession of the Holy Family. Until tomorrow, farewell, little sister.

Janie: Thank you, St. Philomena.

Interpretation of the Vision

December 28, 1997

St. Philomena: *Greetings from Heaven, my little sister.*

Janie: Ave, St. Philomena, my little heavenly friend!

St. Philomena: *My little sister, Our Master is pleased with your response to His request to pray for His Bride during these troubled times. The evil one was desperately trying to distract you from prayer, but with your heroic efforts you placed all your trust in Our Master, and victory was yours.*

Janie: St. Philomena, the evil one was very strong in his attacks this morning, but I prayed very hard to be delivered from his attacks. The Rosary was the weapon that I used against him, and he quickly left.

St. Philomena: *My little sister, you abandoned yourself into the hands of Our Master, His holy Mother and St. Joseph. The evil one hates the Holy Family, and he knew that he could not touch you once you began praying the Rosary.*

Janie: St. Philomena, do you know the meaning of the vision that I had?

This morning God showed me a vision while I was in prayer. I saw the year 2000. I saw the Church, and suddenly I saw a dark cloud over the Church. I said to myself, "I don't understand what this means. I thought the year 2000 would be a jubilee year with much prayer and celebration in the Church. What does this dark cloud represent?"

Then I saw vultures flying in the air but lower to the ground. Then I saw what appeared to be a huge flood. There were thousands of bodies in the flood. Then I saw the vultures eating the flesh off the bodies in the flood. This vision really frightened me, but I received no explanation.

St. Philomena: *My little sister, this is the interpretation of the vision that you saw. The dark cloud over the Bride of Our Master represents the darkness in the hearts of many of the priests and religious, their lack of faith and love for God. Although this will be a time of great rejoicing, darkness will also linger in many of the representatives within the Bride of Our Master.*

The vultures that you saw represent all the demons from the great abyss. The flood represents the sinfulness in many hearts, and the vultures eating off the flesh of the bodies represent the demons that are constantly destroying many souls through their evil temptations. These are the souls that do not believe in God.

Do not be frightened by this vision but pray more earnestly with all your heart for these poor souls and for the Bride of Our Master. Remember, that prayer and fasting deflect much of the evilness in the world. Know that God will entrust you with many more visions. Trust Him always. Until tomorrow, farewell, little sister.

The Vision Concerning the New Year

December 29, 1997

St. Philomena: *Greetings from Heaven, little sister.*

Janie: Peace to you, St. Philomena.

Conversations With St. Philomena

St. Philomena: *Little sister, continue to prepare with strong prayer, for you will suffer from physical illness as the new year begins. Much awaits the world in the coming new year.*

Little sister, behold the vision before you concerning the new year:

In a vision, I saw in our country uncontrolled fires and cities that would be affected by the smoke of these fires. I saw many people who would suffer from physical illness as a result of the smoke caused by the fires. I saw floods, heavenly rains, tornadoes causing much destruction and leaving thousands homeless. I saw earthquakes, hurricanes and temperatures that would cause very hot weather. The floods, heavy rains and tornadoes I saw in many parts of the world.

I saw a great number of teenagers killing one another or anyone who would get in their way. I saw much violence among the youth. I saw the persecution among God's people. I saw apparition sites that would be condemned and greatly persecuted, especially Medjugorje. Marian apostolates would also undergo persecution. True visionaries would be persecuted and the Church would continue to suffer, especially our Holy Father.

I understood that much awaited us in 1998, but that prayer, fasting, Holy Mass, Adoration, praying the Rosary and reading Holy Scripture are our tools for our own conversion and for the conversion of poor sinners. I understood that God's love and mercy are greater than all the corruption and sinfulness in the world.

I saw much more of which I cannot speak, but God allowed me to see this to pray and fast in reparation for all the evil in the world.

St. Philomena will come on December 30 and 31 to pray with me. She said that I would be suffering these next two days in reparation for what I saw in today's vision.

Conversations With St. Philomena

1998

Our Most Holy Mother's Heavenly Visit
January 1, 1998
Solemnity of the Mother of God

St. Philomena: *Greetings from Heaven, little sister.*

Janie: Peace to you, St. Philomena.

St. Philomena: *Little sister, you are preparing for Our Most Holy Mother's heavenly visit. I can see how joyful you are to have the Heavenly Queen come to visit you.*

Janie: St. Philomena, I am very happy. I have much to share with my Heavenly Mother, but first we are going to Holy Mass. Pray for me that my heart may be truly ready for her visit.

St. Philomena: *Little sister, the Sacrifice of Holy Mass will help to prepare your heart. Until tomorrow, farewell, little sister.*

Janie: Thank you, St. Philomena

People Will Suffer from Calamities and Pestilence
January 2, 1998

St. Philomena: *Greetings from Heaven, little sister.*

Janie: Peace to you, St. Philomena.

369

Conversations With St. Philomena

St. Philomena: *Little sister, today I wish to share with you many things and to remind you of what the Heavenly Queen has said to you concerning your suffering. These next few months you will suffer physically, and your physical suffering will be hard for you. You will undergo much physical pain, and you will feel very ill.*

Little sister, Our Master desires that you undergo this suffering most especially for His Bride, to help to prepare you for Lent and to help your country and many parts of the world where people will suffer from calamities and pestilence.

Little sister, this year will be filled with many sufferings as you have seen before in visions.

(At this point I recalled the visions which I was shown, where there would be many tornadoes that would cause much destruction, earthquakes, hurricanes, floods, heavy rains, fires and droughts that would be caused by extremely high temperatures. People would die from this heat; thousands would be left homeless and suffer sickness, and there would be millions of dollars of destruction).

St. Philomena: *Little sister, you have recalled your vision well. Until tomorrow, farewell, little sister.*

Janie: Thank you, St. Philomena.

When You Honor Mary, You Honor Her Son

January 3, 1998

St. Philomena: *Greetings from Heaven, little sister.*

Janie: Peace to you, St. Philomena. My family and I are preparing to attend Holy Mass in honor of First Saturday. Please pray for us so that we will make a good confession.

St. Philomena: *Little sister, you and your family are consoling the Heavenly Queen by honoring her request regarding First Saturdays. Know that special graces and blessings are given to all those who honor First Saturdays. Remember, little sister, that Our Heavenly Queen promises to assist at the hour of death, with graces necessary for salvation, all those who honor her request for First Saturdays. This is a devotion most pleasing to God. Remember, when you honor Mary, you honor her Son. Until tomorrow, farewell, little sister.*

Janie: Thank you, St. Philomena. You help me so much.

Many Blessings As a Family

January 4, 1998

St. Philomena: *Greetings from Heaven, little sister.*

Janie: Peace to you, St. Philomena.

St. Philomena: *Little sister, today Our Master will come to visit you and your family after you return from attending Holy Mass. You will receive many blessings as a family. Until tomorrow, farewell, little sister.*

Janie: Thank you, St. Philomena.

I Will Intercede

January 5, 1998

St. Philomena: *Greetings from Heaven, little sister.*

Janie: Peace to you, St. Philomena. St. Philomena, today is my sister's birthday. Please keep her and her son in your prayers. I love them both very much. They are the closest to me in my entire family, although we don't visit each other much. Pray for both of them. They both suffer much. They are dear to my heart. I will offer my Mass and prayers for them in a special way today.

Conversations With St. Philomena

St. Philomena: *Little sister, I will intercede for your special intentions. Until tomorrow, farewell, little sister.*

Janie: Thank you, St. Philomena.

(Today I was sick and went to the emergency room. I spent hours there. I had a terrible pain on my side. I was very ill).

Graces to Souls Who Visit My Shrine

January 6, 1998

St. Philomena: *Greetings from Heaven, little sister.*

Janie: Peace to you, St. Philomena. St. Philomena, today I ask you to intercede for me so that we will be able to visit your shrine on your feast day. Also, I ask your special intercession for the Rector, so that he may be able to accomplish all that he has planned for your shrine. I know that he loves you very much and that he and Sister X work very hard to bring devotion to you in every way they can. They are both special to me, and I pray for them every day.

St. Philomena: *Little sister, I am always interceding for the Rector and Sister X. They are both dear to me and I am truly grateful for all that they do to spread devotion to me. Let us both continue to intercede for them, and God will take care of all their needs.*
You, my little sister, will visit my shrine on my feast day. Many special heavenly blessings and graces are given to souls who visit my shrine. Until tomorrow, farewell, little sister.

Janie: Thank you, St. Philomena. Thank you for everything.

Today I continued to recover from the pain of yesterday. I am very weak. Also, there is a terrible suffering because of my grandchildren. Please God, protect them.

372

Heaven Chose You

January 7, 1998

St. Philomena: *Greetings from Heaven, little sister.*

Janie: Peace to you, St. Philomena. St. Philomena, I am trying hard to record everything that you share with me. I try to journal everything. I want to share what you tell me, but part of me wants to keep it to myself. I know that there will be those souls who do not believe that what I've written comes from you. In a way I am not concerned about it too much, but it saddens my heart.

I am happy that you visit me, but I, myself, do not desire to have heavenly visits. It's nothing personal, St. Philomena, but these heavenly visitations come with such responsibility. I do not particularly like to write because my hands are almost always hurting. St. Philomena, I am not complaining, but I want to talk about this to you. I spend so much time writing down all the information about my visitations. Then I am also busy with my little grandson, my husband, my sons, and my traveling, always seeing people. Does God really want me to write everything that I receive? I will do so gladly, but only if He wants me to.

St. Philomena: *Little sister, God knows that you have no desire to receive heavenly visitations. This is why you were chosen. You did not choose heaven; heaven chose you to be a humble recipient of these heavenly messages. These messages are to be shared. The Holy Spirit will enlighten you on what to write. God knows that you have the responsibility of your family and how devoted you are to your vocation to the family. God knows that you love the virtue of obedience and of your loyalty and hunger to do His Holy Will. Rejoice, little sister! God is pleased with you. You are to do what He wants you to do.*

Janie: Oh, St. Philomena! I am so relieved. You know it takes so long to write everything, and at times I'd rather be doing something else like watching TV or shopping. I'm just joking, St. Philomena; I just wanted to see you smile. God knows my heart.

373

Conversations With St. Philomena

St. Philomena: *Little sister, your sense of humor is a delight to God, and because of your sense of humor you bring joy to others by making them smile. Your heart is full of God's joy and your sense of humor demonstrates that.*

Little sister, I love you very much. Always trust in Our Master, and He will help you in everything. Until tomorrow, farewell, little sister.

Janie: Thank you, thank you, St. Philomena, from the bottom of my heart.

(Today our grandchildren are spending a few days with us. I am so happy. My physical pain continues. The doctors do not know what it is, but I think that I have kidney stones. I offer this terrible pain for the intentions of Our Lord in all that He is asking of me).

Your Cross Is So Redemptive

January 8, 1998

St. Philomena: *Greetings from Heaven, little sister.*

Janie: Peace to you, St. Philomena. St. Philomena, I am so sad because of the suffering that my grandchildren are enduring. Please keep them in your prayers.

St. Philomena, today I continue to suffer with this physical pain. I feel so weak, but I am praying very much. I embrace everything that God wants to send me.

St. Philomena: *Little sister, your cross is heavy and intense, but so redemptive. I am praying for you. God is pleased with the way that you embrace your suffering. Until tomorrow, farewell, little sister.*

374

Anchor of Hope from Heaven

God Will Give You the Strength
January 9, 1998

St. Philomena: *Greetings from Heaven, little sister.*

Janie: Peace to you, St. Philomena. St. Philomena, please pray for me that God will give me the strength to be strong tomorrow. It is our youngest son's birthday. I want to bake him a cake and have a special family celebration as we usually do. I'm not feeling my best today and I feel dizzy. I offer everything up to God and I embrace my suffering with joy in my heart.

St. Philomena: *Little sister, do not be concerned with your son's birthday. God will give you the strength to have a joyful day with your family. Until tomorrow, farewell, little sister.*

Janie: Thank you, St. Philomena.

A Joyful Day
January 10, 1998

St. Philomena: *Greetings from Heaven, little sister.*

Janie: Peace to you, St. Philomena. St. Philomena, I am doing better and my family does not want me to cook, so I think that we are going out to eat for our son's birthday. Praise be to God! He always takes care of His children.
    Today is also the day that my earthly mother went to heaven. Give her a hug and kiss for all of us. Tell her thanks for all her prayers and that we're doing our best to serve God.

St. Philomena: *Little sister, today will be a joyful day for you and your family. Until tomorrow, farewell, little sister.*

375

Conversations With St. Philomena

For All the Suffering Youth

January 11, 1998

St. Philomena: *Greetings from Heaven, little sister.*

Janie: Peace to you, St. Philomena. St. Philomena, I was so sick during Holy Mass, but I offered all my suffering for Our Lord's Bride, for poor, poor sinners, for peace in the world, and for all the suffering that awaits our world this year. I know that since this year is dedicated to the Holy Spirit, God will help our world through our prayers, fasting and sacrifices.

St. Philomena: *Little sister, you are suffering much, but your love for the Cross is pleasing to Our Master. Know that the Holy Spirit will enlighten your path as you suffer.*

Janie: St. Philomena, it's getting hard for me to write. Tomorrow I will see my doctor. Pray for me.

St. Philomena: *You are in my prayers, little sister. Offer your suffering for all the suffering youth. Until tomorrow, farewell, little sister.*

Janie: Thank you, St. Philomena.

Trust in Our Master

January 12, 1998

St. Philomena: *Greetings from Heaven, little sister.*

Janie: Peace to you, St. Philomena. St. Philomena, my doctor confirmed what I believed to be wrong with me. I have kidney stones and he wants me to rest and drink plenty of fluids. He gave me pain medication, but it makes me so sick when I take it. Again, I offer my pain for the intentions of the Two United Hearts.

My doctor does not want me to travel unless I am near a hospital. I am supposed to go to Glenwood, Arkansas for a few days to give a retreat. The pain is so intense I do not know what to do.

St. Philomena: *Little sister, trust in Our Master, trust in Him. I know that you are in great pain. I love you, little sister. Until tomorrow, farewell, little sister.*

An Inspired Prayer to Our Lady

O Mother of the Redeemer, come to my aid. I abandon myself to your motherly protection. I renew my consecration to your Immaculate Heart. I renounce all that is not of God and renew my baptismal vows.

O Most Holy Mother, I want so much to embrace my suffering, but my physical pain is interfering with the desires in my heart to remain obedient to my suffering. No matter how difficult it may be, all for the glory of God, I offer my pain.

Take me by your hand, my Heavenly Mother, and lead me to the Cross of your Son on Calvary. There I will find my strength. Amen.

The Rosary Is the Remedy

January 13, 1998

St. Philomena: *Greetings from Heaven, little sister.*

Janie: Peace to you, St. Philomena. St. Philomena, I have been offering many Rosaries for the intentions of the Two United Hearts. While I am in bed, during my Holy Hour and throughout my day, the Rosary is my weapon. The devil tries to distract me from prayer, but prayer is my strength and my joy.

St. Philomena: *Little sister, God is pleased that you turn to the prayer of the Rosary for strength. The Rosary is a powerful prayer. Our Heavenly Queen desires that all her children recite the Rosary, so that she can help her children draw closer to God.*
Little sister, the Rosary is a beautiful form of prayer and the

Conversations With St. Philomena

most efficacious means of attaining salvation outside of the Mass. The prayer of the Rosary is the remedy to help cleanse the evil in many hearts. It brings a multitude of blessings to those who pray the Rosary and those for whom the Rosary is being offered. Keep praying your Rosary, little sister. Until tomorrow, farewell, little sister.

Janie: Thank you, St. Philomena.

Abandonment Into His Care

January 14, 1998

St. Philomena: *Greetings from Heaven, little sister.*

Janie: Peace to you, St. Philomena. St. Philomena, today I told my spiritual director what my doctor had said about my not traveling unless I was near a hospital. My spiritual director said this would not be a problem. My physical pain so intense that I really do not want to go, but I will turn to Jesus and abandon myself to His care.

St. Philomena: *Little sister, Our Master is pleased with your abandonment into His care. You will suffer much on this trip, but many souls will be helped. Many blessings will come upon the people who you will be speaking to. Until tomorrow, farewell, little sister.*

God Will Take Care of Everything

January 15, 1998

St. Philomena: *Greetings from Heaven, little sister.*

Janie: Peace to you, St. Philomena. St. Philomena, today I am preparing for my trip to Glenwood, Arkansas. My husband does not really want me to go; he is concerned about me. Please pray for him and me so that we will both do God's Holy Will.

378

Anchor of Hope from Heaven

St. Philomena: *Little sister, God will take care of everything. Rest now, little sister and pray your Rosary for you and your husband. Until tomorrow, farewell, little sister.*

Janie: Thank you, St. Philomena.

Your Desire to Listen to Your Husband
January 16, 1998

St. Philomena: *Greetings from Heaven, little sister.*

Janie: Peace to you, St. Philomena. St. Philomena, thanks for your prayers. My husband is at peace with my going to Glenwood, Arkansas. I am so happy. I love my husband very much and I want to do what he asks of me. Thank you, St. Philomena.

St. Philomena: *Little sister, God is pleased with your desire to listen to your husband. Your family is so blessed. Until tomorrow, farewell, little sister.*

Janie: Thank you, St. Philomena.

A Travel Day
January 17, 1998

St. Philomena came to pray with me. I am traveling and my flight is leaving very early.

A Private Message
January 18, 1998
Glenwood, Arkansas

Today St. Philomena came to pray with me and my spiritual director before my talk to the people.

379

Conversations With St. Philomena

People's Hearts Will Be Healed
January 19, 1998

St. Philomena: *Greetings from Heaven, little sister.*

Janie: Peace to you, St. Philomena. St. Philomena, please pray for me. I feel so sick; my pain is intense and I feel like vomiting. I am keeping this from everyone for I know that God will help me.

St. Philomena: *Little sister, God will help many of the families who will come to hear you speak. Be strong, little sister, and know that people's hearts will be healed. Until tomorrow, farewell, little sister.*

Janie: Thank you, St. Philomena.

Continued Suffering
January 20, 1998

Today I was very sick with the pain on my side. I have hardly been able to eat. I have been vomiting and passing blood. This illness has taken place since January 17th when I traveled to Arkansas. St. Philomena told me that I would suffer so that God could help the families here to draw closer to Him. I haven't shared this with anyone because God is giving me the grace to suffer.

St. Philomena showed me a vision of all the families who are receiving healings. St. Philomena came to pray with me for these families.

Continue to Offer
January 21, 1998
Glenwood, Arkansas

St. Philomena: *Greetings from Heaven, little sister.*

Janie: Peace to you, St. Philomena.

380

St. Philomena: *Little sister, you have suffered much with your illness. Continue to offer your suffering for Our Master's request. You will be able to sleep during your flight. Until tomorrow, farewell, little sister.*

Janie: Thank you, St. Philomena.

God Blessed These Humble Souls

January 22, 1998

St. Philomena: *Greetings from Heaven, little sister.*

Janie: Peace to you, St. Philomena. St. Philomena, I am so grateful to God for giving me the grace to be able to travel to Glenwood, Arkansas. I enjoyed the people there, even if I was feeling pretty sick. I am so happy for this special blessing.
   Many of the people shared with me how much God was helping them. I am so happy. These people are such simple people, and they want to know God. Please intercede for them. As you know, I told them about you.

St. Philomena: *Little sister, I will intercede for all your requests. God, indeed, blessed these humble souls. Until tomorrow, farewell, little sister.*

Janie: Thank you, St. Philomena.

Closer to His Divine Love

January 23, 1998

St. Philomena: *Greetings from Heaven, little sister.*

Janie: Peace to you, St. Philomena. St. Philomena, please pray for me that I may be able to pass these kidney stones. I am drinking plenty of fluids, but nothing is happening. I want to be able to go to

381

Conversations With St. Philomena

Holy Mass and to accept all that God desires of me for my own purification and for poor sinners everywhere. Oh, I suffer this pain so
that sinners will come to Jesus, to His divine Heart!

As I suffer, I bring sinners to Our Lord that He may heal these
souls and have their hearts for His very own. I suffer so that people
everywhere will seek the love of Jesus and amend their evil ways.
Oh, how my own heart burns with love for Jesus! I have such hunger to please Him, by accepting all the suffering which He sends
my way.

St. Philomena, please pray for me and ask Our Lord to grant
me the gift of being able to attend Holy Mass while I suffer with
this physical pain. Sometimes I cannot drive, and there is no one
here at home to help me to Holy Mass.

St. Philomena: *Little sister, Our Master will take care of all your
needs. Know that the more you offer your suffering to Our Master,
the closer you are to His divine love. Until tomorrow, farewell, little sister.*

Janie: Thank you, St. Philomena.

Abandon Yourself to the Sacred Heart

January 24, 1998

St. Philomena: *Greetings from Heaven, little sister.*

Janie: Peace to you, St. Philomena.

St. Philomena: *Little sister, as your pain intensifies, abandon yourself to the Sacred Heart of Our Master. As you open your heart to
receive Him, He will give your heart greater comprehension of
what His heart is giving you. You will have a greater knowledge of
how your suffering is bringing many souls to Our Master.*

I then saw a vision of many souls coming to Our Lord Jesus in
their nothingness and in humility, seeking His love and mercy and

turning from their sinful ways.

St. Philomena: *Little sister, Our Master is giving you His strength and courage and your great and painful suffering for poor sinners. As you embrace your cross, He is bestowing on you much enlightenment to know that He is with you, helping you to carry your cross. Give Him everything. He loves you very much because of your obedience to suffer to save souls. This is such holy work. As you suffer for souls, it gives all of Heaven a delight beyond words. Until tomorrow, farewell, little sister.*

Janie: Thank you, St. Philomena. Pray for me, pray for me.

For All the Silent Requests

January 25, 1998

St. Philomena: *Greetings from Heaven, little sister.*

Janie: Peace to you, St. Philomena.

St. Philomena: *Little sister, know I am interceding for all the silent requests that you have in your heart. As you and your family prepare for Holy Mass, offer your Mass for all the families in the world who have turned from God. Until tomorrow, farewell, little sister.*

Janie: Thank you, St. Philomena.

The Heavens Rejoice!

January 26, 1998

St. Philomena: *Greetings from Heaven, little sister.*

Janie: Peace to you, St. Philomena. St. Philomena, today I called my doctor to make an appointment. I am not passing any kidney

383

stones. As you know, I am very sick in bed. I've been vomiting and cannot eat anything. I know that Our Lord is with me. This is my greatest joy. I am grateful for the intensity of the pain, for this is where I feel united to the Cross on Calvary. This is a beautiful suffering.

St. Philomena: *Little sister, the heavens rejoice, the heavens rejoice! Until tomorrow, farewell, little sister.*

Janie: Thank you, St. Philomena.

Strength During Illness

January 27, 1998

Today I am very sick. St. Philomena came together with the three Archangels to give me strength. Praise be to God!

No Strength

January 28, 1998

Today I am sicker than yesterday. I am in bed. I have no strength. St. Philomena came to pray with me.

All the Souls Being Saved

January 29, 1998

I am feeling worse today. My doctor has scheduled me for out-patient surgery tomorrow. He said that I have a kidney stone that is lodged. St. Philomena came to pray for me. She showed me all the souls that are being saved through my suffering.

Surgery

January 30, 1998

St. Philomena prayed with me before my surgery. St. Philomena told me that Jesus would come. He did in the Eucharist.

St. Philomena, St. John Bosco, St. Teresa, Archangels

January 31, 1998

St. Philomena, St. John Bosco, St. Teresa of Avila and the Archangels have come to visit me. I have not conversed with them, but they prayed with me.

Today I received Our Lord in the Holy Eucharist. What a joy!

For All His Intentions

February 1, 1998

Today I am still in the hospital. I have been very ill. St. Philomena has been with me, praying for me. I continue to pass much blood from the little tube that is inserted in my bladder. This had to be done to keep me from getting an infection. One of the risks of doing this is that it can cause many side effects. I have most of them, including the bleeding. I feel so weak, but again I offer everything to my Lord and Savior for all His intentions. I love you, my beloved Jesus.

Today I will go home, but I am to remain in bed.

In Your Country and In the World

February 2, 1998

St. Philomena: *Greeting from Heaven, little sister.*

385

Conversations With St. Philomena

Janie: Peace to you, St. Philomena.

St. Philomena: *Little sister, you have suffered so much with your illness, but you have been very brave through it all. Know, little sister, that more suffering awaits you. As I shared with you, many things will happen in your country and in the world. There will be terrible crimes committed by young people that will lead to the death of others, major weather problems and disasters, much suffering in the Church, much persecution of true apparition sites and a great division among many Marian apostolates. I tell you this again that you may keep all of this in mind during your suffering. Until tomorrow, farewell, little sister.*

Janie: Thank you, St. Philomena. I embrace all my suffering for my Lord and my All.

Your Will Rejoice

February 3, 1998

St. Philomena: *Greeting from Heaven, little sister.*

Janie: Peace to you, St. Philomena. St. Philomena, I am still bleeding much, but today I have an appointment so that my doctor will take this little tube out. It's causing me to bleed so much. I am also supposed to travel to New Jersey on the 5th of this month. I don't know what to do. Please help me.

St. Philomena: *Little sister, you will continue to suffer, and you will travel to New Jersey. This time will be a great time of much prayer, and Our Master has arranged with you to meet with some of His beloved ones. You will rejoice. The suffering from your illness will leave you, but your suffering will continue until you arrive at your destination. You will pray with many, and there will be physical and spiritual healing. Rejoice! Until tomorrow, farewell, little sister.*

Later today, the doctor removed the little tube. When I got home, my bladder began to spasm. I became so sick, that I called my doctor. I felt like I was dying. I was getting ready to go back to the emergency room to meet my doctor. My youngest son told me, "Mom, I am going to lay hands on you and pray over you." He said, "Tell me where you are hurting." He got some holy water (healing water) that I had brought from St. Michael del Milagros in Mexico. He laid hands on the area that was hurting and put some holy water on me in the Sign of the Cross, and then he said this prayer to God: "O God, please help my mother and take away this pain from her. She is always helping and praying for all of us and many other people that she meets. She is suffering a lot and has been so sick. She is supposed to go to give a talk in New Jersey, but she cannot if she is feeling sick. Please, dear God, help my mother. I love her a lot and she loves you a lot. Help her, dear God, help my mother." I was healed instantly from the spasm in my bladder. I rejoiced with my 17 year old son, and we danced and cried together. I know that our prayer life as parents has an effect on our children and others around us. My husband and I do the best we can to set an example for our children and grandchildren. We teach them the importance of always praying and turning to God for everything and the importance of using holy water and other sacramental tools for spiritual assistance. My little son has done well. Praise be to God forever and ever. Amen.

I was moved by the Holy Spirit to pray the following prayer for parents.

Prayer for Parents

Heavenly Father, I pray for all parents to be loving and prayerful examples for their children. Pour Your love and strength into the hearts of all parents that they may love their children unconditionally.

Father, give all parents the wisdom to know that You are with them in all the sufferings and crosses that come with being a loving parent. Help parents to trust You and to know that Heaven

Conversations With St. Philomena

is at their disposal. Parenthood can be so difficult from time to time. That is why I ask your heavenly blessings and assistance on all parents. It is difficult to love our children when they embrace the evil ways of the world. Stand by all good and lost parents, dear Father, and help us all bring our children to Your love and Your mercy. In Jesus' name I pray. Amen.

You Cannot Hide Your Suffering
February 4, 1998

St. Philomena: *Greetings from Heaven, little sister.*

Janie: Peace to you, St. Philomena. St. Philomena, I ask you to pray for me because I am wondering if people are supposed to know of my suffering. In our conversations we speak much about suffering. I know that I am a victim of love because Heaven invited me to offer myself, but I really don't want my family or people to know of my suffering.

St. Philomena: *Little sister, you cannot hide your suffering, especially from your family. At times your suffering is intense and God wants your family to help you. Other people know of your suffering because they are close friends, and other people will know that you suffer by your writings. This is all God's Holy Will. There are other chosen victim souls that suffer as you. Some are hidden and some are in the public eye. Do not be concerned with this. Prepare and get ready for your trip.*

Janie: St. Philomena, one more thing please. Will I always write everything you share with me?

St. Philomena: *Little sister, on the first day of the fifth month I will share my last public conversation with you. After this day you will not have to write anything for the public to read. I will continue my daily visitations with you. This will not stop until Our Master says otherwise. Until tomorrow, farewell, little sister.*

388

Janie: Farewell, St. Philomena.

Private Messages

February 5 - February 9, 1998
New Jersey

St. Philomena visited with me, but the messages were for all the people that I visited with. There were many conversations and physical healings during these days. My physical illness disappeared as soon as I got off the plane in New Jersey. I suffered the Passion of Our Lord in reparation for the people there.

You See the Conditions of the World

February 10, 1998

St. Philomena: *Greetings from Heaven, little sister.*

Janie: Peace to you, St. Philomena. St. Philomena, today I am feeling much pain in my soul. I know that our Holy Father suffers much and that there is much persecution among priests and religious. I can truly feel much pain in my soul. I also can see visions in my soul of the sufferings in the world. There appears to be a rumble in different parts of the world where cries of anguish fill the air.

I see in my soul where there is much fear and panic. People are destroying one another, and there is no safety in the streets in many parts of the world. I see chaos and bloodshed.

I see where food and supplies will run out, which will give way to conditions of famine.

I see in my soul where nations will be crippled by disaster after disaster, and because of these disasters the nations that are under attack with disasters will have to turn to other nations for help.

I see so much suffering in the world.

I see where the playground for many of our youth has come to reflect the spirit of Sodom and Gomorrah, where fornication, abortion, drugs, homosexuality, prostitution, violence, and unbelief in God prevails. Oh, what suffering I feel in my soul!

I see in my soul the destruction of faith in many families and in the Church.

I see millions of children who suffer from neglect by their parents, the rise of divorce and the brokenness in the family of the Church and the family.

I know that I've seen this before, St. Philomena, but today these visions are piercing my soul with pain.

St. Philomena: *Little sister, God is allowing you to see the conditions of the world. He wants you to offer all your sufferings and prayers for what He is showing you today. Remember, prayer is the remedy that will heal many unconverted hearts. Until tomorrow, farewell, little sister.*

Janie: Thank you, St. Philomena.

Pray for the Visions Yesterday
February 11, 1998

St. Philomena: *Greetings from Heaven, my little sister.*

Janie: Peace to you, St. Philomena.

St. Philomena: *Little sister, continue to pray for the visions which God allowed you to see yesterday. Little sister, much prayer and many sacrifices are needed to overcome all the evil in the world. Until tomorrow, little sister, farewell.*

Janie: St. Philomena, I will pray for all these intentions.

That Happy Event With the Heavenly Queen
February 12, 1998

St. Philomena: *Greetings from Heaven, little sister.*

Janie: Peace to you, St. Philomena. St. Philomena, pray for us, for everybody is so busy preparing for the 9th anniversary of Our Lady with us. We are all so excited. Please pray for X. and X. His X. is so ill and suffering much. They are both dear to our family.

St. Philomena: *Little sister, I will intercede for you as you prepare for that happy event with the Heavenly Queen. I will intercede for your dear friends and their loved one. Until tomorrow, farewell, little sister.*

Janie: Thank you, St. Philomena.

Banish the Excessive Fear

February 13, 1998

St. Philomena: *Greetings from Heaven, little sister.*

Janie: Peace to you, St. Philomena. St. Philomena, I am still troubled with the visions in my soul of February 10. I know that there is so much suffering in the world. This makes me sad.

St. Philomena: *Little sister, many souls suffer because they have no relationship with God, their heavenly Father. Many souls do not believe in prayer. Without prayer souls do not know God, for God is prayer.*
Little sister, God is so loving, and He wants to banish the excessive fear which souls have of Him. He wants His children to know that His joy lies in His children. He is where all hope, all love and all safety lies for His children. He wants to bring hope to every nation in the world. For those who hope in God, peace and security is theirs.
Little sister, God has one concern: to watch over all His children and to love them. He wants His children to trust Him and to turn to Him with all their needs. Many souls have become so materialistic, and they never turn to God, so they suffer much.
Little sister, God wants to be with His children. He wants the salvation of all His children, not their condemnation. It is souls

391

Conversations With St. Philomena

who turn away from God's love and mercy; He never turns away from His children. Many souls choose the evil ways of the world instead of a relationship with God. No matter how evil souls may be, God loves them all with unconditional love. Until tomorrow farewell, little sister.

Janie: Thank you, St. Philomena.

A Blessed Time

February 14, 1998

St. Philomena: *Greetings from Heaven, little sister.*

Janie: Peace to you, St. Philomena. St. Philomena, we are very busy with the celebration tomorrow. I have friends coming over and I will spend the night at X's house. I am so excited with all our special friends in Christ that come to help us celebrate.

St. Philomena: *Little sister, you will have a blessed time with all your friends. Until tomorrow, farewell, little sister.*

Janie: Peace to you, St. Philomena.

Private Prayer

February 15, 1998

St. Philomena came to pray with me this morning.

Private Message

February 16, 1998

St. Philomena came to all of us (i.e., our friends). There was a private message.

Graces From Their Heavenly Queen

February 17, 1998

St. Philomena: *Greetings from Heaven, little sister.*

Janie: Peace to you, St. Philomena. St. Philomena, I am still so excited about my visit with Our Lady. It was such a joy!

St. Philomena: *Little sister, many received a multitude of heavenly blessings and graces from their Heavenly Queen. She touched many hearts. Until tomorrow, farewell, little sister.*

Janie: Thank you, St. Philomena.

They Will Pierce Your Heart With Sorrow

February 18, 1998

St. Philomena: *Greetings from Heaven, little sister.*

Janie: Peace to you, St. Philomena.

St. Philomena: *Little sister, prepare with strong prayer, for in the remainder of this month and throughout the next two months, you will endure yet another physical suffering. Our Master is asking your continual "yes" to suffer for His Bride and for many things that are yet to happen in your country and throughout the world. You will understand more about the importance of Our Master's request for you to offer yourself as a victim of love when these things take place.*

These next few months will be hard for you. Keep in mind what Our Holy Queen said to you about your suffering: that it would also be manifested in a physical way. Little sister, pray much so that you will remain united to Our Master's love. Know that your prayers will help you to endure your own suffering.

Little sister, you will undergo many hard trials. You will be rejected and be persecuted by people very close to you, those with

393

Conversations With St. Philomena

whom you have a close relationship. Their attacks on you will be brutal, and they will pierce your heart with sorrow. Your suffering will reflect Our Master's suffering and persecution. He, too, was rejected by His family and close friends. He was called a drunk, a crazy lunatic. They said that He was possessed by Satan. Much will be said of you as well, and some will come from your own relatives as well as close friends.

Janie: St. Philomena, it's a little scary to know that my close friends would do this kind of thing. Who can I trust? I share so many things with my close friends.

St. Philomena: *Little sister, continue to ask God to enlighten your heart and soul through the power of the Holy Spirit. Put all your trust in God, and when these sufferings come to pass, rely on God and the guidance of your spiritual director. He will help you during these times. Are you willing to accept yet more physical suffering? This suffering will be manifested in terms of physical illness.*

Janie: St. Philomena, I am ready to accept anything which God wishes to send me. I know that I have my sure refuge in His love and mercy. I offer myself into His most Holy Will. I am totally His to do with as He wills. He has complete charge over my life.

St. Philomena: *Little sister, for the next few days I will come only to pray for you as you will be suffering. Until then, farewell, little sister.*

Janie: Thank you, St. Philomena.

Severe Physical Suffering

February 19 - February 22, 1998

No message was given since I was suffering from a physical illness. St. Philomena came to pray for me from February 19th through February 21st. On the evening of the 18th, I was sick with a severe pain on my side. This pain was intense and came quickly. After three hours of suffering, my husband rushed me to the emergency room.

I was very ill and had uncontrolled vomiting. The medications which I was given could not control my vomiting. I couldn't have anything for pain because the doctors did not know what I had. I was given a number of tests including a Cat scan, but the doctors couldn't find anything.

After six hours of continuous suffering, the hospital called a stomach specialist. He came and immediately informed the staff of what I had. I was suffering from acute appendicitis. The specialist said that I had to have immediate surgery. He told my husband and me that I was lucky that he was called in time; otherwise my appendix would have ruptured and I could have died. I was hospitalized for three days. During my stay at the hospital Our Lord and the three Archangels came to visit me.

Today my husband and I are scheduled to fly to Palm Springs, California to visit our close friends and to give private talks. I am feeling very sick, but my doctor said I could go if I felt like it, but to get plenty of rest. I feel safe because my husband will be with me.

Private Visit

February 23, 1998
Palm Springs, California

St. Philomena came to me today, but our visit pertained to me and our close friends.

Your Suffering Is Helping Many Souls

February 24, 1998
Palm Springs

St. Philomena: *Greetings from Heaven, little sister.*

Conversations With St. Philomena

Janie: Peace to you, St. Philomena.

St. Philomena: *Little sister, you have suffered much as you continue to recover from your surgery. Rest, little sister. Know that your suffering is helping many souls. Until tomorrow, farewell, little sister.*

Janie: Thank you, St. Philomena.

Our Master Will Come to Visit

February 25, 1998
Palm Springs

St. Philomena: *Greetings from Heaven, little sister.*

Janie: Peace to you, St. Philomena.

St. Philomena: *Little sister, today as you continue to suffer, Our Master will come to visit you. Prepare for His coming. Until tomorrow, farewell, little sister.*

Janie: Thank you, St. Philomena.

Private Visit

February 26, 1998
Palm Springs

St. Philomena came to pray with me for people to prepare for the season of Lent. I am still feeling sick.

The Blessing of Friendship

February 27, 1998
Palm Springs

Today St. Philomena came very early with Our Lord. We

prayed together for all the unbelievers. Today my husband and I fly home. I pray that God continues to bless our dear friends, X and X. I love them so much, and they are so good to us. Their friendship is a treasure to us. I will miss them dearly. They took such good care of us. Thank you, Lord, for putting X and X in our path. Their friendship is truly a gift of love.

Weak From Surgery
February 28, 1998

Today St. Philomena came to pray with me and for me. I am still weak from my surgery. I cannot drive, so I rely on the assistance of my family to take me to Holy Mass.

Heal the Woundedness: In the Hearts of All Unbelievers
March 1, 1998

St. Philomena: *Greetings from Heaven, little sister.*

Janie: Peace to you, St. Philomena.

St. Philomena: *Little sister, today let us pray for all the unbelievers in your country. Let us ask God to hear our prayers and to heal the woundedness in the hearts of all unbelievers. God wants to help His children, but he cannot if His children do not ask Him to help them. Sometimes it is difficult for these souls to turn to God, for they have no one to pray for them. Our prayers will help them. Let us bring to Our Master all those souls who do not believe in Him, especially in your country. Remember, little sister, it is through the unbelievers that Satan destroys many innocent souls. Pray for all the unbelievers in the world. Until tomorrow, farewell, little sister.*

Janie: Farewell, St. Philomena. I will offer my prayers for all the unbelievers in the world, beginning with my own relatives who have abandoned their faith.

397

Conversations With St. Philomena

Priests and Religious Who Have Given Up

March 2, 1998

St. Philomena: *Greetings from Heaven, little sister.*

Janie: Peace to you, St. Philomena.

St. Philomena: *Little sister, today you are suffering for the Bride of Our Master and it is a most intense suffering for you. Be reassured that your suffering and sacrifices will transform the hearts of many priests and religious who have wandered from the true path which leads to Heaven.*
You have suffered, little sister, with joy in your heart. Allow Our Master to use your suffering to bring back those priests and religious who show no respect for the Most Holy Eucharist, for the priests and religious who have given up the holy sacrament of confession, for the priests and religious who do not possess the courage to stand strong and to profess their faith. Pray and suffer, little sister. The Bride of Our Master is in much need of prayer. Until tomorrow, farewell, little sister.

Trust in His Strength

March 3, 1998

St. Philomena: *Greetings from Heaven, little sister.*

Janie: Peace to you, St. Philomena. St. Philomena, today I need your prayers to help me to prepare for my trip to San Antonio, Texas. I am still recovering from my surgery, and I am feeling weak.

St. Philomena: *Little sister, know that God is taking care of all your needs. Trust in His strength. During this holy season of Lent your suffering will continue to increase. God will give you the grace to help you to suffer in reparation for poor sinners. Until tomorrow, farewell, little sister.*

Janie: Thank you, St. Philomena.

398

These Families Are Heavenly Treasures

March 4, 1998

St. Philoména: *Greetings from Heaven, little sister.*

Janie: Peace to you, St. Philomena.

St. Philomena: *Little sister, join me in praying for all the families who are dedicated to praying together. These families are heavenly treasures whose prayers help to convert other families who do not believe in God. Until tomorrow, farewell, little sister.*

Janie: Farewell, St. Philomena.

In a vision I saw many families praying the Rosary and there was a multitude of angels around them. Family prayer is a strong force for the conversion of the world and for bringing about family unity.

Embrace the Sacrament of Reconciliation

March 5, 1998

St. Philomena: *Greetings from Heaven, little sister.*

Janie: Peace to you, St. Philomena.

St. Philomena: *Little sister, offer your prayers today so that more people will believe in the Sacrament of Reconciliation. Many have abandoned this sacrament because they do not understand its power for renewal of the soul. So many experience misery because sin has brought darkness in their souls. Pray that they will repent and embrace the sacrament of Reconciliation. Until tomorrow, farewell, little sister.*

Janie: Farewell to you, St. Philomena.

Conversations With St. Philomena

God Has Stooped Down to You

March 6, 1998

St. Philomena: *Greetings from Heaven, little sister.*

Janie: Peace to you, St. Philomena.

St. Philomena: *Little sister, you have endured much suffering these past months for love of Our Master's Bride and for love of all families. You are concerned about the unborn and the immense suffering of the holy souls in Purgatory. You spend much time offering your prayers and sacrifices to God for your own soul and the evil in the world.*
    Little sister, you are doing well on your spiritual journey. You suffer in reparation for poor sinners and you wage spiritual warfare to save souls. Little sister, your simplicity is pleasing to God. God has stooped down to you, the poorest of His creatures, to talk to you and through you to all families in the world.
    Little sister, God speaks to you and through you to the family using simple words. He wishes that His children return back to simplicity and embrace purity in their lives. God loves all humanity and He wants to bless all His children. You, little sister, in your littleness understand this about God. This is why you pray and suffer so much for souls. Until tomorrow, farewell, little sister.

Janie: Thank you, St. Philomena.

A Fountain of Living Water Which Never Dries Up

March 7, 1998

St. Philomena: *Greetings from Heaven, little sister.*

Janie: Peace to you, St. Philomena. St. Philomena, today I ask that you tell me about God's love for humanity. Yesterday's conversation was so full of joy and hope for the work that I do to win souls for God.

400

St. Philomena: *Little sister, the love of the Father for humanity is like a fountain of living water which never dries up. To all who turn to Him, He pours His infinite and merciful love into their hearts. His heart is full of love and this loving heart is open to all. No one is turned away.*

In His heart lies that eternal love that calls out to humanity to return to the One Who loves them with immense love. His love is that spring where all can come to quench their thirst. From His heart comes immense love and this love is the remedy that humanity needs to amend their evil ways. Little sister, pray for all of humanity so that through your prayers and the prayers of all the faithful, unconverted souls will convert. Until tomorrow, farewell, little sister.

Janie: Farewell, St. Philomena.

Special Family Intentions

March 8, 1998

St. Philomena: *Greetings from Heaven, little sister.*

Janie: Peace to you, St. Philomena. St. Philomena, please pray for my family for our special intentions. We are preparing to go to Mass.

St. Philomena: *Little sister, I will intercede for your special family intentions. Until tomorrow, farewell, little sister.*

Janie: Thank you, St. Philomena.

Grateful for All Your Hard Efforts

March 9, 1998

St. Philomena: *Greetings from Heaven, little sister.*

401

Conversations With St. Philomena

Janie: Peace to you, St. Philomena. St. Philomena, today I am preparing for the meeting of the Confraternity tomorrow, so keep us in your prayers.

St. Philomena: *Little sister, I am so grateful for all your efforts to promote devotion to me. You have prayed and worked very hard for the Confraternity to come into being. You discerned well and you remained steadfast while you were contemplating the format of the Confraternity. Know that it was I, St. Philomena, who prayed for you to bring about this Confraternity. I will always be with you, little sister, as you continue to work for my cause.*

Always remember to keep Father Braschi in your prayers. Always remain under the guidance of my sanctuary in Mugnano. This is very important. Work very closely with him and God will bless all the work that you do to spread devotion to me. Until tomorrow, farewell, little sister.

Janie: Thank you, St. Philomena. I will do all that you ask of me. I love and respect Fr. X very much. I know that he dedicates his life to promoting devotion to you and protecting your name.

I Am Always Near

March 10, 1998

St. Philomena: *Greetings from Heaven, little sister.*

Janie: Peace to you, St. Philomena. Dear St. Philomena, thank you so much for your intercession. The meeting of the Confraternity went well. All your devotees are so happy to come together and learn about your spirituality and your life. It is truly a learning experience for all of us. We are all trying to be as courageous in our faith as you were. We are all praying for ourselves and our loved ones to embrace the virtue of purity. We are teaching our children the virtues of purity and chastity. For all this we are grateful to you.

402

St. Philomena: *Little sister, I am always near to those souls who have devotion to me and who call upon my help. I, St. Philomena, salute you, little sister, in all that you are doing for me. Until tomorrow, farewell, little sister.*

Janie: Thank you, St. Philomena.

A Time of Immense Grace

March 11, 1998

St. Philomena: *Greetings from Heaven, little sister.*

Janie: Peace to you, St. Philomena. St. Philomena, today I ask for your intercession so that I may continue to endure my daily suffering with peace in my heart. I try not to complain, so please help me through your prayers.

St. Philomena: *Little sister, do not be unhappy. You are not complaining, but your cross is intense. Remember the reading of Holy Scripture, "To those whom God has given more, more is expected of them." Little sister, Heaven has chosen you, a poor humble soul, to cultivate the hearts of poor sinners through your own suffering. Remember that your suffering helps other souls to repent.*
Little sister, your suffering is helping many souls to prepare for the time when God the Father will pour His mercy into the hearts of all His children. This will be a time of immense grace. Hearts will be purified and redeemed as never before.
The suffering in the world will continue to intensify as much calamity and pestilence will engulf many parts of the world. There will be much division between countries, and countries will retaliate by using their weapons to destroy one another. Many people will be wounded and others killed.
Little sister, know that the coming year is a year of great preparation for souls to embrace the third millennium with joy in their hearts. (I had a vision at this time that 1999 would be a year of great preparation for the world. I did not understand too much of

this, only that it was a time of great preparation.)
Little sister, continue to embrace all that God sends you to help souls to draw closer to God. Until tomorrow, farewell, little sister.

Janie: Thank you, St. Philomena. I will pray more and more every day.

Remain Prayerful and Faithful
March 12, 1998

St. Philomena: *Greetings from Heaven, little sister.*

Janie: Peace to you, St. Philomena. St. Philomena, please pray that I may have God's holy wisdom. Many people talk to me about the things to come, the great chastisement, the purification, the great enlightenment of souls. Many people are fearful, some worried and fearful for their unconverted loved ones. I encourage them to pray everyday and to trust God in the present moment. I tell them to remain focused on today and to offer their prayers and sacrifices for poor sinners. I don't know what else to tell them.

St. Philomena: *Little sister, your guidance comes to you from the Holy Spirit. God's children are to remain prayerful, trusting in the love and mercy of God for themselves and for their loved ones. Prayer is what the world has forgotten, therefore evil has settled in many hearts. When souls begin to pray again, hearts will begin to change. Continue to encourage souls to pray for world peace and remind souls how much God loves all His children. God's love is greater than any other force in the world. Encourage souls to remain prayerful and faithful to God at all times, and their fears and worries will vanish from their hearts. Encourage souls to read Holy Scripture, especially Matthew 6:25-34. Until tomorrow, farewell, little sister.*

Janie: Thank you, St. Philomena.

Strengthened by the Holy Spirit

March 13, 1998

St. Philomena: *Greetings from Heaven, little sister.*

Janie: Peace to you, St. Philomena. St. Philomena, pray for me today. I will be going to San Antonio, Texas for the weekend. Pray for all the people that I will be witnessing to. I am not feeling too well because of my suffering. Pray that I will be strong throughout this weekend.

St. Philomena: *Little sister, do not worry. You will be strengthened by the Holy Spirit and God will touch many hearts. Offer your suffering for the intentions of Our Master and His Most Holy Mother. Until tomorrow, farewell, little sister.*

Janie: Thank you, St. Philomena, especially for helping me to fast for this weekend.

Special Intentions

March 14, 1998
San Antonio, Texas

St. Philomena came to me this morning. We prayed for the special intentions of the people that I would be speaking to.

Attack of Satan

March 15, 1998
San Antonio

St. Philomena came to me this morning to pray and to give thanks to God for all the people who were touched by my testimony.

After my retreat and talk in San Antonio, we drove back to Austin, Texas. During the retreat there were many conversions and healings. We prayed all the way home. When we arrived at my

Conversations With St. Philomena

house, I got out of the car and I felt a strong force behind me that pushed me as I was getting out. I was about to land on my head but my angel helped me and I only injured my hand.

St. Philomena and my guardian angel told me that Satan was so angry with me for helping to bring so many people back to God that he wanted to hurt me by causing an injury to my head, but through the intervention of my guardian angel Satan did not succeed.

Because of the injury to my right hand, I can write very little. I will see the doctor on March 17. I will write as much as I can.

For All Families of the World

March 16, 1998

Today St. Philomena and I prayed for all families throughout the world.

Prayer Can Reduce Disasters

March 17, 1998

Today St. Philomena showed me in a vision how many disasters our world will experience as calamities and pestilence. Prayer, according to St. Philomena, can reduce many of the disasters. We prayed together for a good while.

Hand Injury

March 18 - April 19, 1998

Yesterday, I had my hand x-rayed and then saw a specialist. The specialist said that my hand was broken in the center of my palm up to my wrist. He said it is a very tender area. He put me on restrictions and he said that I must follow these restrictions if I wanted my hand to heal. I told him that I do much writing. He said I was to do no writing at least for six weeks, until I see him again. I asked God for the grace to write whatever I am supposed to write. My hand will be in a small cast.

St. Philomena came to pray with me for all the sick people in the world. St. Philomena encouraged me to follow my doctor's advice so I will not be writing until April, after I see my doctor. I will then give a summary of my visitations with St. Philomena. I will offer this time for myself, my family and all families, the holy souls, the Church and the unborn. I know that is by the grace of God that I can write and endure the pain in my hand.

Visions of the Schism

April 20 - 26, 1998

I saw my doctor on the 17th. He said I haven't healed completely, so I have to continue the restrictions that he asked me to follow. I have suffered much during this time, especially during Holy Week, but St. Philomena has been so kind and loving with me.

Our Lord asked me to pray and fast from Wednesday and Holy Thursday to Good Friday in reparation for His Bride and poor sinners. Our Lord came during these three days. St. Philomena and the three Archangels were with Our Lord.

During this time, I have been shown visions of the turmoil in the world. I have seen the persecution in the Church whereby many priests and religious will abandon their vocations. Many priests and religious will fall into temptation and cause many to suffer. (The suffering will be among the other priests and religious who are being obedient to our Holy Father). I saw how the schism will divide many in the Church; the spirit of apostasy will be ever so strong. I have been asked by St. Philomena to offer all my suffering and sacrifices for the visions which God allows me to see.

I find it so hard to write about the persecution in the Church because I know that many who read this will not believe, especially if they are priests or religious. Some will believe. I write out of obedience to God, for my responsibility and my duty is to God first. I am also aware that there will be those who will not believe that St. Philomena is coming to share parts of her life with me, but I must write about all that St. Philomena has shared with me.

These past weeks have been very intense in suffering, but I have been able to endure everything because St. Philomena has helped me in my suffering. That is why God sent her to me, to give me courage during suffering and to encourage me to remain faithful to God during my suffering. I love St. Philomena so much, so much. I am grateful to God for St. Philomena.

Live in Spiritual Poverty

April 27, 1998

St. Philomena: *Greetings from Heaven, little sister.*

Janie: Peace to you, St. Philomena.

St. Philomena: *Little sister, you have suffered much during these few weeks. During Holy Week your suffering was intense as you prepared to undergo the Passion of Our good Master. You did not complain, but remained true to the divine union that God has called you to. God Himself chose a few souls to be with you as you suffered in the Passion on Good Friday, including a priest. These chosen souls were able to pray for you as you underwent the Passion. Your suffering has continued and you have remained faithful to God.*

Little sister, in a few days I will give you our last conversation for you to write and share with God's children. I will continue to visit you daily, but you will not have to write our conversations. You have done well in writing all that's required of you, even though your hands hurt most of the time. You give so much of yourself, little sister, and God is pleased with your attitude of service to others in spite of your intense sufferings.

Little sister, continue to abandon yourself totally to Our Master. Remain simple and little in the eyes of God, pleasing Him by your good and simple life. Remain a little child, trusting God in everything as a small child trusts her parents.

Little sister, live in spiritual poverty, looking to God for every-

thing. Live in His love without worrying about anything, and your heart will be filled with His joy. Until tomorrow, farewell, little sister.

Janie: Thank you, St. Philomena.

All Who Take Care of My Shrine

April 28, 1998

St. Philomena: *Greetings from Heaven, little sister.*

Janie: Peace to you, St. Philomena. St. Philomena, I am glad that I can write without too much pain. I don't like taking my pain medication because it puts me to sleep. St. Philomena, I am getting excited about our pilgrimage to your shrine in August. We will be there for your feast day. Tell me will we have a good time there? I cannot wait.

St. Philomena: *Little sister, you and those who join you on this pilgrimage will receive many blessings and graces. There will be many crosses as well, but the crosses will help to prepare you and make your faith stronger. Fr. X will be very happy to see you, and you will spend much time with him.*
Little sister, always remember to pray for him. He takes such good care of my shrine and is most kind and generous to all who visit there. He has dedicated his life to God and lives to serve God totally, and part of that service is to spread devotion to me and to protect my name. He is very dear to me, and I intercede for him and all who take care of my shrine.
Little sister, many special things will happen when you visit my shrine. You will feel closer to Fr. X, and he will have a special place in your heart, as he has in mine. Until tomorrow, farewell, little sister.

Janie: Farewell to you, St. Philomena. I love you.

409

Conversations With St. Philomena

This Journey of Dying to Self

April 29, 1998

St. Philomena: *Greetings from Heaven, little sister.*

Janie: Peace to you, St. Philomena. St. Philomena, today I can write again without too much pain. What can I do for you today, my little Philomena? You have helped me so much during this time that you have been visiting me.

St. Philomena: *Little sister, you have done much for me as you spread devotion to me. You have helped many souls to have devotion to me. I am known in many parts of the world, but your love and devotion to me has made me more known. I am deeply grateful, for through my intercession I am able to lead many souls to Jesus and Mary. This brings much joy to my heart. Little sister, you have done much for me. What may I do for you?*

Janie: St. Philomena, help me to die to myself, so I can be united totally to the hearts of Jesus and Mary and to the love of St. Joseph. Help me to always console Jesus and Mary by doing the Holy Will of the Father. Help me to remain little and poor and humble, for I realize that such a spirit of poverty and humility will always make me lean on Jesus, rather than on myself. Help me to totally depend on Jesus for everything. My soul so hungers for perfection. This is why I must die to myself completely, so that Jesus may truly be my Master, Teacher, my All. Help me, please help me, St. Philomena to die to myself, so that I may experience the fullness of God's love in my life.

St. Philomena: *Little sister, know that God has heard your cry. He will help you to draw closer to Him, but this drawing closer to Him will cause you much suffering. Your purging will be intense, and you will be plunged into the furnace of His divine love.*
In this journey of dying to self, He will give you self-knowledge that will trouble your heart, for you will not think that it's possible to experience such joy and hunger for God's love. At other times

410

you will experience darkness, when you do not understand what is happening to you, and this time of darkness will be most painful. Remain steadfast and pray for courage to suffer all this. Little sister, I tell you this now so that you will remember all this when it takes place. I will be praying for you during these periods.

Little sister, heaven chose you before you were born. You have suffered all your life. God has given you many gifts at a very young age. You knew and understood things that others did not. You began having what the world refers to as "interior locutions" as a small child. You heard God's voice in your soul, but you did not understand this. Your own mother and family did not understand why you seemed so different from your brothers and sister. They persecuted you and abused you. Little sister, the devil also tried to scare you as a child. You could see him and knew when he was around.

Little sister, I share all this with you now to confirm that your experiences with Heaven began at a very young age. Do you remember this? Little sister, I share this with you, for one day you will write the story of your life. Remember that as a child of six years, you told your mother often that one day you would write a book about your life? This will happen, and God will send you the Holy Spirit to enlighten you and help you to see yourself as a child. You will remember everything with the help of the Holy Spirit.

Janie: St. Philomena, I do remember everything which you are telling me. I have been told by a bishop, who spoke to me about parts of my life, that I should write about my life because it would shed light on my present heavenly experiences. The only worry I have is that it's so hard for me to write at times, because of the pain in my hands. How will I write all this? I do trust God, but in my humanness I question this.

St. Philomena: *Little sister, God will make everything happen according to His Divine Will. Now my little sister, you have listened and have written everything. Rest now. Until tomorrow, farewell, little sister.*

Conversations With St. Philomena

Janie: Thank you so much St. Philomena. I will ponder everything we shared tonight. I love you.

St. Philomena: *I love you, little sister. Good night.*

Janie: Good night, St. Philomena.

Feel Joy in Your Heart For Your Master

April 30, 1998

St. Philomena: *Greetings from Heaven, little sister.*

Janie: Peace to you, St. Philomena.

St. Philomena: *Little sister, today you will have the visit of the three Archangels. You will receive many special graces as you visit with the Archangels.*

Janie: Little Philomena, I am very excited and I am still thinking of all that you shared with me last night. It was wonderful and a little scary, but my trust is in my Jesus.

St. Philomena: *Little sister, you will always have the love and guidance of Our Master and His Most Holy Mother as long as you trust in their intercession.*

Janie: St. Philomena, I will always trust my Jesus, even in the darkest moments that await me. My Jesus is everything to me. I am so in love with Him. He lives for me and I for Him. He died for me and I will die to myself for Him. I carry my Jesus in my heart and there He remains hidden. My Jesus commands me, telling me everything that I must do.

St. Philomena, I feel such love in my heart for Jesus and I will share this love with all who hear me. All I need is the love of my Jesus in my life, this divine love that does not need to use words to

412

communicate. His Spirit lives in me and that is all I need. I love Jesus.

St. Philomena: *Little sister, the Holy Spirit is truly showering you with many special graces. This is why you feel joy in your heart for Our Master. Little sister, you will have a very joyful day. Until tomorrow, farewell, little sister.*

The Last Public Conversation

May 1, 1998
The Feast Day of St. Joseph the Worker

St. Philomena came with St. Joseph.

St. Philomena: *Greetings from Heaven, little sister.*

Janie: Peace to you, St. Philomena.

St. Philomena: *Little sister, today you shall write the last public conversation.*

Janie: Yes, St. Philomena! But will I be able to share some of our conversations as you continue to come to me?

St. Philomena: *Little sister, you may share as the Holy Spirit guides you.*

Janie: St. Philomena, today I recommend to you the prayer group, their families and all who have devotion to you. Please always keep us in your prayers.

St. Philomena: *Little sister, I will intercede for each member of this prayer group, their families and all who have devotion to me. Little sister, I have shared many things with you and now you are ready to make these conversations public. You will be persecuted, and you will suffer for those who will refuse to believe in these conversa-*

413

tions. Remain strong through all this. I, St. Philomena, will be with you.

Always encourage families to pray together and to teach their children about purity and holiness. Remember that a pure heart has no desire to sin. Encourage families to trust God and to turn to Him in all their needs.

Remember, little sister, what I have shared with you about the pestilence and calamities. Ask families to protect themselves through their prayers. Remember that prayer is the remedy for the conversion of poor sinners. Never forget that God's love and mercy are greater than any pestilence, calamities, wars, or anything that exists in sinful hearts. Always abandon yourself to the love and mercy of God. Always! Remember to pray for Fr. X and my sanctuary in Mugnano, Italy. Pray for this intention, always.

Janie: St. Philomena, I will share everything you told me. Tell me what title should I give your book?

St. Philomena: *Little sister, I will honor any title you choose. I am grateful to all for their devotion to me. Until tomorrow, farewell, little sister.*

Janie: Thank you, St. Philomena for all these conversations. God's blessings upon all those who will read these conversations. I love you, St. Philomena.

St. Philomena: *I love you, Janie, my little sister. Thank you for writing everything which I have shared with you. Thank you. God's blessings upon you, your family and all of God's children. Blessings to all.*

[Note: Janie has continued receiving daily visits from St. Philomena and the Three Archangels, St. Michael, St. Gabriel, and St. Raphael, but with messages of a personal nature, accompanied by special intentions that the Holy and United Hearts of Jesus and Mary desire Janie to pray and suffer for.]

Conversations With St. Philomena

Appendix

The Cord of St. Philomena

The cord is made of wool, linen, or cotton. It is red and white in color with two knots at one end of the cord. The red and white colors, as well as the two knots, honor St. Philomena's double crown of virginity and martyrdom. The cord is tied around the body as a girdle. Although no ceremony is necessary for conferring or wearing the cord, a priestly blessing should be imparted upon it. The Roman Ritual does contain a blessing for the cord. The following prayer is recommended when first wearing the cord:

O St. Philomena, who has endured death for the sake of Jesus Christ, graciously obtain for me patience in this illness, and if it is the will of God, grant that on putting on this Cord, blessed in your honor, I may recover health of body, in order to labor with greater fervor for the sanctification of my soul. Amen.

Through the wearing of the cord the faithful venerate St. Philomena and seek to obtain perfect chastity of heart, body, and soul. Additionally, the devotee is encouraged to pray daily the following prayer:

O St. Philomena, Virgin and Martyr, pray for us that, through your powerful intercession, we may obtain that purity of mind and heart which leads to the perfect love of God.

The Sacred Congregation of Rites has granted a full plenary indulgence on the following days to those who wear the cord: 1)

417

Conversations With St. Philomena

The day that the cord is first worn, 2) May 25, the anniversary that St. Philomena's body was discovered in catacomb of St. Priscilla, 3) August 11, the Feast of St. Philomena, 4) December 15, the anniversary of the approval of the cord, and 5) most remarkably, at the moment of death.

The Oil of St. Philomena

Tremendous intercessory miracles have been associated with the oil from the Tomb of St. Philomena, including restored sight, hearing, speech, physical mobility, and mental health. The oil is perpetually burned before the tomb of St. Philomena at her shrine in Mugnano, Italy. It is dispensed throughout the world and can be obtained from the Mugnano Shrine or other authorized St. Philomena Centers.

The Chaplet of St. Philomena

Authored by the *Cure of Ars*, St. John Vianney, the Chaplet is another form of devotion to St. Philomena. The Chaplet is prayed by reciting the Apostle's Creed, three Our Fathers in praise of the Holy Trinity, 13 Hail Marys honoring St. Philomena's 13 years on earth, and concludes with the invocation, "O St. Philomena, Virgin and Martyr, pray for us."

Novena to St. Philomena

A novena, or nine consecutive days of prayer, is another popular devotion to St. Philomena. Traditionally, the Creed and the *Glory Be* are recited three times in honor of the Most Holy Trinity prior to the novena prayer. The following prayer is one of many approved versions:

Oh faithful Virgin and glorious Martyr, St. Philomena, who

works so many miracles on behalf of the poor and sorrowing, have pity on me. Thou knowest the multitude and diversity of my needs. Behold me at thy feet, full of misery, but full of hope. I entreat thy charity, O great Saint! Graciously hear me and obtain from God a favorable answer to the request which I now humbly lay before thee. (Here mention your specific intention). I am firmly convinced that through thy merits, through the scorn, the sufferings and the death thou didst endure, united to the merits of the Passion and Death of Jesus, thy Spouse, I shall obtain what I ask thee, and in the joy of my heart I will bless God, who is admirable in His Saints. Amen."

Novena Prayer To Saint Philomena

O faithful virgin and glorious martyr, St Philomena, who works so many miracles on behalf of the poor and sorrowful, have pity on me. Thou knowest the multitude and diversity of my needs. Behold me at thy feet, full of misery, but full of hope. I entreat thy charity o great Saint. Graciously hear me and obtain from God a favourable answer to the request which I now humbly lay before you *(here specify your petition)*. I am firmly convinced that through thy merits, through the scorn, the sufferings and the death thou didst endure, united to the merits of the Passion and Death of Jesus thy Spouse, I shall obtain what I ask of thee and in the joy of my heart I will bless God, who is admirable in His saints. *Amen*

The Great Devotees

Leo XII. Declared Saint Philomena, The Great Thaumaturgist of the 18th century.
Gregory XVI. Named her Patroness of the Living Rosary and conceded to her the Universal cult.
Pius IX. Miraculously cured by the Saint. When he became Pope, he made a pilgrimage to her sanctuary on November 7, 1849.
Leo XIII. While Cardinal, made two pilgrimages to the Sanctuary.

He sent a very beautiful Cross to the rector of the Sanctuary.

St. Pius X. Elevated the Pious Archconfraternity of Saint Philomena on May 21, 1912, into a Universal Pious Archconfraternity. He loved to hear talk of her and sent various gifts to her Sanctuary. Among these gifts is a magnificent gold ring carrying a large precious stone.

The Servant of God, Sister Maria Luisa of Jesus. A fervent devotee of the Saint, she founded in Naples the religious order of the Sisters of Our Lady of Sorrows and Saint Philomena.

The Holy Curé of Ars. A great devotee of Saint Philomena, he diffused devotion to her throughout France.

Yen. Pauline Jaricot. Foundress of the Living Rosary and Propagation of the Faith, she was miraculously cured by Saint Philomena on August 10, 1835, and put her forward as the Supporter of Missionary Priests.

Blessed Bartholomew Longo. A devotee of the Little Saint, he placed under her patronage, Opere Pompeane.

St. Peter Juilian Eymard.

St. Peter Chanel.

St. Anthony Mary Claret.

St. Madeleine Sophie Barat.

St. Euphrasia Pelletier.

St Francis Xavier Cabrini.

St John Nepomucene Neumann.

Blessed Anna Maria Taigi.

INDEX: by Topic and Message Date

Conversations With St. Philomena

Abuse of children and young people:
    May 9, 1996; May 25, 1996; June 3, 1996; June 7, 1996;
    June 9, 1996; November 11, 1996; December 10, 1996;
    January 7, 1997; April 20, 1997
Adoration:
    June 26, 1996; September 1, 1996; September 23, 1996;
    November 6, 1996; January 3, 1997; May 2, 1997; May 22,
    1997; June 6, 1997; June 21, 1997; July 27, 1997; September 16, 1997; September 23, 1997; October 1, 1997; November 25, 1997; December 5, 1997; December 18, 1997;
    December 22, 1997; December 29, 1997
Anchor of Hope from Heaven:
    May 1, 1996; May 31, 1996; November 11, 1996; April 21,
    1997
Apparitions condemned:
    January 17, 1997: December 29, 1997
Army of Mary:
    June 21, 1996
Birth Control:
    May 20, 1997
Calamities:
    June 9, 1996; January 18, 1997; October 15, 1997; January
    2, 1998; March 11, 1998; March 17, 1998; May 1, 1998
Cardinals:
    June 4, 1996; May 28, 1997; July 12, 1997; September 18,
    1997; October 9, 1997
Cardinals, bishops, and priests:
    May 28, 1997; September 18, 1997; October 9, 1997;
Celebration of Holy Mass:
    August 21, 1996
Chaplet of St. Philomena:
    October 22, 1996
Children:
    May 1, 1996; May 2, 1996; May 3, 1996; May 6, 1996;
    May 7, 1996; May 9, 1996; May 21, 1996; May 23, 1996;
    May 24, 1996; May 25, 1996; May 29, 1996; May 31,
    1996; June 3, 1996; June 5, 1996; June 7, 1996; June 9,

1996; June 11, 1996; June 12, 1996; June 20, 1996; June
21, 1996; June 23, 1996; July 13, 1996; July 17, 1996; July
22, 1996; July 29, 1996; August 3, 1996; August 14, 1996;
September 8, 1996; September 21, 1996; September 23,
1996; September 27, 1996; October 2, 1996; October 10,
1996; October 11, 1996; October 20, 1996; October 31,
1996; November 5, 1996; November 6, 1996; November
11, 1996; November 12, 1996; November 16, 1996; November 20, 1996; December 1, 1996; December 4, 1996;
December 6, 1996; December 7, 1996; December 8, 1996;
December 10, 1996; December 22, 1996; December 23,
1996; January 1, 1997; January 2, 1997; January 7, 1997;
January 11, 1997; January 13, 1997; February 3, 1997; February 4, 1997; February 17, 1997; March 9, 1997; March
10, 1997; March 11, 1997; April 9, 1997; April 19, 1997;
April 21, 1997; May 6, 1997; May 11, 1997; May 20, 1997;
May 21, 1997; June 19, 1997; June 29, 1997; July 20,
1997; August 7, 1997; August 9, 1997; August 16, 1997;
September 3, 1997; September 11, 1997; September 18,
1997; September 19, 1997; September 20, 1997; September
22, 1997; September 23, 1997; September 25, 1997; October 16, 1997; October 19, 1997; October 22, 1997; November 1, 1997; November 9, 1997; November 12, 1997; November 20, 1997; November 23, 1997; November 28, 1997;
December 7, 1997; December 9, 1997; December 27, 1997;
January 10, 1998; January 13, 1998; February 3, 1998; February 10, 1998; February 13, 1998; March 1, 1998; March
6, 1998; March 10, 1998; March 11, 1998; March 12, 1998;
April 27, 1998; May 1, 1998

Children out of wedlock:
May 20, 1997
Confession:
May 3, 1997; March 2, 1998
Consecration to the Sacred Heart of Jesus and the Immaculate Heart of Mary:
October 6, 1996

Contraception:
October 13, 1997
Conversion:
May 5, 1996; May 20, 1996; May 25, 1996; June 12, 1996, June 17, 1996; July 12, 1996; July 20, 1996; July 29, 1996; August 18, 1996; August 26, 1996; September 4, 1996; September 11, 1996; September 16, 1996; September 18, 1996; September 26, 1996; September 27, 1996; October 9, 1996; November 12, 1996; November 24, 1996; January 1, 1997; February 3, 1997; March 1, 1997; March 5, 1997; April 22, 1997; May 25, 1997; June 16, 1997; June 17, 1997; June 19, 1997; June 20, 1997; June 21, 1997; June 26, 1997; August 16, 1997; August 17, 1997; August 18, 1997; August 19, 1997; August 27, 1997; September 4, 1997; September 18, 1997; September 23, 1997; October 14, 1997; October 16, 1997; December 5, 1997; December 6, 1997; December 29, 1997
Cord of St, Philomena:
May 27, 1996; October 22, 1996; October 23, 1996
Country [U.S.A.]:
May 20, 1996; September 23, 1996; July 3, 1997; July 28, 1997; September 18, 1997; December 29, 1997; January 2, 1998; February 2, 1998; February 18, 1998; March 1, 1998
Crisis of faith:
October 15, 1997
Daily Mass:
September 23, 1996; November 10, 1996; January 3, 1997; February 24, 1997; June 3, 1997; July 4, 1997; November 12, 1997
Devastation:
October 15, 1997
Devil:
June 1, 1996; November 18, 1996, November 23, 1996; December 15, 1996; January 9, 1997; January 11, 1997; January 17, 1997; March 14, 1997; April 23, 1997; May 27, 1997; May 28, 1997; June 12, 1997; June 23, 1997; June 26, 1997; June 29, 1997; July 26, 1997; July 30, 1997; Sep-

tember 18, 1997; September 20, 1997; October 21, 1997; October 23, 1997; October 25, 1997; November 7, 1997; November 9, 1997; November 12, 1997; November 15, 1997; December 14, 1997; December 17, 1997; December 18, 1997; January 13, 1998; April 29, 1998

Disasters:

February 2, 1998; February 10, 1998; March 17,1998

Disobedience to the Vicar of Our Master:

September 18, 1997

Divine Intervention will come upon the world:

October 15, 1997

Division among many Marian apostolates:

February 8, 1998

Division within the Church:

June 25, 1996; September 3, 1996; July 11, 1997

Divorce:

May 3, 1996; November 28, 1997; February 10, 1998

Drugs:

June 24, 1996; June 27, 1996; September 5, 1996; September 25, 1996; November 5, 1996; November 16, 1996; June 30, 1997; February 10, 1998

Earthquakes:

December 29, 1997; January 2, 1998

Eucharist:

May 11, 1996; June 4, 1996; August 13, 1996; September 1, 1996; September 24, 1996; November 4, 1996; November 10, 1996; January 3, 1997; January 9, 1997; July 27, 1997; August 7, 1997; October 9, 1997; October 12, 1997; October 13, 1997; October 14, 1997; October 21, 1997; October 25, 1997; December 5, 1997; January 30, 1998; January 31, 1998; March 2, 1998

Eucharistic:

May 1, 1996; June 26, 1996; January 17, 1997; July 27, 1997; September 17, 1997; October 1, 1997; November 24, 1997

Euthanasia:

October 13, 1997

Conversations With St. Philomena

Evil of the technology of humanity:
May 23, 1997
Fallen priests:
July 28, 1996; July 29, 1996
Famine:
February 10, 1998
Father Gobbi:
June 21, 1996
Fatima:
October 6, 1996
First Fridays:
January 3, 1997; January 4, 1997; May 2, 1997; June 6, 1997
First Saturdays:
October 6, 1996; November 2, 1996; January 4, 1997; February 1, 1997; May 3, 1997; June 6, 1997; August 2, 1997; November 1, 1997; December 6, 1997; January 3, 1998
Floods:
December 29, 1997
Forgive:
May 3, 1996; May 21, 1996; June 1, 1996; June 5, 1996; June 13, 1996; June 24, 1996; November 12, 1996; July 3, 1997; July 28, 1997; August 18, 1997; October 4, 1997+
Forgiveness:
June 1, 1996; June 13, 1996; May 21, 1997; November 28, 1997
Fornication:
June 24, 1996; September 5, 1996; September 25, 1996; November 5, 1996; June 30, 1997; February 10, 1998
Great apostasy:
October 15, 1997
Great chastisement:
March 12, 1998
Great purification:
October 15, 1997
Halloween:
October 31, 1996

Hell:
>May 31, 1996; May 20, 1997

Holy Father:
>May 8, 1996; June 10, 1996; September 16, 1996; April 2, 1997; April 6, 1997; May 29, 1997; November 10-11, 1997; December 29, 1997; February 10, 1998; April 20-26, 1998

Holy Mass is the greatest prayer to God:
>November 4, 1996; October 6, 1997

Holy Mass is the source of all healing:
>August 7, 1997

Holy Mass is the ultimate prayer:
>August 7, 1997; October 6, 1997

Holy Sacrifice of the Mass:
>August 7, 1997; October 13, 1997; October 14, 1997; January 1, 1998

Homeless:
>June 18, 1996; November 16, 1996; November 27, 1996; October 15, 1997; January 2, 1998

Homosexuality:
>September 5, 1996; September 7, 1996; March 10, 1997; February 10, 1998

Infanticide:
>October 13, 1997

Leaders:
>September 23, 1996; September 26, 1996

Marian apparitions:
>January 17, 1997

Marian Movement of Priests:
>June 21, 1996

Masonic activity within the Church:
>July 11, 1997

Masonic cardinals, bishops and priests:
>May 28, 1997

Medjugorje:
>June 3, 1996; June 28-29, 1996; July 1, 1996; July 2, 1996; July 3, 1996; July 3-5, 1996; July 4, 1996; July 5, 1996;

Conversations With St. Philomena

Priests and religious abandoning their vocations:
April 20-26, 1998
Priests, Bishops, Cardinals and Religious:
June 4, 1996
Prostitution:
September 5, 1996; November 16, 1996; March 10, 1997;
February 10, 1998
Purgatory:
November 2, 1996; November 2, 1997; November 16,
1997; March 6, 1998
Purification:
February 9, 1996; February 11, 1997; April 11, 1997; May
31, 1997; October 15, 1997; January 23, 1998; March 12,
1998
Purification of poor sinners:
Feb 9, 1996; April 11, 1997;
Rosary:
May 12, 1996; June 26, 1996; July 30, 1996; September 1,
1996; September 23, 1996; September 26, 1996; November
6, 1996; November 12, 1996; December 6, 1996; March 1,
1997; April 18, 1997; April 19, 1997; May 21, 1997; May
25, 1997; June 23, 1997; July 28, 1997; October 18, 1997;
October 19, 1997; October 21, 1997; November 25, 1997;
December 2, 1997; December 6, 1997; December 18, 1997;
December 21, 1997; December 28, 1997; December 29,
1997; January 13, 1998; January 15, 1998; March 4, 1998
Sacrament of Reconciliation:
May 3, 1997; July 28, 1997; March 5, 1998
Sacred Heart of Jesus:
October 4, 1996; October 6, 1996; January 3, 1997; June 6,
1997; August 12, 1997; December 5, 1997; December 6,
1997
Sacred Heart of Jesus and Immaculate Heart of Mary:
August 12, 1997; December 6, 1997
Sacrifice of the Mass is the greatest prayer:
November 2, 1997

Satan:

May 4, 1996; May 6, 1996; May 13, 1996; May 14, 1996; May 31, 1996; June 14, 1996; June 17, 1996; June 19, 1996; June 20, 1996; June 23, 1996; July 28, 1996; September 5, 1996; September 7, 1996; September 13, 1996; September 20, 1996; September 21, 1996; September 25, 1996; September 27, 1996; October 9, 1996;1997; May 19, 1997; May 20, 1997; May 23, 1997; June 1, 1997; June 12, 1997; June 16, 1997; June 18, 1997; June 20, 1997; June 30, 1997; July 28, 1997; September 5, 1997; September 9, 1997; September 20, 1997; October 18, 1997; December 17, 1997; December 18, 1997; February 18, 1998; March 1, 1998; March 15, 1998

Schism:

May 30, 1997; September 18, 1997; April 20-26, 1998

Shrine to St. Philomena in Italy:

August 1, 1996; August 6, 1996; August 27, 1996; September 24, 1996; October 22, 1996; October 27, 1996; October 28, 1996; October 29, 1996; March 14, 1997; March 31, 1997; April 1, 1997; April 2, 1997; April 3, 1997; April 7, 1997; April 8, 1997;1 10, 1997; 4, 1997; August 11, 1997; August 13, 1997; April 28, 1998

Sodom and Gomorrah:

February 10, 1998

Spirit of apostasy:

January 17, 1997; May 30, 1997; April 20-26, 1998

Suicide:

October 13, 1997

True Presence:

June 4, 1996; January 3, 1997; January 9, 1997; September 17, 1997; October 9, 1997; October 13, 1997; October 25, 1997; November 24, 1997; November 25, 1997; December 5, 1997

Two Hearts:

October 6, 1996; February 6, 1997; March 8, 1997; April 1, 1997; June 6, 1997; December 6, 1997

Unborn:

> May 2, 1996; May 7, 1996; May 24, 1996; May 25, 1996; June 7, 1996; June 20, 1996; July 22, 1996; September 21, 1996; September 23, 1996; May 20, 1997; July 30, 1997; October 5, 1997; October 6, 1997; October 8, 1997; October 18, 1997; October 19, 1997; March 6, 1998; March 18-April 19, 1998

Vicar of Our Master:

> April 6, 1997; September 16, 1996; September 21, 1996; November 14, 1996; November 27, 1996; January 9, 1997; April 1, 1997; May 24, 1997; May 28, 1997; July 12, 1997; September 18, 1997

Violence:

> May 9, 1996; June 7, 1996; June 9, 1996; July 20, 1996; September 4, 1996; September 5, 1996; October 10, 1996; November 5, 1996; June 30, 1997; August 9, 1997; December 29, 1997; February 10, 1998

Warning from God to the World:

> June 9, 1996

Weather:

> December 29, 1997; February 2, 1998

Your President:

> September 23, 1996; September 26, 1996